I0827320

trouble with thinking

a memoir in a mind field

GK Jurrens

GKJurrens.com
gjurrens@yahoo.com
eBook ISBN: 978-1-952165-41-2
Paperback ISBN: 978-1-952165-43-6
Hardcover ISBN: 978-1-952165-44-3
Audiobook ISBN:
v.250525 (u.260124_1519)
r.**260310_0905**

"FORGIVE YOURSELF

FOR NOT KNOWING EARLIER

WHAT ONLY TIME COULD TEACH."

– RAVI SHAH

I certify this entire journal, including its cover, to be "A.I.-free," that is, the author—a *certifiable human*—wrote all 82,176 words and designed all original artwork organically, *not* written or created by artificially intelligent software.

Contents

Disclaimer

Foremost, I am a novelist. As such, I strive to entertain you with facts as the beating heart of this anthology, ***not*** merely as dry diary entries of perfectly regurgitated moments in precise chronological order. I refuse to simply record them with cold impartiality. That's not me.

Rather, I'll share a selected collection of hopefully entertaining anecdotes *as I remember them*, and in my conversational style. Like any novelist, however, I *am* prone to taking certain artistic license. And what's missing? A lot of people, places, and other important things in my life that may make it into the next volume, assuming I live that long.

If you're okay with this context, I encourage you to explore these pages for what they represent. I have much to share with you.

~

It might amuse you to peruse my poetic version of the required legal gibberish as portrayed in my book that describes the sexy anatomy of poetry, along a small collection of my own verses, essays, and original images, ***The Poetic Detective***:

While barristers dismay, should I neglect this little tome,
Which decries all connection to real folks, or home,
I faithfully echo these silly words so prescribed,
Lest anyone think I've fallen to taking bribes,
Or spuriously slandered he who thinks too seriously,
And rends his savagery upon me far too furiously.
Should anyone object to this tome rendered in said verse,
I say to one and all, pound said sand and be so cursed.
So sayeth said law.
*Amen. That's all.**

---

* While this is a memoir, any similarity to actual persons, behaviors, places or events should be considered coincidental and fictional *except where contraindicated.* This offers me a veneer of legal protection. You get that, right?

Prologue

ENOUGH! I'LL JUST KILL MYSELF. YEAH, ONE QUICK JERK OF THE wheel, and....

WAIT, what?

I'm not sure I'm able to tell you now why that notion nearly ended it all for me during the summer of 2006 in a rental car on a lonely North Carolina highway. I was living a life most only dared to imagine. Not that I was rich by any measure. But my dream job earned me more salary, bonuses, and stock options than 99% of the people on the planet, not to mention recognition.

A thousand employees scattered around the globe loved and respected me. Well, most of them, anyway. At least the ones I hadn't fired—yet. My beautiful family, a live-aboard boat during Minnesota summers, and a winter condo on the Gulf Coast of Southwest Florida awaited my return. Yet, here I was contemplating... the... unimaginable—suicide by internal combustion.

If I'd had a pistol in the car that balmy night in rural Chapel Hill, this would be a blank page, an error of lethal omission.

I START my journey down a narrow memory lane en route to my sometimes-dubious past not with my weird and wonderful childhood, but by first sharing with you this particular moment of personal crisis in August 2006 at age 57. I'd scrambled to the summit of my career, but considered ending my life that night. Only for a second or two, mind you. This is not to impress you, or to warn you, but to share what you already know:

A handful of key ticks in time irrevocably changes
the direction of our lives,
either by commission or by omission.
They are best not forgotten.
And we are never the same.
IF we survive.

I call them *pivotal moments.* We *pivot* in one direction or another. We can't go back. They instantly become immutable, defining another piece of who we are and who we will become. Sometimes, such a moment happens *to* us. They may confuse our compass or forge our resolution. They set us on a different path from the preceding minute on our individual one-way trip through time. And our lives will have changed forever.

I'd like to share with you a selection of such moments from my rather convoluted past that molded me into, well, a relatively contented egomaniac with residual self-esteem issues. *Only* because I survived that moment in 2006, as an example. *And* I've survived other important moments before and since. Each changed me, my perspective, and my understanding of the world around me, as well as how people perceive me differently as a result. Like the key moments in your own life.

I should also tell you up front what you will *not* find in these pages. This book is not intended to be a complete autobiography, nor a genealogical documentary. This is only my personal story told in a selection of very personal *beats*.

Hey, whatever drove you to buy this book, thanks for being here. I'm deluded enough to believe you'll find this account of my meager life's pivotal time capsules thought-provoking, maybe even entertaining. I had considered waiting until after I'd died to write and publish these notes to offer you a complete account, but didn't think that a practical strategy.

So, as I finish writing this manuscript early in 2026, I'm grateful to still be alive. No thanks to flirting with various oddities and dangers over the years—some self-destructive, some constructive—each more times than I care to count. In most cases, I placed myself in jeopardy due to my inquisitive nature to perpetually try or learn or experience something new. Not that I'm fearless, but possibly a tad reckless, maybe a bit dim, too. I was always game for anything.

But why a memoir, and why now?

Well, others have observed I've led an interesting life and that I should write about it. This felt awkward, at first, but the egoistic thread in the fabric of my personality soothed that uneasiness once I started. Somewhat. So, what you see is what you get.

Further, I find as I age, my memories have aged with me. And they morph ever so slightly with each telling. Having said that, I try to be faithful to them.

This journal has been coming together for several decades. So why publish it now? Somehow, despite my best efforts, advancing age now overtakes me, though I'm delighted to report that is not the state of my mind. Whether or not you find this of interest, at 76 years sassy, I'm *still* tempting fate far too often. But the time has come for me to share my story, albeit from an unusual vantage point. You'll see.

You may even discover dubious pearls of wisdom I've distilled over a lifetime of salvaged screw-ups.

As I've mentioned, you now hold in your hands a selected collection of pivotal moments that I've somehow survived financially, emotionally, spiritually, and physically. A menagerie of sometimes-intense personal stories, experiences, practices, and even a few confessions.

I squeezed them into the pages of this essay from the unusual life of an ordinary kid; although perhaps no more remarkable than your own. I predict at least some of these anecdotes will fascinate you. Others will likely mirror your own. Many will not. That's a promise.

This book's main character was raised on the wrong side of the tracks, as some say. They also say he thrust himself into extraordinary and frequently perilous circumstances time and time again. As he matured and aged, he then reveled in hedonistic immaturity once more, as if life's lessons were to be ignored, even flaunted. He now whimsically flourishes in both often-conflicted memories and the surprising aftermath of all his shenanigans, which he characterizes as ***trouble with thinking***.

Sorry about referring to myself in the third-person. That happens sometimes. It's the novelist's narrator entangled in my resolute-Dutch and stubborn-German DNA. Yes, my great-grandparents were immigrants from the lowlands near the German-Dutch border and spoke *low (non-aristocratic) German*. Some even dare to suggest we're of *peasant heritage*, and damn proud of it.

Also, not to be underplayed, if I'm being brutally honest with you, I've often wondered if I experience undiagnosed ADD—Attention Deficit Disorder—or even mild autism. I'm big on self-diagnoses, as you'll soon discover. Oops, is that my first confession?

Until a few months ago (as I write this), my only home for the last few years had been a 20-year-old 43-foot bus shared with Kay, my soulmate of 56 years. What a grand adventure!

Before nearly a decade in the bus, we earlier lived aboard and voyaged for a few thousand miles in an old 51-foot pilothouse motorsailer—a seriously slow and very traditional sailboat (acres of varnished teakwood) with a big-ass diesel engine, and 20 tons of usually reliable comfort and convenience, depending on coastal or offshore weather. I'll share with you more on all of this later.

But we are not without means. Remember the old saw, "All those who wander are not lost"? We committed to such a peculiar but inspirational lifestyle by choice. The nomadic lifestyle of itinerant vagabonds was right for us. We'd lived aboard and voyaged part-time for 13 years in our boat or on others' boats on a couple of continents.

Another decade in and around our diesel-powered bus after that continued our quest to streamline our daily life to its essentials, and we reveled in that. Bottom line? We've lived like most only dare to dream. Kay and I committed to this itinerant pastime, but now we're preparing to write the next chapter in our saga.

We cling to a growing bundle of cherished moments, like family, friends, and faith. But no way have I forgotten other magic memories long-abandoned by the side of a twisted road with deep ditches: experiences such as dope smuggling, hitchhiking, boat delivery captain, student pilot, SCUBA diving, skydiving, motorcycle touring, sea kayaking, two post-hurricane recoveries, marine law enforcement, search and rescue, high-functioning alcoholic, and the conflicted life of an international high-tech executive, among other delightful (and a few dreadful) bygone misadventures. I'll bore you with stories about a few of these within this journal, focusing on those that changed my life's course, some abruptly.

. . .

In the past ten years, however, my primary focus has been to write and publish 19 books comprising 14 full-length novels (fiction) spanning five genres. Also, a book of poetry, original images, and essays. Plus, four audiobooks, three of which I self-narrated and produced. Oh, and let's not forget a couple of coffee table books no longer in print. On second thought....

I cling to the delusional self-image of a relatively fit young(ish) scoundrel of higher-than-average intelligence who still seeks out many more norms to annihilate. Although this old dude ain't really all that smart, I refuse to give up. Ever.

With this as my canvas, you'll soon gather I have found great joy in painting with words for you a picture of this life (so far) I consider well-lived. I offer you a curated series of quirky snapshots—of pivotal moments. I now look back at these as a mine field successfully navigated—emotionally as well as physically. Especially emotionally. I think of these as my *mind field.*

Fair warning. Within the coming pages, you will witness a few of my most personal disclosures, looking back on select moments of a long—in human terms, anyway—and edgy existence. After seven-and-a-half decades of living larger than I deserve, I continue to reduce my routine to what's important for me *within each moment*—physically and spiritually—no matter what's going on around me. And no, it's not easy. But it *is* fulfilling.

My journey will amuse, annoy, delight, or baffle you. I might even piss you off. *But I will not bore you.* Note that I only plan to share a few more memorable personal experiences from my perspective. *Will it open an entertaining window into a dark room where you just might find yourself staring back at you from the shadows?*

This journal may offer you nothing more than a few incredulous chuckles or snide snickers, and that's okay by me, too. Or you'll offer a nod to similar predicaments from your own past or present, maybe scratch your head at how I reacted. Because with any worry of pretense now a distant mirage in my rearview mirror, I've analyzed why I made certain decisions throughout my mottled past, as embarrassing as some were.

And I offer you how my understanding of how those decisions has evolved with greater insight in their telling all these years later. That's what a memoir should be—*a literary-based archeological dig into one's life in search of significant artifacts that lend their value and insight to the present, and to the future. For their authors, and perhaps for a few of their readers.*

While I do not intend to alienate anyone, certain biases *will* reveal themselves. Skim over these unapologetic heart flowers—or turd blossoms, depending on your perspective—if they offend you. I'll understand, but I will not apologize. Regardless, I take comfort in knowing every one of us shares more similarities than differences.

From experience, I will offer meager explanations, or excuses, for each of my possibly self-delusional beliefs at the time, and why I sometimes *still* struggle—my... ***trouble with thinking.***

Chapter 1

End of Days

I NOW REVEL IN CONTEMPORARY CONCEPTS SO FOREIGN TO MY dear parents' rather simple system of stout beliefs. This will be a good level-set for you before venturing any further in my humble story. Many are commonplace today. For example, Daddy'd often say, "*Divorce?* What in the h-e-double-pitch forks is *that* all about? What part of *'til death do us part'* don't folks understand? So, they just give up on each other, on a sacred vow made in front a God and everybody? Cripes sake, anyway?"

In today's world, Daddy would no doubt be *jumpin' an outhouse jig,* though dancing was never allowed, which made the admonition all that much more profane. He'd express in no uncertain terms outrage that over 50% of today's marriages end in divorce. "And marrying outside the church, like to a *Catholic*? Holy gosh a'mighty!" I never divorced, but I *did* have the gaul to marry a Catholic. Yeah, a Romeo and Juliet kind of thing!

Both of my parents passed away over 40 years ago as I write this. But if they were alive today? Mom and Daddy both would think the *end of days* was upon us. What with so many children (anyone under

25) or adults that live in sin (premarital sex). And same-sex sex, much less same-sex marriage? "Days a Sodom and Gomorrah, Lord!"

As a teenager, I can still see Daddy leaning forward, perched precipitously on the edge of his old rocker. He'd mercilessly *pound* the heels of his white-knuckled fists on the wooden armrests while watching something offensive on the old black and white television as he witnessed some travesty, yet another assault, on his rigid beliefs. And that happened a lot. That chair took a brutal beating over the years.

But for all his bluster, Daddy was hard candy with a gooey center. Mom always sat next to him. She'd shake her head from side to side with a tiny smirk in her bejowled cheeks as she struggled to manipulate her crochet needles. She often painfully labored on such projects, either for one of us kids, someone else in the family, or most likely, for some charity.

Speaking of charities, after Dad passed away and I was an adult, Mom complained she'd been audited by the IRS yet again. They audited that crippled widow several years in a row. Uncle Sam was convinced she cheated on her taxes by claiming over 50% of her meager income went to charities. I analyzed her finances, and she did indeed donate that much, mostly to TV preachers later indicted for fraud. It took two threatening phone calls to the IRS before they relented.

My parents raised us five kids as Baptists, which I think is about as Protestant as you can get. Not only were we Baptists, but *First* Baptists, whatever that meant. And not only were we First Baptists, but we were First Baptists that subscribed to the rigorous dogma of the GARBC, or the *General Association of Regular Baptist Churches*. Regular? And oh boy, that was *not* to be confused with the *American*

Baptist Association **or** the *General Association of Baptists*. Further, we never *ever* mentioned "them *Southern Baptists!*" Or God forbid, *Pentecostals!* At least, that's my childhood recollection more than half a century down the road.

That fervent fragmentation invariably generated heated discussions over what comprised acceptable dogma. Looking back, it felt to my younger brother and me like we were darn-near Amish, not that we knew what that was until a few decades down the road. As I reached early adulthood, I almost mustered the courage to ask, "Seriously, people?" But I dared not out of respect. And fear.

At 16, though, I'd reached a tipping point. I lamented looking back on my childhood, that had dripped with mortal fear of dying before the *Second Coming of Christ*. They forbade us kids going to movies, from playing cards, or hanging out with girls other than those from *First B*. Violation of these, or countless other dire dogmas, were all damnation-worthy offenses. We dared not question our faith. And here I'd thought God bequeathed us free will to think for ourselves. But apparently, that was only allowed if we would only think well-vetted, praise-worthy thoughts.

But I'm jumping ahead. Let's start from a rather absurd beginning, but absurd in a way that I think will surprise you.

Chapter 2

On the Farm

WHEN MOM AND DADDY WERE YOUNG AND SINGLE, AMERICA trembled through an era of extremes. Millions perished. Not one, but two pandemics swept the globe following the *Great War* that ended in 1918. God did not spare America.*

Then, on October 29, 1929—*Black Tuesday*—the free-and-easy *Roaring Twenties* gasped a sudden and traumatic death. But the emotional reverberations and illicit vices it spawned did not. Hundreds hurled themselves through skyscraper windows, and tens of thousands across America surrendered their souls on *Black Tuesday*. Of those who survived its seismic after-shocks, many drowned their sorrows, but even more were unwilling to do so. Some, like our parents, turned to their faith, more than ever.

Then the world slipped from bleak to worse. The skies dried up and scorched the earth below. Shadows deepened over the creased land that once offered her keepers bounty for their labor. Farmers took reckless shortcuts hoping to save their acreages by eking out more crop yield. Many could not. Instead of the new decade ushering

* This chapter is a factual excerpt adapted from my novel, ***Black Blizzard***.

in fresh hope, quite the opposite became the new reality—with no end in sight.

~

Then Armageddon descended like a dark angel on the Great Plains of Oklahoma, Nebraska, and western Iowa the summer of 1931. As time stalled, millions of Americans merely subsisted in the clutches of escalating squalor—starving and displaced from their homes. Hundreds of thousands more sought to re-discover Eden—elsewhere. *Anywhere* else. Those who stayed struggled for a breath of air free from dust and despair under a drab sky that mocked their foolhardiness. And yes, most stayed put for fear of *the sickness*.

But even with faces swathed in handkerchiefs, and those lucky few who owned goggles for covering their eyes against the grit, they could not fill the hollow pit where a solid meal and contentment once settled. However, during zero-visibility dust storms they called *black blizzards,* a larger issue remained—the simple task of breathing more air than dirt.

Banks and private lenders alike gasped for their own survival. They called in notes on homes and farms and businesses that were no longer viable, hoping to turn an economic vacuum into an opportunity for their own salvation. Somehow, a few ordinary folk still held some wealth—in land, livestock, inventory, or precious metals. Many more leaned on the only two things of substance left—their faith and their community. Otherwise, the future might be too bleak to contemplate.

~

This dystopian landscape then became my parents' dour beginning as a loving couple, and for raising a family. Polio struck Sophiena, my mom, circa 1919 at the age of 8. She survived, but it crippled her. Yet, she prevailed. My father Ed—we called him Daddy

—was a dreamer, a concept guy, who struggled to deal with the cold realities of his harsh life. Yet, he too prevailed. Oh, and God saddled *him* with congenital cardiovascular disease, some of which I am proud to say I inherited. I too shall prevail.

While hoisting a stupid grin, Daddy used to say, "we may not have a pot to piss in, but we got a bowl to eat out of." Mom was a hard-core realist and kept Daddy's feet firmly planted in the very dirt he worked with his calloused and cracked hands. He didn't have the heart for it, though to my knowledge he never said that out loud. The older kids all knew, or thought they did.

Mom and Daddy made life work. They always found a way to feed us. And they raised the five of us in two different *litters,* a decade apart. They grounded us on a solid basis of faith that crafted our own work ethic and spiritual outlook.

Chapter 3

Getting By Just Fine

Mom and Daddy, God-fearing Iowa farmers, often survived without knowing the source of their next meal. I'm told that early in their marriage they subsisted on what they grew. That, however, didn't make the mortgage payments, especially during America's Great Depression when they began their adventures as a couple and as parents.

But their kids never went hungry. We did not grow up on meat and potatoes. Meat was expensive, so Daddy sold the meat he raised to pay bills instead of butchering it for food. So, we ate a lot of casseroles. They're called *hot dishes* here in the Midwest. That meant lots of starches, carbs, and maybe some fatty meat they'd buy that lasted longer and was cheaper than lean meat. Mom often cooked with lard. Sometimes during the tighter times in my childhood of the early 1950s on the farm, I'm told we sometimes ate lard sandwiches because they filled bellies.

After I began sprouting my own memories, our family hot dishes included potatoes, possibly a little fatty hamburger, and canned mushroom soup. But vegetables? It's funny. I can't remember *ever* eating vegetables other than potatoes, although that's a possible blind spot in my fading recollections.

IT WAS no surprise Daddy suffered his first heart attack out on the farm at age forty-five. I was three years old. My younger brother had just been born. Of course, I have no memory of that. Daddy's third major cardiac event took him at 72. I am now four years older than that. Food for thought is all.

Both my parents were... rotund. They struggled with that, but didn't know how to combat it. They never knew much about nutrition, or it wasn't a priority. Hell, they didn't even know about the importance of annual physicals back then. I envision Daddy exclaiming, "What the heck is *that* all about? Some fancy town folk's tomfoolery?"

They didn't even really understand why dental hygiene, or sunscreen, or regular exercise, were important. Daddy'd say, "*Exercise?* Shucks, son, we get plenty a that workin' the doggone farm, and we get darn little back for it, other than to feel good about ourselves by avoidin' all that town life."

THEY'D DRAG their keisters out of bed from under the covers long before dawn every morning. For more than half of each year, I'm told the blankets' top edges formed ice crystals where their visible breath condensed and froze beneath their noses during frigid Iowa winters... on really cold nights, anyway.

Mom would struggle to reach down to slip her crippled bare feet into her cold and clunky orthopedic shoes. Couldn't walk a step without them. She suffered with her hunched and crooked back, misshapen feet, and was further plagued by an atrophied right hand and wrist, all from her battle with polio twenty years earlier. I imagine Daddy down on at least one knee on a rough wood-planked floor caressing her fragile feet her into those shoes and lacing them up for her, just so she could walk. And maybe he'd crack one of his silly jokes while he did so, just to cheer her up. She was the center of his world, and he hers.

She'd wobble as she made her way to the kitchen adjacent to their bedroom. Maybe Daddy helped her stoke the ancient kitchen stove they called *Old Blackie* with chunks of wood he'd chopped, cut to length, and split the previous fall. From family stories decades later, I envision Mom bunching up newspaper, or crumpled pages torn from the Sears-Roebuck, to get the fire going. Thin pages from last year's free catalog also doubled as toilet paper in the outhouse through the mudroom door and out back a ways.

Sometimes, if they were lucky and had planned it just right, the previous night's embers got the morning fire flared up more quickly. They hoped for that because the coffee'd come to a boil faster. Mom sometimes forgot to open the flue in the stovepipe that ascended through the kitchen ceiling, rusty from rain that had leaked in around its perimeter and stained the cracked plaster. They'd close the flue at bedtime to save embers that survived the evening's fire. But forgetting to open it in the morning before piling on a fresh chunk or two of box elder filled the kitchen with smoke.

My older sisters, almost a decade my senior, regale me with stories of how Daddy—Ed—snorted playfully whenever this happened. He'd grin because our mom, his—*town girl*—likely never had to stoke a stove as a child, then a proper young lady, in her parent's fancy house in town. She was still learning what it meant to be a farm wife. It took Mom a while to internalize the routine of this laborious life.

Sometimes, Daddy would have already pulled his bib overalls atop his long johns, which kept him from freezing during the night. He'd throw on some boots in the mudroom and bolt for the barn to relieve their few cows'—*the girls'*—milk-swollen utters. He'd invariably emanate the *fragrance of nature,* as he called it, upon his return to the kitchen even after shedding his boots in the mudroom.

Without uttering a word, he'd often peck Mom on the cheek with a devilish grin, and maybe give one of her ample breasts a squeeze from behind. He'd think we kids didn't see. He'd crack open the window between the kitchen and the mudroom to fan out the rancid odor of smoldering box elder that was only half-dried. The well-cured oak wasn't wasted in boiling morning coffee, of course. They'd reserve that for longer-lasting overnight fires.

I'm told Daddy had much to say about exercise as a separate activity. From what I knew of my dad later in life, I still envision him declaring, "Those darn-fool town folk and their crazy ideas. Exercise? Hah! Get 'em out here splittin' wood, sloppin' hogs, milkin' the girls, maintainin' equipment, and workin' them horses draggin' a plow around the field. I'll show 'em exercise, a'right. Be in bed dead to the world by sunset!"

Our parents remained largely sedentary most of every long Iowa winter, getting little exercise indeed. They didn't know what they didn't know. Those flawed saints did what they had to do, and that was plenty.

Daddy'd told the older kids that Mom's transition from town to the farm had been traumatic, especially since she'd piled *that* major lifestyle change on top of her considerable physical infirmities. But she was a trooper. She'd wobble-stumble over the lumpy frozen mud in the yard in her clunky prescription shoes to fetch the morning's eggs from the coop with a tablecloth-lined tin pail she could barely grip, even with her good hand.

And Mom would work her way through a mountain of farm

laundry every week—a lot of it. She'd pump well water and boil it on *Old Blackie* for use in the rickety manual tub-and-ringer washer on wheels in the mudroom. Before hanging the clothes outside to dry, she'd have to drain the same *warsh water* turned gray after multiple loads. Daddy had run an old rubber drain hose out into the yard as a convenience through a hole in the back wall near the floor.

But the task that must have challenged Mom's semi-functional hands the most? Constant repairs to the family's clothes they couldn't afford to replace. Darning socks, hand-sewing busted hems, and other sundry repairs that must have taken endless hours slaving with needle and thread using her crippled hand, I'm told.

Besides caring for my younger brother and me when we were little, my sisters, both a decade older than us, told me recently that Mom struggled just to reach up to the backyard clotheslines with her bad back and junk shoulders. But she'd do so dozens of times every laundry day, often in the bitter cold. She'd need to reach way up and push those clothespins down hard enough onto the line to prevent the laundry from falling or blowing across the muddy yard. All with her crippled hand and bad back? Impossible, but doable.

I often pondered an old, faded photo, before it was lost in a flood, of Mom hanging laundry. She tied her scarf tightly over her hair and ears, knotted under her chin. An old wool coat draped over her rounded back. One cheek puckered against the effort in that photo, and against what must have been... constant pain?

My heart broke every time I stared at that curled and faded picture. I imagine what might have been going through her mind. Did she resent that strange new and impossible lifestyle, or was she simply grateful to be with the man she loved? Or both? Did she experience even a moment of self-pity, or did she relish the stalwart farmwife persona that she staunchly portrayed to the world? At least to us kids.

I also recently learned from my sister, Yvonne, something I had never known. Mom was a strong woman, but that did not prevent her from suffering through more than one emotional breakdown, for which Daddy actually hospitalized her. Details remain sketchy, but that shook my own emotional foundation learning that a half-dozen decades after the fact. Perhaps this is not my story to tell, but it is part of me, so maybe it is.

Chapter 4

Mean Old God

As a young boy, I was *convinced* very few things were possible. My parents nurtured us best they knew how given their own hardscrabble history. They worked *so* hard and *so* long. Plus, they were just *so* much older than us. Mom gave birth to me in her late thirties when Daddy was in his early forties. Three years after *that* my brother Roddy came along!

The story I've been told? My birth that late in their lives was an accident. But they didn't want me to be lonely. Both of our births were... problematic. I almost died. I guess that makes such an event my first fate-driven pivotal moment.

As to my early life on the family farm in northwest Iowa before we lost it to the bank? I have so few memories of those days. One moment I do remember, however, that could have ended my short life, but didn't? I fell five or six feet off a tractor fender, face downward, onto the upturned razor-sharp tine of a six-inch tractor mower blade. That little misadventure speared my tongue as that huge tine (compared to my tiny head) entered my tiny mouth. The not-so-tiny hole in my tongue reminds me of that moment to this day, 71 years later. Yes, I survived the tender age of five. Another moment!

. . .

A FEW YEARS LATER, I must have been seven, circa 1956. I remember a story from my barely legible childhood journal, more like crayon pictures with words scratched around the margins. We had already *moved to town,* as the farmers used to utter that like a curse—their voices dripping with dread—to Rochester, Minnesota. My little brother and I nearly suffocated inside the well-insulated walls of a minuscule information silo during those formative years. At least that's my view now.

As a frightened kid, I'd pray *every single day* to an uncaring God who'd created a cold and cruel world: "Please, I don't want to die today." My favorite companion was a warm pipe in a corner of the stairs in our old house....

~

A CRYSTALLINE TEAR meanders down my upturned cheek for no particular reason. I've been on my bony little knees for a long time, elbows resting two stairs up, as I lean into them. My white-knuckled hands remain clamped together under my reddened chin, rubbed raw with worry. I gaze upward at the shining gates of Heaven, receiving no sign that anyone is listening. "I guess that's all I got for now, God. Amen."

I long for warmth and dread another bout of being afraid some more. I will *not* chew my nails anymore now that the bleeding has stopped. Roddy, my younger brother, likes to sit and talk sometimes. "Hey, GG!" That's what he and my two older sisters and older brother call me sometimes. "What do you think about our house? It's a good house, right?" I'm guessing kids are teasing him.

"That's easy. I really like going up the stairs to our room." I like how those stairs turn to the left just a few steps up, and then turn again to the right near the top. I don't tell Roddy I find those stairs interesting, and a kind of refuge. I do tell Roddy, "Ya know, in the corner near the bottom of the stairs is that big old bare pipe, a metal chimney, maybe? It's warm on cold days, even warmer at night. Right, Roddy?"

He just nods, no doubt wondering where this stupid story is going. I continue. I guess I need to talk. "Yeah, those stairs sure are steep and not very wide, huh? Almost like a ladder. It's easier if ya put your hands on the steps in front of ya to kinda climb on all fours, ya know? I turn a little sideways as I climb, especially now that I'm bigger. Wonder why Mom stores lots of books 'n stuff there." I open the door to the stairs and point, ever the knowledgeable big brother. "See? This is where I hide a lot from an awful death."

"Yeah, you're scared a lot, GG."

"You too!" I whine, inflecting my voice first up, then down, then up again. "It's sorta weird our only bathroom is at the top of the stairs." I nod up through that open door. "Mom's polio from when she was a kid? Did you know she can't walk a step without them clunky shoes. And one hand doesn't work so good. Looks kinda weird, too, huh? She never goes upstairs. That's why Daddy put a toilet in their bedroom off the front room right next to their bed. Or was that always there? Anyways, it's a good house, Roddy. It really is."

He smirks, already having moved on. "Daddy's even older than Mom, isn't he? It's weird how their bedroom is right off the front room, with that funny brown folding door they push open to one side —like a accordion."

"Yeah, 'n Mom always takes a bath with a big ole sponge 'n soapy water at our big ole kitchen sink. If it isn't too dark out, 'member how she asks us to go play outside or watch TV, during? Sure is dark a lot."

Roddy picks up on that. "We watch a lot of TV! It's funny. But this *is* a good house, huh, GG?" Something else is bothering him. I'm not gonna ask. I got plenty of my own stuff to worry about.

I say, "Yeah. Don't know about you, but I spend an awful lotta time on those stairs, next to that warm pipe. Winter's so darn long. I sit close, even leaning on that pipe, sometimes. Then I'm even warmer inside, too, even though the house is awfully cold a lot. Mom always says we're all blessed. So why don't I *feel* that way? Am I bad?"

"Aw, GG, you think way too much. We're just poor. That's what my friend from school says, anyways. And Mom prays a lot, so she talks a lot about being blessed, about God 'n Jesus 'n stuff. So what?"

"All's I know is, being alone is really nice, scrunched up next to that warm pipe. Gives me time to think. On my own, ya know? And I *do not* think too much! I just need to keep track of a lotta stuff. Even though Mom works hard at her nurse job all day, and Daddy's janitor job while we're sleeping, it's always so hard to get alone, 'cept on the stairs next to that warm pipe."

"GG, if thinking makes you sad cuz you pray a lot, why pray, except when Mom says we gotta?"

"Well, I guess it makes me not as scared 'a dyin', ya know? Mom's always talking about the *Second Coming* 'n all. Dunno. Don't you get scared like that, Roddy?"

"Nah. Not sure what all that church stuff means, anyway. I'm gonna go play. See ya!"

I KEEP THINKING, ya know? About my feelings about the house now that he got me going. There's a nice big window at the top of the stairs inside the bathroom with no door. There's always dusty air up them stairs. Funny about that. I can see how it just floats around in the sun. *Wouldn't it be nice to float around in the air like that?* An ugly, old light bulb hanging down from the ceiling up there helps me see the floating dust at night.

I always think about how Mom says I'll go to Hell if I think about the wrong stuff. Don't even have to say it out loud to be a sin! Lots of ways to go to Hell, I guess. Yeah, she taught me to pray before I learned how to walk, according to Carol, my older sister. I remember always praying to a mean old god, even though I'm afraid he'll do bad things to me and Roddy, or make us just die. That's what you do—you pray for all of that stuff to not happen.

I always thought my brain worked pretty good—I can think of a lot of really bad ways to die. Mom tells me and Roddy maybe that won't happen for a long time. But if it does, dying's only the beginning. I'm always afraid of dying in weird and awful ways. I just know there'll be a forever with no girls, or grape soda, 'n stuff. That's always in my brain.

It's as if Roddy is still sitting there with me on them stairs, listening to me even though he went out to play. The street lights aren't on yet. Probably playin' *kick the can* with Joe 'n Mary Donney from around the corner, even though they're Catholics.

Am I praying again, or just talking to myself? Sometimes, it's hard to tell the difference. I'm thinking about a lot of stuff God doesn't understand. I depend on these stairs. This pipe is always warm and friendly and will never kill me or all the people on Earth, just for thinking about girls. These stairs and this warm pipe are my best friends, besides Roddy, a course. 'N maybe Charlie Donney, even though he's a Catholic, too. I like 'em and can depend on 'em. I sure can't depend on that mean old God. I guess it's Mom's job to keep us scared of sinning and hanging out with Catholics. Isn't her fault. That's just her job.

Sometimes I cry myself to sleep. I just feel so darn bad for the end of the world and everybody at the hand of that mean old God. So, why do people look forward to that *Second Coming,* anyways? Why are they so anxious to give up on living 'n stuff? Is it so bad that they wanna just *quit*? Does everybody think like that?

Even though I'm bigger now, I still think good stuff about that old house. I never did find out why Roddy was so worried whether we had a *good house.* It's gone, now, just an empty lot with a lot of weeds.

Chapter 5

Rebellion

At 13, I just knew *The End* had to be very near. It was *always* near, maybe any day. Every year the news reported *wars and rumors of wars, and earthquakes.* Signs of the *Second Coming of Christ* when the world must end, at least for all believers. I guessed the rest would just have to live with Hell on Earth after that. The Holy Bible's Book of Revelations *proved* it to be true and was *always any day now* to all believers, like our *actual* lives were little more than nasty foreplay for the next life, whatever that *might* be.

I lived in near-debilitating fear of the end of this dirty vessel of sin —my body and my dirty thoughts. Plus, looking back, I got mad about the curse that *mean old God* branded me with *before I was even born* —something somebody labeled *original sin.* That damn-near crippled me emotionally. I'd pray every morning and every night, sometimes quietly to myself, even years later at school whenever a girl passed by. But then I prayed for God to wait until after I could have sex with a girl, any girl, at least once... maybe more. Then it would be okay to destroy the world, I supposed.

I hungered for even a taste of just one worldly pleasure, even though that was bad, and I'd probably go to Hell for all of eternity. I thought, *What if Hell isn't as bad as Mom says?* And then guilt would suffocate me again for even considering such a thought. Seemed there was little hope of escaping *some* flavor of damnation, no matter what.

A couple of years later, I feared I would explode. I really just wanted a little earthly light before eternal darkness and righteousness, maybe even a little short-term spiritual freedom in return for never-ending subservient salvation. That would be okay too, I guessed.

Then I blasted through my 16th birthday like a horny rocket on solid fuel. My world tilted precariously on its various axes and sped up past the point of spinning me out of control, at least enough to achieve escape velocity. My orbit of fear and subservience and blind belief had to be broken. I'd decide for myself. *Yeah, I'll take control.*

From that point on, trouble followed me like a mean old rail yard dog, never to be kicked loose without getting bitten. Sometimes, it even drew blood. Yeah, I was old enough to think in metaphors, like some country song lyrics, but didn't yet know that word. I realized years later that moment of decision was yet another pivot point, for better or worse.

That decision to rebel, to pursue freedom, to plot my own course, opened the aperture of my beliefs to a universe of possibilities. It delivered the freedom to make a ton of awesome mistakes I never would have dreamed conceivable. My life got messier, but I had indeed taken control of my own vessel (of ***alleged*** sin). I felt... liberated. And a lot less afraid all of the time. I wouldn't realize until much later, however, how much *more* afraid my poor parents had become... for me.

1966 STARTED a chain reaction in my life. Most adults around me remained hung over from the fifties, trying hard to jump directly to the seventies, but failing miserably. Sex, drugs, and rock 'n roll made their nationwide debut—worldwide, too, for all I knew. I no longer quite knew what to think of life in general, and more specifically, of my own. Smaller and smarter than most kids, I spent much of my time wanting stuff I didn't have, and less time figuring out how to get it.

I had suddenly become fearless, except no way would I mess up my (now) fairly good-looking face in a fight. Besides, fights were for people who couldn't think fast enough to turn enemies into friends. I learned that the first time I got punched in the gut and thrown to the ground so hard I bit through my lip and vomited. That elicited a vow to never *ever* get punched again. In general, though, I discovered how to navigate what had become the beautiful mess of my young life. At least I thought I did.

I'LL REMIND you that my parents had lost everything before I arrived on the scene. Then, with five kids in tow, they started over in their 50s. We moved from a crappy little farm outside the little town of George in northwest Iowa to a crappy little house in Salem Corners, near Rochester, Minnesota.

Losing the farm and starting over nearly killed them, especially Daddy. He had always seemed larger than life, but people—mainly Mom—repeatedly reduced him to the role of a small thinker and a menial laborer... you know, all that practical stuff. That was my impression, and probably not a fair one. I had a lot more in common with Daddy than with Mom.

She was the realist. You know the type. He'd survived two cardiac events, as the docs called 'em, starting in his 40s soon after I was born. Despite her physical problems, our mom returned to school to complete her nursing degree in her 50s so we wouldn't starve while

Daddy regrouped. Already in his late 50s or early 60s when we moved to Rochester, Daddy scored a job cleaning urinals for a contracted janitorial service. But his spirit would not be broken. After all, those urinals were at IBM!

LATER, in high school after a sudden growth spurt, I was neither small nor weak. I'd become the good-looking six-footer whose specialties included scoring mediocre grades with almost no effort, and demolishing friends' or family cars. Mostly though, I obliterated my own motorcycles bought with money from a huge newspaper delivery route on my bicycle with a big-ass wire basket in front for the papers. Remember newspapers and smart-ass kids delivering them? At least it was honorable work. And legal.

Later, I could afford bigger and more powerful motorcycles with money I earned working several of those mindless jobs only teenagers will work. I shattered numerous bones in the process of crashing my acquisitions, all the while nurturing my considerable ego. Yes, I still believed in my invincibility despite my dented and tarnished armor. I'd come a long way from those stairs in our parents' house, even though I still slept in the same bedroom at the top of those same stairs most nights.

ALTHOUGH NOT BY MY DOING, all my plaster casts were the coolest, as they featured the most signatures with little red hearts and other stuff from kids at school. Some were even garnished with a drop or two of perfume. Girls just offered, which was fortunate, because despite my reasonable looks and being tall, my shyness still plagued me.

You know those guys who constantly check the status of their hair and clothes in every reflective surface? Yeah, that was me. I tried to be subtle, but failed. Add a raging hormone-induced interest in girls, and I seemed to have become the all-American recipe for a fairly average small-town kid. Nothing more. At the time, though, I *knew* I was just too damn large for life.

I continued to be enamored of myself, yet I *still* lacked substantive confidence around girls. On the rare occasion, I dated good little Baptists with whom my job-exhausted mother still found time and energy to arrange meet-ups after Sunday morning or evening services. Or at Wednesday Bible study before I refused to attend. Cold fish, all. Yeah, Mr. Sensitive, alright. Nope. I'd become the textbook definition of a narcissistic little prick. But in my own defense, I *would* come to realize that a mere half-dozen decades later.

Yeah, at 16, I shattered not only my left femur, adding to a still-growing collection of fractured bones worn like badges of foolish honor, but also my parents' hearts. I'd seceded from the family's most-devout faith. Definitely party time for ole number one.

Besides, nobody fell for that religious crap anymore, did they? Now mature as hell—yet another self-diagnosis—I needed to make up for lost time. Once unshackled from an obsolete Christian prison, guarded by mythological bars and immovable wardens, my social life soon achieved breakout status.

Chapter 6

Car Killer

My early teen years had been passing me by in a fog of mediocrity. Although it came back into focus once in a while, for a few standout moments. Though I was physically invincible, I still craved acceptance. Then, invincibility almost killed me and my friends.

I can't vouch for every detail of this near-death experience—one of several—but it's close. Yes, the three of us had been drinking. No, we weren't of legal age at 16. New to driving, our buddy, Rod (not my brother), piloted an old Mercury. Or was it a Chevy? No matter. It sure sounded like a fast car with a big-ass V8 and a *four-on-the-column* shifter. I recall each of us craving a need for speed, though none of us said that out loud. More of an unscratchable but persistent itch. I can't even tell you where we'd been earlier that night or how we scored the booze.

We careened through Silver Lake Park. Rod drove along the lake's curvaceous perimeter road as if possessed by feral abandon. But me on the passenger side, and my friend Bill in the middle of the front seat? Not so much, though we'd never allow such cowardice to surface. A vortex of wind noise swirled around us through the rolled-down windows. The summer evening intoxicated us, along with the beer and whiskey we'd been swilling. Bill hollered over the thunderous roar of the big engine. "Boy, this thing sure has a lot of power!"

He and I both clutched the metal dash with white-knuckled grips, already hurtling through the darkness. Not sure what we were expecting, other than naked fear knowing our buddy *Crazy Rod*. He growled, "Ain't nothin'. Watch this." He downshifted with violent abruptness milliseconds before stomping on the gas pedal to challenge a tight curve around the old Isaac Walton League cabin. I don't think we careened up onto less than four wheels, but it had to have been close, at least within the expanse of my fertile imagination six decades later. Neither do I remember if that car was equipped with seat belts. Even if it was, we weren't wearing them. Another potential act of cowardice.

I drank in delicious first-hand terror with my two intoxicated neighborhood buddies—slow-motion trauma. Decelerating from somewhere on the high side of 55 MPH to a dead stop in less than a second or two. This experience felt similar to a few other pivotal life-or-death moments in my teenage years and beyond—this wasn't the first, nor would it be the last. None of us should have survived that night, but we did. After all, ***we were invincible.***

Time didn't quite stop. That was the surreal illusion that engulfed me. Whatever this phenomenon is called, I'd experienced it before when a lady T-boned me on my motorcycle with her car's front bumper several months earlier. She'd blown through a stop sign at speed on West Center Street. I saw it coming in full slo-mo, and with intense curiosity, observed the sequence, powerless to twist fate toward my favor. *It's a beautiful thing, this cosmically choreographed ballet—foreplay to a violent embrace. But the pain and blood and many weeks of rehab? Not so much.* Fortunately, I healed quickly in my youth.

I forget a lot, but the seconds leading up to that almost lethal event with two of my besties 60 years ago? I will never forget that cinematic frame-by-frame phenomenon. The front of Rod's heavy sedan folded around that massive tree trunk that remains scarred to this day. The car's ass-end left the ground. Just a touch of vertical deceleration—and a whole lot of horizontal—followed.

Then, a warm curtain of blood descended into my eyes a few seconds after I snapped back from planting my nose on the dash and the top of my skull into the windshield that both gravity and I had just shattered. Part of it, anyway.

Nor will I ever forget the strong sense that I was part of something unique and special—proof of my immortality, and more importantly, of belonging. We sat there stunned, listening to the background soundtrack of hissing and crackling and the ticking of cooling metal. We bled together, a fraternity of adolescent desperadoes.

Most of all, that night of invincibility meant camaraderie. Did that mean I was a *danger junkie*? Surely not. Or was that what it must be like to bond with others in combat? I hadn't a clue. Not back then. As I recall, after the initial shock, I think we coughed up a little laugh, a sneer into the Grim Reaper's shadowy leer. Or maybe a nervous chuckle at the ridiculous proposition that we had all survived. Or most likely, simply a veneer of false bravado instead of crying like babies in front of each other.

Now, I'm not saying I sought to re-experience that euphoria again and again. But thirteen motorcycle accidents, plus "totaling" my mom's 1962 Buick Le Sabre while under the influence of some damn fine weed, all before the age of eighteen? And I'm still alive to regale you with these idiotic tales? Evidence suggests I *was* invincible, immortal, an exception to the professed frailty of man. Especially as a hormone-inflated teenager. ***Or*** I was just damn lucky!

Chapter 7

Great Expectations

I had emerged from my parents' primordial ooze, and at last, possessed of an insatiable curiosity about… everything, including the nature of faith. We were fortunate to experience what is now called poverty. Back then, we *got by just fine, thank you very much.* The only commodity we had plenty of? Faith, stronger than hope, that things would be okay, even get better. When I was younger, anyway.

Then, a sense of stark contrast struck me when I witnessed my affluent schoolmates wanting for nothing, yet wanting more. I took nothing for granted. Eventually, however, faith did not satisfy me anymore, either. I expected more, too. Much more.

So, let's talk about expectations. During my elementary or junior-high (middle) school years in the mid-to-late 1950s, teachers assigned students a set of *personal* expectations reduced to a seemingly simple number. We don't discuss this much now, but those expectations hit me in my mid-teen years.

Remember IQ tests? *IQ = Intellectual Quotient.* It's a two- or three-digit numerical test score that allegedly represented my relative level of intelligence compared to my peers. About two-thirds of the population scores between 85 and 115. And 2% each score above 130 and below 70. My score? 150. What the hell was I supposed to do with *that*? By the way, I married a woman who I later learned scored 151. Of course, I did.

These scores are *estimates* of intelligence at best. As a frame of reference, one estimate put Albert Einstein's IQ at around 160, although that's a guess since that genius never took the test like Kay and me and almost everybody else in school at the time. So, these were qualitative tests designed to measure the diversity of human intelligence, initially used to measure mental retardation, now called a developmental disability.

Researchers had also added questions that gauged attention, memory, and problem-solving skills. They likely measured me on the *Stanford-Binet Intelligence Scale*. This test was used for decades to quantify the mental abilities of millions of people around the world. If you dare take it yourself, here's your chance: https://www.stanfordbinettest.com/#google_vignette. I do not care to subject myself to that again. Shouldn't have changed that much. Intelligence is intelligence. Although I must admit I do not feel as sharp as I once did, even though I engage in mental gymnastics most every day. Besides... *why?*

But back then... so what? Well, these IQ scores set a certain academic level of expectation. A rather burdensome one. In retrospect, I had paid little attention to that silly triple-digit number that proved to be prophetic. In all humility, I did seem to possess a singular focus. My credo, however, later became *10% inspiration, 90% perspiration.* And I *have* enjoyed learning new things for as long as I can remember, even when that was not a cool thing to do.

For example, who learns to play a trumpet when the *only* cool instruments were guitar and drums? Further, what kind of social retard plays in the *high school marching band?*

I gave this whole IQ thing very little thought. But later, I realized that was the reason my parents signed me up for *accelerated* classes in junior-high and high school. Yeah, that placed even more pressure on me to perform, but it still didn't really occur to me until much later how significant that was to my development at that age and beyond. So, thanks Mom and Dad, I guess. I do think it helped later to have that on my resumé, even though my grades were far from stellar back when my head was still firmly implanted in my ass. Limited visibility down there. In retrospect, had I taken it seriously, I could have earned a year or two of college credits in high school. 20/20 hind-end-sight.

And learning to play the trumpet? Who'd have guessed that would come in really handy a couple of years later, in California, of all places!

Chapter 8

Boy Meets Girl

There is no doubt that one particular Friday night in the summer of 1966 changed my life forever. I probably remember it a bit different than anyone else. Does not matter. Magic does that to a borderline romantic like me.

Still suffering from the residuals of a Thursday night hangover, I repositioned myself in the backseat. There might have been others in the station wagon's third seat behind me. Memory fails. We hurtled through the darkness to an after-party once the high school mixer at the Armory had gone dark. Even the dim dome light laid spurs into the flanks of zebras thundering through my dusty brain. Not the kind from a zoo, mind you, but the real deal from Africa, or wherever. I had rehearsed this too-cool commentary in case anyone asked. Yeah, I know.

The bench seat of Dale Scobie's not-quite-mint candy-apple-red (I think) fifty-seven Chevy Nomad, upon which I half-reclined, was not that comfortable. Maybe it was Steve Rowe's car. Doesn't matter, either way. I had hitched a ride, as usual. I owned only a motorcycle myself. The cheap circular wire-rimmed shades helped to staunch the flow of blood hemorrhaging from my eye sockets, but more because I thought they looked cool. Shades of John Lennon, you understand.

~

"Hey, isn't that Kay Boyce?" Next to Dale in the front bench seat, reliable Bob Humphrey—Hump—had spotted a tall, attractive brunette walking in the opposite direction on the sidewalk. I peered over the bottom edge of the right rear door frame and the rolled-down window.

The warm and intoxicating summer night outside was only somewhat visible from my semi-reclined position of self-induced misery. I retrieved a distant elementary school memory of Kay Boyce. Yeah, a Catholic girl from St. Francis Parochial School down on Fourth Street. I attended Holmes Public School at 11th Avenue and Center Street.

This girl? Everything bounced. She wore her silky dark hair longer on the sides, parted in the middle and short around the back of her neck, framing her slender Gracie Slick face. Except for *Herb Alpert's Tijuana Brass*, the *Jefferson Airplane* was my favorite band, after all. Their lead singer, Gracie? Aw, man. Now, this girl? Shades of Gracie!

She wore her miniskirt longer than most, but it did not hide those slender, muscular legs. Kay looked more like a gymnast than a rock singer once you took the time to see her. Of course I had ignored her in elementary school, being Catholic 'n all. But now she demanded attention.

"Hey, Kay! Need a ride?" Hump barked as we rumbled past. Small town. Plus, Dale's muffler was holier than the Pope. She turned to toss a vivacious wave. Recognition dawned in her eyes as she flipped her gaze. Her hair followed, bouncing. Gangly Hump understood she was *way* out of his league, Adam's apple 'n all. But he appreciated she liked him as a friend, sometimes protector and defender. Made him feel a little like a knight. No hiding that.

Chivalry lived. Hump'd do anything for the likes of Kay Boyce, even though he was a *pill*—a doctor's kid—and the rest of us were *hoods-slash-nerds,* but definitely not *pills* or *jocks*. Rather, most of us were part-time delinquents—*hoodlums,* some older folks said. It's what we understood. Hump grew up on Pill Hill in Southwest Rochester, but hung with our crowd from the southeast side. Never figured out exactly why. I guess he liked our bad-boy vibe tempered with a bit of intelligence. See how this worked? Good, because we didn't at the time.

The sporty Nomad wagon rolled to a stop quite far from the curb. Dale's ragged brakes squealed in protest. He meant to get them fixed. Saving up, he'd said.

Kay chirped, "Sure! A ride would be cool. Just hiking home from the worst date ever! Thanks for the rescue." That last word came out a bit more heartfelt than we expected. We'd learn later we had indeed rescued her from a rapidly developing situation. Don't ask.

Hump grinned like a horny puppy, swung the squeaky door open, hopped out, and waved her in with a formal bow and an inviting sweep of his left arm across his waist. She chuckled at his knight-like gallantry and folded her lithe frame into the front bench seat between her tenth-grade Mayo High School classmates. Hump slammed the heavy door after sliding a little too close to Kay with some effort, and away we roared.

Despite her considerable but wasted athletic talent and girl-next-door allure, Kay Boyce wasn't popular. No money for popular-girl clothes, and too busy working after school to afford or care much about girly shit. They said she was the bright spot in a dim white-trash family, not that anyone deserved to say that. Small town. Before Kay had slid into the car, Hump had also conceded that she spoke her mind more readily than most guys *or* girls could handle. He'd say, "Ya wanna know what Kay Boyce is thinking? All ya gotta do is *listen,* man!" Didn't want her to hear. That would have been... unknightly.

Now, three crowded in front, one in back, Dale said, "Kay, you know Gene back there, don'cha? Why not hop in back?" Still reclined in the backseat, it would have taken every inch of my six-foot height to meet Kay's eyes *if* we'd both been standing. She had to be at least five-ten. A damn Amazon. I'd read about 'em. Even fantasized a little.

Kay materialized next to me in the backseat as I struggled to sit up, at least partway. Had she just glided *over* the front bench seat? In a *skirt?* It happened so fast that none of us guys were sure.

A storm gathered with crushing momentum. I muttered, "Hullo." Dragged off my shades. Our eyes met. Thunder rumbled. Hoping she'd hear over the rage of hooves pounding in my head and Dale's perforated muffler, I whispered, "C'mere. Wanna tell you a secret."

Rochester wasn't that big a town with a population less than a hundred thousand. She must have thought me cool, but full of myself. She was not wrong. Instead of presenting her ear to receive some silly secret I've long since forgotten, she did a head fake. Not sure why. Surprised me with an abrupt but wet kiss that landed warm and soft. Lilacs? Lightning! But now no other sound whatsoever, other than her shallow, rapid breathing. So warm. I'd stopped breathing.

Oh, crap. What now? My unaccountable lack of confidence with the fairer sex pressed down on my chest with inexorable force, especially with this otherwise now-unapproachable creature. I need not have worried. Kay gently led me through the dark and scary forest. Clouds parted. The moon and stars became our only audience in that backseat. We moved as one through our introductory dance of meaningless and profound whisperings and warm gestures.

Despite my diminished capacity, we muttered what seemed like relevant trivialities while Dale drove toward her house according to her distracted instructions. Dale missed a few turns. Still, we arrived way too fast. No sooner had the Nomad rolled to a stop than the right rear door flew open, as if she were a caged bird eager to once again take flight. After chirping a lilting "Bye!" over her shoulder, Kay flipped that laughing hair and was... gone. My entire universe collapsed into a desolate and lonely hole of dark energy.

Chapter 9

Boy Courts Girl

The next day, I arrived at Kay's house after quizzing everyone I knew about her address. No Boyce in the phone book. Weird. I found out much later her previous boyfriend, my friend Bill who'd recently shared a serous tree-scarring with, encouraged all our friends not to help me find Kay's house. He still loved her, and she him, but more like a brother. It took some effort to find her. I was not to be deterred. Her parents' house turned out to be even tinier and crappier than my own. Parked my motorcycle. I knocked—much louder than I intended.

And then, there she was, silhouetted by the sunlight from her kitchen window. Drenched her hair and sweatshirt-draped shoulders. I felt like I had lumbered over the finish line of a marathon with a hangover just moments earlier. I *hated* running, but loved what I saw, now sober with a painful headache. Hungover or lovesick? I considered turning and leaving. But then, breathing became an issue. My feet seemed glued to her stoop.

"Gene! What are you *doing* here?" She executed a furtive glance over her bare left shoulder, peeking out from that oversized sweatshirt, her hair swinging in response, both back, then forward. Did I see *fear* in her eyes? She noticed my trepidation since I suddenly looked like the star performer in the theater of wounded egos. But her endearing grin broadcast I had not misread her the night before. She blamed her unexpected reaction on her hard-ass stepdad who hated any boys who showed an interest.

"Why? Is he jealous?" An innocent joke. It looked as if her chest might explode. She huffed me into an abrupt silence with a flushed face and a tender hand on the center of my chest. Her gentle gesture didn't match her wild eyes. My confusion escalated. We conspired to escape for a ride. I left alone, conflicted.

Five minutes later, as agreed, she met me down the block and hopped astride my 305cc Honda Scrambler. I'd paid cash for that baby with my paper route money, but mostly with money from my new job as a dishwasher at the Townhouse Restaurant, which paid a lot more. She bent close behind me on the bike's bench seat with her arms wrapped around me. We left her house behind. I thought, *Jeez, it's even smaller and dumpier than mine.* I'd noticed... only just.

"Gene!" she shouted over the pounding beat of the twin-cylinder engine. "Are you okay? Your heart is jumping like a jackhammer!"

Am I more embarrassed by her warm hands pressed against my chest or her observation about my heart rate through my t-shirt? So, I chuckled and cracked the throttle wide-open with my right hand. The bike leaped forward.

"Shift!" she cried with glee over the scream of my unobstructed exhausts. At the crescendo of the next gear's RPMs, she'd playfully punch me in both kidneys to punctuate the same command: "Shift!"

I hollered over my left shoulder, "So, you ride a lot, Kay?"

"This is my first time!" she shouted as we flew over 60 MPH down the center of a two-lane residential street. My suggestive but witty retort died in my throat, because that was where my heart was wedged, blocking the blood flow to my brain.

I kept imagining her clinging to me, naked, except for her knee-high socks and penny loafers, of course. Her generous boobs pressed into my shoulder blades through her sweatshirt. After a powerful surge forward, I hollered, "I'm glad you like it. I'm a bike guy, big time! Don't even own a car. *Love* to ride."

Then came the low growl in her voice, her lips pressed into my ear. "I bet you do," she smirked. She didn't mean what I meant. She continued, "Uh, Gene, we're being followed by a car with pretty red flashing lights. Do we keep going until we get to hear their pretty siren?"

"Aw, crap... hey, so worth it!" I sped up, thinking only with my little head. Well, not *that* little. Not anymore. I sensed more than saw her impish smile. She thought I was fun *and* funny.

DESPITE THE SENSE of ease with which our relationship began, we soon discovered we were polar opposites. No chance of success as a couple. None. Whatsoever. We were both strong-willed, and each of us always wanted to *be the boss* within our instantly tumultuous relationship—a source of incessant bickering.

To make matters even worse, she was a Catholic! I was Protestant. Her family drank and smoked. Mine were teetotalers and convinced both iniquitous vices, *and* Catholicism were Satan's tools. She came from an abusive, dysfunctional, broken home. Worse, her mom managed the roughest bar in town—the Roxy. By contrast, though also dirt-poor, my family was a nurturing, smothering nuclear family of huggers, teetotalers, and Bible-bangers.

I was her Romeo; she was my Juliet. Our budding romance seemed cursed from that first furtive kiss. The *only* common denominator as our relationship developed? Our depressing economic and social status. Well, that and sex.

Chapter 10

Hood or Pill?

Unlike Kay and most of my neighborhood friends, except for Hump, I *crossed the tracks,* metaphorically speaking, to mingle with a handful of *pills* now and then—doctors' kids. Rochester *was* Med City after all—home of the world-famous Mayo Clinic. And I was just a *townie.* But making friends with most anyone had become my superpower—how's *that* for ego?

Looking back, I guess most thought of me as a non-violent *hood,* or maybe a smart kid who hung out with *hoods,* but would rather be a *pill.* A *grass is greener* thing. I felt a pull. **More** *trouble with thinking.* Yeah, I was conflicted. Now, though, it sounds ridiculous. Some pills liked hanging out with a bad boy from *the hood* who didn't mock or threaten or intimidate, but just wanted to be a friend. In return, as a hood/nerd, they lent me a veneer of respectability. We even joined forces in a band we called the *Brass Tax. Yes,* I had befriended a small group of *pills*—and they me—in what would become a musical group, but more importantly, a gang of lifelong friends.

We considered Herb Alpert—*the man*—our musical hero. He was big news back then, even though he played a trumpet, not a guitar. I blew a mean, beat-up old cornet, a short trumpet, in the high school band, too. That is, when I wasn't smoking cigarettes, or dope, or getting speeding tickets, or breaking my own bones using internal-combustion-powered machinery, or conspiring with Hump to pilfer his dad's costly single-malt scotch.

As I allegedly matured, I crossed any and all racial, religious, or cultural boundaries with ease. Though I never suffered fools, I still got along with most everyone. It became clear that few kids my age possessed this skill. But as a teenager, I still remained desperate to belong.

Even in high school, some dealt me a few nerd-antidote cards—because I still possessed the heart of a loner who was too damn smart for his own ego. I even disproved a few of my classmate's old adage (roughly paraphrased), "If you were unfortunate enough to be musically inclined, the only cool instruments in the '60s were the guitar or drums. And the only cool music was rock!" I called bullshit. Then, I walked the talk. Yeah, we used the word *cool* a lot!

The *Tax* even scored a few paying gigs and a local TV appearance on Bernie Lusk's Cancer Telethon. That was big stuff for a half-dozen high school kids in our mid-'60s small town. The white-collar kids *kahooted* with the interesting blue-collar kid from *The Hood*. I knew I was a token. Didn't care. Went both ways. I *always* had fun being a renegade, as long as it didn't involve extravehicular violence.

Chapter 11

Plotting Escape

It was warm for southeastern Minnesota in early December 1968. Life sucked. I didn't dig Shakespeare, but I'd heard a line somewhere, out of context, maybe in a Monty Python comedy sketch: "Now is the winter of our discontent." Yeah, discontent. My parents didn't have any money, but my brother Rod and I never went hungry. My older brother and two sisters were like a generation ahead of us. So, it was me and Roddy.

Now 18, and despite doing okay in a few *accelerated* classes for the smart kids, I'd graduated from Mayo High School with nothing surpassing adequate grades. I reflected on that phenomenon. Blamed it on *hormone impedance.* After all, how well was I going to perform in physics class? I had spent most in-class time penning love notes *on all sides of cardboard boxes* to my sweetheart, the girl one year behind me with the fabulous legs and the shitty home life and an attitude she used to kick my emotional ass on a regular basis.

Somehow, Mom and Dad had scraped together enough coin to pay for my first quarter's tuition at the Rochester Community College after my post-high-school summer of screwing off. Lacking any semblance of enthusiasm, I begrudgingly agreed to attend RCC, less than two miles from our family home. So far, nobody in our clan had graduated from college. I guess I was their beacon of academic hope

That could have been an exceptional situation. Still living at home, so no expenses to speak of. And the launch of my future was being handed to me, but this idiot remained too self-absorbed and petty to see it for what it was—a precious gift. Of course, that never occurred to me. Mom and Dad must have sacrificed a great deal for me to be sitting here in the RCC Student Union drinking cheap coffee with two new friends. God, talk about stupid!

ACROSS FROM ME, Sebastian said, "Are you guys diggin' this crap?"

Rafe looked at the two of us across the round table. "Living with my parents who bitch at me all the time? To study my ass off for required classes I hate? For stupid teachers who know less about life than me? Yeah, right, man."

As the three of us hunkered over our coffees, I rolled my eyes. "So, what are we saying?"

Sebastian hoisted onto his face a conspirator's grin that peeked its way through his red peach-fuzzy whiskers. "What say we score a ride and head west?" I wasn't sure what he meant and said so. Sebastian grinned bigger and bent over the table as if to impart some high-holy secret. "We pool our coin, buy a cheap car, go to the coast. That's where the action is!"

Rafe leaned in too. "Like, now?"

"Like *right* now. This minute. I know a chick with an old Merc she's selling. 25 bucks. You in, Geno?"

Holy shit. We're doing this? I mumbled, "Um, sure. Why not?" Yeah, a another rebel without a clue *or* a cause. I *felt* this was right, despite *knowing* it was not.

Sebastian jumped up so fast his chair toppled over behind him and clattered to the shiny floor. He whooped, "Hell, yeah!" Quite a few heads around us turned, startled. And he hustled toward the door, with me and Rafe in tow. The five-minute walk to my dad's 1960 American Motors Rambler station wagon in the parking lot gave us time to build up a suitable head of steam.

Sebastian could talk the rust off a shiny sewer pipe.

Chapter 12

Witches Brood

We pulled up to the rented house of Sebastian's *friend.* He looked up toward the back of the second-floor apartment with exterior steps that ascended all the way to the third floor. *Is somebody watching us?* We parked my dad's wagon in an overgrown gravel parking space 50 feet behind this beat-up dark-green house with faded yellow trim. Sebastian whispered, "Now these three chicks are kinda out there, ya know what I mean?"

I said, "No, man, I do *not* know what you mean."

He looked over his shoulder before continuing, as if to ensure nobody overheard him. "Okay, they're kinda like... witches, I guess? I don't believe in that shit, but they do. You'll see. We get the car and we get the hell outa here, okay? Here's ten bucks. You guys got another 15 between ya?"

I coughed up nine dollars, including some change. Rafe handed Sebastian another seven dollars. We had more than enough with that, plus another $18 and change between us for food along the way. For fuel, though, we'd be *livin' off the land.*

~

Cass was their... negotiator. Looked to be our age, or a few years older. She liked bright-colored beads. Wore them on both wrists, several strands around her neck, and had strings woven into her dyed-blonde dreadlocks. She also wore a set around her waist and on each ankle. She tapped the toes of her bare right foot as if impatient or pissed that we interrupted... something. Bare feet? In December? And it was damn cold in here. *Huh.*

Her wide and colorful but faded headband matched her equally faded paisley skirt that almost reached her beaded ankles. That headband left her prominent forehead bare, but covered her ears. Couldn't miss her nose ring—the first one I'd ever seen. Well, not so much a ring. Had two opposing crescent moons dangling below her pierced nose. *Weird shit.*

She wore a short, black, threadbare blouse with long puffy sleeves with a waist line showing off her *muffin top*, her chubby tummy, and belly button ring with two more crescent moons opposite each other, but this thing had a short string of black beads dangling from it. My first of those, too. She wasn't very attractive, but I couldn't peel my eyes away. I just stared.

She half-whispered, as if she were in church, or something, but we could all hear. "We'll take twenty-five dollars and not a penny less. Be warned, though. *Ole Blue* burns more oil than gas. If you're okay with that, let's see the cash." She swung two keys connected by green twine in front of Sebastian before continuing. "And lay the few items in the trunk on the grass. We'll deal with those after we're done up here. Deal?"

Her impatience pressed down on us. The air got thicker and heavier, as if their little *coven* had been in the middle of something important when we'd banged on their door unannounced. Must have been the huge plume of incense, or whatever it was, curling up from the floor toward the ceiling that then hung up there like a little storm cloud. The other two girls sat cross-legged on the floor facing each other with some other strange shit scattered between them, surrounding that brass incense burner the size of a lacy-looking soccer ball.

The pair just stared up at the three of us, as did Cass, their vacant expressions unnerving. They gazed at us like a trio of adolescent cockroaches not worth even a half-assed stomping. A big old floor-standing clock in a dark corner ticked like a monster metronome. I noticed both of its hands dangled uselessly down over the six as if they had grown too apathetic to do their job. Like time didn't really matter, but the rhythmic ticking did. Other than that, and the *negotiations, a* quiet blanketed the room like a tomb.

Sebastian paced. No, he swaggered. They didn't appear impressed, now more bored than annoyed by our intrusion. The place stunk. I didn't wanna know. Our fearless leader purred, "Sure, ladies. No problem, assuming it ain't hot."

Cass looked insulted. She chuffed. "The slip is in the glove box."

"Okay, then. But since we're gonna be buyin' a lot of oil, how about you leave us a couple a bucks and take twenty?"

I'd never seen Sebastian move so fast. He threw most of our paper money on a small table next to Cass, snatched the keys hanging from her left index finger, and bolted from the room. *What?* Rafe and I looked at each other with scrunched foreheads and squinty eyes, our hands hanging dumb by our sides. We then realized this had been his plan all along. *Son of a bitch! Never a dull moment with this guy.*

We followed suit. Scurrying from the room like cockroaches skittering away from the light, we scrambled down the outside flight of wooden stairs. I ran to my dad's wagon. Cass screamed something from a now-open second-floor window. *Something about fire and smoke and the fox's spirit? Sounds like Latin or something tossed in there, too. Is she putting a* ***curse*** *on us? Shit!*

Sebastian and Rafe had stopped for a second to listen to what Cass screamed, but then piled into *Ole Blue* like two highwaymen. Fired her up. Spit gravel and grass all the way out of the small parking area. My dad's Rambler caught the brunt of it. I followed. I thought, *A helluva way to start tripping together!*

Chapter 13

Heading West

Each of us had already thrown a backpack together. I'd jammed mine full of important stuff before we'd headed over to *Witch Central.* My second-hand military surplus rig bulged with a bundled-up Marine dress uniform jacket I'd picked up at the Salvation Army for $2. Plus, a wool cap, and a big-ass bag of peanut M&Ms I stole them from my little brother Roddy's stash at home. He now wanted to be called Rod. *But never Rodney!* Same weird name thing with me. They'd saddled me with *Eugene.* I *only* used that on my driver's license... because I had to.

My old used trumpet (paid for by my parents, of course), and a pair of old hiking boots wouldn't fit inside, so both hung from a pair of carabiners near the bag's bottom. Those carabiners had come with the knapsack. We'd left these packs in my parents' detached garage, accessible via an alley in the back. Rafe had scored a couple of five-gallon gas cans and a six-foot chunk of garden hose from his dad's garage. We'd also stashed that *refueling equipment* earlier.

Sebastian pulled our new ride into the alley while I parked my dad's car out front on 7th Avenue SE. Left the keys in the enclosed front porch where he'd find them. I bolted outside, around the house's side yard, and into the alley. So we loaded all our stuff into the Merc and took off like thieves in the night, even though it was early afternoon.

Fortunately, the witches had provided us with more than a half-tank of gas. Sebastian pointed *Ole Blue* west on US Route 14. But only after we scored a five-gallon jug of bulk oil from a local truck service center out on Highway 63 South, not far from Rochester's only truck stop. It was also a good thing Sebastian had cheated the witches. That oil wasn't cheap, but the guy took pity on us with an old can and reclaimed oil. We didn't know about that or proper viscosity, not that we'd have cared.

Sebastian hollered out the window at nobody. "*Goodbye, Minnesota. Hello, California!*" as we left a mighty trail of blue smoke that disappeared almost as fast as us.

OLE BLUE not only billowed smoke behind us but also from beneath her belly. A hole in the floorboards between the front and rear bench seats revealed the absence of a tailpipe and muffler. No wonder she belched thunder and spat sparks. The exhaust pipe had rusted off somewhere forward of the front seat. Smoke filling the car in minutes became problematic. The solution? Too cold to leave the windows rolled down. So we liberated a stop sign from its post on a country road somewhere near Albert Lea, Minnesota, with a rusty screw-driver we found in the glove box.

The sign was too big for the hole, so one side perched atop the transmission hump in the middle of the floor back there. But we made it work. The gas and oil cans wobbled atop that canted sign. Much of the smoke now followed the path of least resistance under the car instead of into it.

We siphoned gas from parked cars in each of several small towns along the way. But not too small, mind you. Sebastian said lots of nosy people populated really tiny towns, which were like a village-wide neighborhood watch on steroids. There lived little old ladies who couldn't sleep with nothing better to do than to spy on everyone, including the likes of us, he said. We found *that* out in Manhattan, Kansas, of all places.

SEBASTIAN STOOD WATCH. I grabbed one of the gas cans from the backseat floor. Rafe flipped open the gas filler lid and unscrewed the cap on a five- or six-year-old Pontiac's gas tank. He fed one end of the short hose into it. I set the can down on the asphalt between the car and the curb. Unscrewed its cap. Rafe started sucking. It took four or five deep inhales.

Unfortunately, as so often happened, he took in a partial lungful of not only vapors but liquid. Started choking as he stuffed his end of the hose into the can. The gas flowed, aided by gravity and a natural siphoning action. But now, Rafe's loud choking and wheezing caught somebody's attention. He topped off his ruckus by vomiting the contents of his empty stomach on the frozen boulevard.

The next thing we knew, a brilliant porch light caught us by surprise. But we needed that gas. So we stayed put. We froze while the hose and gravity did their magic. Freezing in place rendered us invisible during the commission of our crime. Or so we imagined. Then, that damn porch light started flashing. But we needed that gas. It started flashing faster yet. *But we needed that gas!*

An old lady opened her storm door. She shouted through the screen door, "Get out of here, you hooligans! I've called Sheriff Tully! Now, scoot!"

The cat was out of the bag, as they say. We figured that for a small-town sheriff to get dressed, crawl into his prowler, and drive on over there, we still had a few minutes. I waved to the old lady and shrugged. Rafe blew her a sarcastic kiss. Then we both wheeled around toward the narrow street while the gas still flowed into the can. The scent of marijuana hit both of us at the same time. *What the hell?*

Sebastian got up off his butt from the far side of the Merc with a shit-eating grin in response to the old woman's alarm. Turns out we'd chosen our target vehicle directly under a streetlight. We could see him quite well. He was... *smoking a joint?*

Rafe said, "Some lookout *you* are, Se*bastard.* Gimme a hit!" Meanwhile, I jerked out both ends of the hose, dribbling gas down the front of my jeans, and hoisted the now-heavy can into the backseat of the Merc. We'd parked directly behind the Pontiac. I tossed the hose on top of the can. Within the next 60 seconds, we'd piled in and beat feet out of Manhattan, chuckling at the name of this one-horse town, and at the thrill of not getting arrested.

Every 50 miles or so, the dash's oil light alerted us. We'd stop, transfer a gallon of oil into a garden watering jug from the five-gallon oil can on the backseat floor. After popping the hood and pouring oil into the filler until it overflowed (yeah, I know *now* that's not how it's done), we'd stow the mess and roll on.

A well-oiled routine.

Sebastian was taller than the rear bench seat was long. He'd hang his legs onto the floor to get comfortable as he slept while Rafe or I took turns driving. But the gas and oil jugs occupied most of that space. To silence his moaning and groaning, we threw the oil can, our oiling jug, and one of the two gas cans into the trunk. We'd not opened it until then. I did so by sticking my index finger in the hole where the lock used to be and tugged. Pinched my finger, but it popped the latch.

When the lid screeched open after the latch released, the three of us stood on the side of that county road and... stared. More in shock than in surprise. That's when we remembered Witchy Woman's command: ... *lay the few items in the trunk out on the grass. We'll deal with them after we're done up here.* Rafe repeated those words to us. He'd remembered Cass's words verbatim.

I said, "Oh, shit. She was shouting some sort of curse at us out the window, something about... *fire and smoke and a fox!* I thought it was because we cheated 'em out of a few bucks for the car. What if *this* is why she was so pissed?" I down-nodded toward that crap in the trunk.

Sebastian said, "This is way beyond weird, guys." We stood there, gaping at a board about a foot wide and a little over two feet long. Nailed to it was... the stretched-out skin of a... baby fox? It looked... fresh. It even stank a little. Beside it lay a set of small colored bottles and several bundles of grass or some kind of herb.

Decades later, I realized that must have been sage. I *now* know people use sage in a spiritual practice called *smudging*. In many traditions, sage smoke carries prayers to the spirit world. It's used in rituals to invite guidance from ancestors or higher powers. This herb carries deep spiritual significance that spans many cultures. It's not just for cooking—it's a powerful tool for cleansing, healing, and connecting with higher energies or dissipating negative energies within a space. So they say.

But back then, those large, fragrant bundles of dried, grassy-looking stuff just seemed... mystical, especially lying close to that dead fox's skin all splayed out, nailed to that plank. Sebastian made sure the bundles weren't weed. And that carton of six tiny bottles with cork stoppers? We also wondered about a purple garment—a robe?—piled there, too. Fertile young imaginations ran amok that day!

. . .

But we came to our senses with a few flippant remarks—a reasonable defense mechanism. Rafe slammed the trunk lid *way* harder than necessary. We shrugged, laughed at our own silly wonderings, piled into the big two-door oil burner, and continued our trek west.

Chapter 14

Fire in the Hole

I TOOK MY TURN DRIVING FOR A COUPLE OF HOURS BEFORE stretching out on the backseat. Profound fatigue had plagued me ever since we'd left Rochester. Didn't much like the feeling. A dark cloud suffocated us, like the sun setting way too early on a December day, and imagining Old Man Winter forbidding it ever to rise again.

Was I burdened with guilt at abandoning my college studies only a few weeks in, after my poor parents scraped together the bucks to pay for it? Or was it something else? Honestly, the memory of those feelings eluded me at the time, but scraped at me later. That night, I drifted off to sleep in the backseat with nightmares of a family of young foxes squealing at me for desiccating their destiny and for burning them alive. They just wanted to drink coffee in the RCC Student Union. *What?*

The air in my nostrils seared my nose hairs. A fit of violent coughing awakened me. I lay on the backseat facing forward while my entire body jostled violently. Took a few beats before I recognized the gas can's shape silhouetted by... *flames?* The Merc wandered all over the road as Rafe drove. Had he *fallen asleep?* Sebastian had. I saw him slumped against his passenger window, snoring.

I hollered, "Rafe! Wake up! We got a fire back here!" The car danced its way toward the wrong ditch. And we were *speeding up!* I punched Rafe's shoulder. Hard. He lurched awake as he jerked the wheel. I hollered again, "Fire!" That roused Sebastian, too. Took a few seconds, but Rafe wrestled us back to the right side of the country road and slammed on the brakes. We skidded to a stop on the gravel shoulder.

By that point, the three of us coughed non-stop as our lungs protested the now-smoke-filled car. We were explosively expelling those poisonous fumes. I had to wait for the guys to swing open one of the car's two doors. Until they did, they held me hostage back there with that fire and smoke. I beat on the seat back with a fury born of respiratory distress.

They left both doors wide open as they each tumbled out on all fours. I pushed the back of the split front bench seat forward and stumbled out through the driver's door. Collapsed down onto my hands and knees, too. Took a few beats before there was a break in our coughing.

Finally, with wild eyes, I wheezed, "Hey, we gotta put out that fire before that near-empty gas can lights up. That'll take out the whole car!" Rafe grabbed one can, I snatched the other from the passenger side. Their handles were almost too hot to hold.

Sebastian: "We don't have any water!"

Me: "Fuck water. Piss on it!"

Rafe: "What? Oh, yeah!"

Sebastian: "Both sides. Geno, you get the passenger side. Hose 'er down!"

We got to it. And it worked! A car slowed as it passed by. Although columns of smoke billowed out of both *Ole Blue's* doors, the scene must have been too bizarre to consider stopping.

We'd not made a pit stop in a while, fortunately. Our reserves dampened the burning carpet fibers that dangled down through the hole in the floor enough to kill the worst of the flames. The metal sign covering the hole smoked hot enough on the passenger's side to bubble the paint. But not too hot to pluck it out of the car from the roadside.

Having emptied his bladder first, Rafe ran to the trunk, popped it, and grabbed the strange purple robe. He beat the now-exposed carpet that still smoldered around the edge of the hole. With the windows rolled down, we closed the doors and collapsed in shock and exhaustion at the edge of the ditch for the better part of half an hour.

Sebastian broke the prolonged silence and said, "Well, that was interesting."

I took time to cough one last time and croaked, "Coulda been a lot worse than the stink of hot urine."

Rafe muttered, "Fuckin' witches...."

Both Sebastian and I responded in chorus. "*What?*"

"It's that curse, man! Isn't it obvious?"

I said, "Oh, bullshit, man. Old car, naked exhaust, carpet dingleberries... do the math, dude!"

Rafe looked worried. "We shouldn't a oughta crossed them witches. I'm tellin' ya!"

Sebastian said, "Whatever. Let's rip out that carpet, get our sign back in place. From now on, we keep *all* the fucking cans in the fucking trunk. Chuck that other shit out."

Rafe's eyes grew as wide as his taught face allowed. "No, man, we gotta send that stuff back to 'em with an apology. Get 'em ta lift this curse! No more screwin' around with this shit, here. This is serious, you guys."

Sebastian hauled himself up out of that ditch, exposing twin wet spots where his skinny rump crunched and melted the frosty grass. Brushed off his crusty jeans, smirked at Rafe and said, "You for real, man?" He marched over to the still-open trunk, grabbed that board, and tossed it way out into the ditch. Same with the bundles of weeds, although he paused as if he considered smoking it before a half-assed series of tosses. Like that's all they deserved. The colored bottles followed. Picked up the charred purple thing from the ground by the passenger's door, gave it a kick. "Okay, let's went, gents."

And off we gents went.

~

Over the next couple of days, Rafe grew increasingly agitated. Not because the entire car stunk of roasted piss. That had mostly cooked off. Both Sebastian and I noticed his crazed eyes and jerky gestures. Sebastian said, "A'right, what's goin' on, man? You look like you got a cattle prod jammed up your rectum. You're not still thinkin' on that witchy shit, are ya?"

Rafe had taken to chewing a plastic beef jerky wrapper from a snack he'd devoured days earlier. Bunched the whole thing in his mouth except for the very end of that long skinny thing which he clutched in his fist. He'd then slowly pull it out between his clenched teeth like he was stretching taffy. He'd repeat this several times a minute, non-stop, for *hours*. His eyes darted around like he was being hunted, and sleep eluded him. When it didn't, he'd jerk awake in the backseat loud enough that we'd hear his whelp over the roar of *Ole Blue's* tumultuous exhaust.

I half-shouted back to him from the front passenger's seat, "Alright, Rafe. Spill."

He half-screeched and half-whined, "It's those fuckin' witches, you guys. We shouldn'ta oughta disrespected that stuff in the trunk." Neither Sebastian nor I laughed at his outrageous fear. The whole weird episode weighed on our minds, too.

Chapter 15

Wiccans

I SHARE THIS NEAR-CATASTROPHIC EPISODE WITH YOU BECAUSE I still visualize this entire fire 'n smoke 'n pissin' 'n witchy thing with crystal clarity 60 years later. I'd later conjure an opinion about how the power of our beliefs shaped our actions that night so long ago, especially Rafe's. We'd clung to a Halloween-like stereotype of witches, their motivations, and the seemingly *magical* effects that words and intentions could have on three stupid teenagers a thousand miles distant. That was all we knew.

I've since learned most folks who practiced what we called witchcraft back then were likely *Wiccans*. *The Craft* is a common name for the spiritual and magical practices of *Wicca*. Besides spell work, Wicca is an intensely personal, nature-centered path of growth, healing, and empowerment through creating and leveraging sacred energies within and around us.

For example, Wiccans, Native Americans, and others use sage to purge negative energies in a space. They employ tinctures—liquid extracts—made by soaking parts of plants, such as leaves or roots, in alcohol or vinegar to draw out the potency of their active compounds.

Usually stored in small bottles, like the ones we'd found in *Ole Blue's* trunk.

Herbal medicine often uses tinctures, too. In fact, I now know many wiccan practices have much in common with modern holistic medicine, also called integrative medicine by respected medical institutions like the Mayo Clinic. But *witchcraft's* unfortunate stereotype has turned popular ideology against Wiccans and their practices.

I've since connected several other similarities between Wicca and Christianity. For example, a *spell* may be another word for *prayer.* And the practice of Wiccan *intentions* shares more similarities than differences with Christian *devotions.* Likewise, if we didn't know better, we'd never associate the positive and now popular and broadly accepted practices of *mindfulness and meditation* with Wiccan concepts. Yet, there it is. *Perspective!*

Had we only known back then.

Chapter 16

Denver

Two days later, we arrived in Denver. Sebastian had a friend who'd moved there from Rochester. Of course, when we arrived, a party raged. While I had been dating Kay, she grew angry when I told her I was going on an open-ended road trip... without her. So, we *broke up*. But she still tugged at my heartstrings. A lot.

Sebastian's friend hooked each of us up with one of his female friends at the party. I sat and talked with a nice girl. Her name was Rina, or Rena. Something like that. We'd smoked some weed, and I was pretty high, as I recall. Rena wanted to escape the noise of the crowded apartment's living room. Other than the bathroom, that meant the place's only bedroom. *Uh-oh.*

1968 was the year that found its way into the history books as the infamous *Summer of Love.* Lots of folks, far more than ever before, treated sex as little more than an enjoyable recreational activity. A surrogate for love. Not me. I was taught differently. Summer had passed, but it was still 1968. And I found myself almost a thousand miles from home with a beautiful girl sitting on the side of a bed looking up at me suggestively. *Shit!*

"Um, look, Rena. You are totally awesome. I'm just a kid from

Minnesota that's still got it bad for a girl back there. Make sense?" I shrugged and puckered one cheek with a half-assed smirk of apology.

She looked shocked. No, surprised. Then, her expression softened in the next instant. "Wow. Hey, um, that's pretty cool, G. Wanna just talk for awhile? I don't wanna go back out there yet." She patted the spot next to her on the bed.

Not sure why, but after saying nothing with a whole lot of words, we lay down on the bed, shoulder to shoulder, staring at the ceiling and... dreaming. Out loud. It remained an open question whether this hick from the cornfields of Minnesota felt embarrassment or pride that he'd held the moral high ground. Either way, we had a pleasant conversation, not that I recall a single word of it. And then we fell asleep.

The next morning, I awoke recalling the previous evening. Rena was already awake and propped up on one elbow, staring at me. *Uh-oh,* I thought again. She said, "Hey, you look awful. Wanna go grab some breakfast and maybe do a little shopping?"

"Um, I don't have any money."

"Oh, that's okay, G," that's what she called me, "I have some. C'mon."

She bounced off the bed, ruffled and flipped her long and straight reddish-blonde hair, never once glancing at the huge mirror on a nearby dresser. *Interesting.* I did. *Ugh!*

Turned out Rena's father owned six major-league department stores in the Denver area. Not sure if I was a stray she'd adopted. Maybe that was her thing. But after a nice breakfast in a diner a few blocks away, we took a taxi to one of her dad's stores, a huge multi-level affair in a fancy mall. She bought herself a few things, and a few more for me. A sweater and a scarf, maybe? Rena winked and conspiratorially muttered, "Friends and family discount." Again, memory fails on the details, but I became convinced this was all a dream.

It was chilly, but we did a lot of walking and talking. She struck me as lonely, although I didn't understand why. I suspect she enjoyed having a boy for a friend who was interested in more than just getting into her pants. I must have filled that need.

~

Living with a bunch of friends who shared costs in those days was the most natural thing in the world. We returned to the apartment where we'd met, and the party still simmered with my buddies Sebastian and Rafe still taking part. But after a few days, their enthusiasm dwindled, especially for Rafe. He pulled Sebastian and me aside. "Guys, I called my parents this morning to see if they'd wire me some cash. They told me I got a frickin' draft letter!"

"What's that?" I truly had no idea.

"You kidding, Geno? That's when you gotta go to Vietnam and shoot people, man! Or get dead yourself. Into the Army for two entire years! Aw, I am so totally screwed."

Sebastian looked him over before slant-glancing at me. He muttered, "Yeah, me too. I been ignoring it."

Rafe looked incredulous. "You can't ignore that, man! You don't report within 30 days, they throw your ass in jail! Oh, man, what're we gonna do?"

Sebastian didn't miss a beat. He'd obviously already put some serious thought into this. "Gotta find me first. We go to Canada, man. Keep-outa-jail-free card. Right now we're closer to the border than we are to Frisco, anyway. We cross, they can't touch us."

"*What?* You nuts?"

"Dude, you rather get your ass shot off somewhere in a jungle? I'm gone. You guys with me, or not?"

I listened with wide eyes and a dropped jaw, not contributing a single word to this surreal discussion. Sebastian had decided. Had this been his plan all along? Probably. Rafe looked like he was suffering. He had always loaded his emotions with a hair trigger, like with the whole witch thing. Finally, he said, "Oh, what the fuck. Let's do it. I ain't goin' to no war. That's bullshit, anyway. How about you, Geno?"

This decision flew in the face of my every belief. Siphoning gas was one thing. But leaving the country? Running from the law? I didn't know the word at the time, but I'd be a felon—a serious criminal. I did know this was a huge deal. No doubt about that.

After five seconds of stewing, I muttered, "Naw, not me, man. I ain't been drafted, I don't think. Gonna hang here with Rena for a minute. Then keep heading west. Spot me ten bucks for my share of the Merc, and we're good. Okay?"

They both looked a little disappointed, but not a lot. We weren't much more than casual travel buddies, anyway. Besides, they both looked over at Rena and grinned. They got it. Or they thought they did.

They left the next day, and I was stuck in Denver without wheels. I told Rena. She said, "What'll you do now, G?"

I fudged my situation a little—an escape strategy—even though I didn't really need one. "Well, I'm supposed to meet some folks in San Francisco in a week, but I don't know how I'm gonna get there, now."

She looked a little sad, but then she grinned. I'll never forget what she whispered so nobody else in the apartment heard. They were all out of it, anyway. "What good is being rich if I can't help a friend. You scared of flying?" She pecked me on the cheek, popped up from the floor, and said, "I gotta call Daddy's travel agent."

Yup, it was a dream, alright. Shit like this just didn't happen to this kid raised on the wrong side of the tracks from the cornfields of Minnesota. I am still not entirely convinced that really happened. Who knows? Maybe I'm *still* dreaming.

Chapter 17

Penniless in San Francisco

Three days later, Rena and I shared half a joint in the backseat of a taxi before saying goodbye at the Denver airport. The driver didn't object, as long as we shared the occasional hit with him. A sign of the times. I remember thinking, *We'd never get away with this in a Rochester cab,* although I'd never been in a cab in *Rotch*.

Rena pecked me on the cheek. That had become kind of her thing. Like a big sister. I was okay with that. We promised to keep in touch, but never did. Just like I never heard what happened to Sebastian and Rafe.

I arrived at the San Francisco International Airport after a two-and-a-half-hour flight—my very first time on an airplane. Nothing more than a blur in my altered state of semi-consciousness, though. Rena didn't settle for anything but the best dope. Moderation was deemed over-rated in those days.

Sitting in the arrivals terminal with my backpack on the floor between my knees, it was as though the colossal airport had paralyzed me. Must have sat there for a couple of hours. I considered stoking up the joint Rena gifted me. Glad I didn't. It grew dusky outside. I had almost no money. I wouldn't take a cash handout from Rena, even though she'd stuffed a few bucks in my pocket. Accepting that plane ticket was bad enough.

But now, no way did I have enough for a twenty-dollar taxi into the city. Sixteen bucks and change, a ratty old backpack with a few clothes, a pair of old boots, and a banged up trumpet. All the essentials. Except Rod's peanut M&Ms were long gone, even though I valiantly tried to ration them—just two per day— like they were worth their weight in gold. You'd have thought I was shipwrecked on a deserted island without essential malnourishment.

Hitchhiking was common, but not on a densely traveled four-lane urban highway with a 70-MPH speed limit like the 101 into the biggest city I'd ever threatened to visit. And certainly not at night, during a rainstorm, on a road where the shoulder fell off into a frickin' ravine. Oh, and the signs proclaimed that hitchhiking was illegal here. I remember thinking that was the deepest and darkest ditch I'd ever seen, like a west coast earthquake had opened up the earth parallel to the 101. The traffic's headlights and taillights streaked by above me at what seemed the speed of light. I never felt so alone, and yeah... scared shitless.

I held my thumb high, but had no idea whether anyone even saw me in this madness, much less my stupid little thumb. Before I left the airport to find a ride, somebody told me it was about twenty miles into the city. *Twenty miles? Of* ***this***? I'd wasted more than an hour of daylight just to hike out to the highway after getting lost a few times wandering the maze of heavily trafficked airport roads. And now, I feared getting flattened like a bug on somebody's grill. I felt that small and insignificant. But then, I got lucky, or so I thought at the time.

An older sedan slowed and pulled toward me at the precipice of the ditch-slash-abyss. I ran up to the car's rear ditch-side door, stumbling on the gravel slope bordering that concrete slab, and grabbed the door handle. Yanked it open against the wind, and hoisted first my pack onto the backseat and then my skinny little keister.

I sat beside a pretty big guy back there. He and the two bruisers in the front seat gave me a ride into the city, alright, but for the entire way, these characters tried to... *seduce me!* A real 1968 San Francisco welcome, I'd learn later. My first encounter with what we called *homos* in high school. Another stereotype to be feared. So, as soon as I saw plenty of lights around the car, I asked them to let me out.

They had transported me into the city, as promised, but I had no idea where I was. Didn't matter. Time to escape that damn car, not that they were overly aggressive or anything. I'd learn later my fear had made me irrational. Got to where I levied a threat. "You guys don't wanna get charged with kidnapping, do ya? How 'bout you let me out, now, 'kay?"

The car screeched to a halt, the right rear door flew open, and I tumbled out. Landed on my butt on the asphalt. But I had been liberated. And damn clever, I thought. Yeah, they were pissed. Coulda handled that differently, but coulda gone real bad, too. Dumb, small-town teen. Had I led them on without realizing it? I didn't think so, but this was *such* unexplored territory for me.

Must've been close to midnight, but still lots of folks out and about. Asked a few passersby for directions—most only knew their own neighborhood. One woman said, "Why you wanna go *there,* boy?" She said it was too far to walk. So, I asked a bus driver who stopped to pick up a bunch of folks. I had enough coins for the fare.

By 2 am, and three or four transfers later, I found my Minnesota friend's apartment. She'd told me to definitely look her up if I ever escaped the frozen tundra. After humping up five flights of stairs in the ancient building on the corner of Haight and Broderick, I knocked on a green door. Flashed back to the witch's green house and shivered. I heard thumping music. Not loud, but it sounded like a party. Later, I'd learn it was just another weeknight. Some scruffy dude answered the door. Too tired to offer him anything more than a weak smile, I mumbled, "Claire here?"

"C'mon in, man. She's over there." His return smile seemed genuine.

I spotted my friend on a lumpy old couch covered with what looked like a horse blanket. She stopped talking to a hairy dude and swung her unfocused gaze toward the front door where I still stood. She spotted me from across the smallish room filled with at least eight others, all engulfed in a pungent haze. Most looked older. *Real hippies!* But what did I know? No small-town crowd here.

She squealed, "Gene? You *made it!* I never in a million years thought…." She got up, rushed over, and threw her arms around me. Crushed me! Claire reminded me of Janis Joplin—not real pretty, but she lit up a room big-time.

I said with as much enthusiasm as I could muster. "Hey, Claire. *Really* good to see you. Listen, I gotta sit dow—" The room tilted. My vision dimmed before…. I must have fainted or something. Next thing I know? I'm lying on that lumpy couch with a cold washrag on my forehead. Some tall guy with the longest hair I'd ever seen on a dude stood over me. He wore a blue shirt with a *US Post Office* patch on his right shoulder. But the guy also wore the most colorful and blousy pants I'd ever seen on a guy. Damn-near a floor-length dress. Somehow, he pulled it off.

He twanged with a southern accent, "Hey, little man, you shore do make an entrance!" He chortled and patted me on the shoulder as I lay there staring up at him. "Name's George. You're Gene. You might-could need sustenance, little man." Not a single question in the bunch. "Welcome!"

Claire sat cross-legged on the floor, rubbing my shoulder. "Safe to assume you need a place to crash, Gene?" She grinned, already knowing the answer.

"Um, yeah. Guess so."

"Okay, George?" She looked up at George, the tall mail carrier who looked tropical or oriental or Hawaiian, and Indian from the waist down. He grinned and nodded. "But he'll have to chip in." He looked at me but spoke to Claire. I was her friend.

"He's good. I'm sure he understands. Right, Gene?"

"Sure. Whatever I can, you guys." I then realized George was right. I must have grown weak from lack of food and water. Nothing to eat since early the previous morning at the diner in Denver with Rena. And lots of exertion since. And stress. Eating and drinking had been low priorities after my first-ever flight, plus avoiding getting squished on the 101. Not to mention almost getting screwed by a trio of hairy monsters, *and* surviving my first experience with public transit. Oh, and *then* hoofing up five flights of stairs to top it off? Stupid, in retrospect.

George paused, nodded, and grinned again. "Good enough, partner. Ain't a fancy pad, but we stay warm and dry here by hunkerin' down together."

So began my partnership with a mailman, a record salesman, Claire who busked her violin music around the neighborhood parks for loose change, plus a few others who didn't work. Well, not regular jobs, anyway. They panhandled to those who visited the hood to take pictures of the hippies, or to score some dope. Friendly folks, this bunch. I felt like I belonged with these free spirits. At least a helluva lot more than I ever did with Rafe, Sebastian, or anybody at the Rochester Community College. But I missed Kay.

Chapter 18

Drafted!

Two days later, I pawned my old boots for a couple of bucks to chip in for a ten-pound bag of rice for *the pad*. Later, I hocked my trumpet to help rent a storefront. The horn didn't get played much these days anyway. Too much other cool stuff happening. Plus, one of the three valves no longer worked. I think my tumble out of the gay-mobile took its toll on my old horn.

Claire's merry little band of do-gooders fancied themselves performing an important public service. I now considered myself one of them. That thrilled me. And now we had a dingy little shop from which to provide that service. We collected information on the current draft laws, which turned out to be a challenge. The information around them changed often back then. We also compiled key contacts for jobs in select Canadian cities for those willing to leave the country permanently. And we developed contacts at the local news outlets for those who resisted but stayed to face prison and make a show of it.

I remember our feral outrage at what we perceived as political gamesmanship with the lives of kids just like us. The term our group used to describe the Vietnam *conflict?* A *political football.* How American, right? But this was no game to us. This was much more than an abstract intellectual concept for the group—and now for me. We all had friends or family who were getting drafted and killed in this immoral one-ring circus. Yes, we strongly believed this, and we acted accordingly within the scope of our First Amendment *obligation.*

EARLIER IN 1968, reports said that the enemy —as defined by some politicians after we invaded Vietnam—slaughtered a thousand of our boys *every week.* They were victims in a huge operation called the *Tet Offensive. Tet* was a major military campaign launched by North Vietnamese and Viet Cong forces on January 30, 1968, coinciding with the *Tet* holiday, their lunar New Year. We were determined to help those who had been drafted make an informed decision.

These extraordinary casualties and nationwide protests that captured media attention turned public opinion against this conflict on the far side of the planet. That was the beginning of the end of American involvement in that prolonged war. It took several more years, though. U.S. involvement in the Vietnam War ended on January 27, 1973, with the signing of the Paris Peace Accords, although the last American troops didn't leave Vietnam until March 29, 1973.

INDULGE ME IN A BRIEF FLASH-FORWARD. They had drafted me in early 1969. Not long after the *Tet Offensive* enraged the youth of America while I was still in San Francisco speaking my mind. Then, they honorably discharged me after four years of service in February 1973, the same time the war ended. It seems silly to say so, but I felt I had played a part, however small, in ending that travesty by *participating* in history. But that wasn't the end of it.

Without exception, everyone who survived one or more tours *in-country* came back irrevocably changed, none for the better. That holds true for most veterans who survive the carnage of combat. I can't help but to mention here the depth of my personal sorrow concerning the concept of war. General Dwight D. Eisenhower, our thirty-fourth president, said,

> **"I hate war as only a soldier who has lived it can, only as one who has seen its brutality, its futility, its stupidity."**

I quote the genius Albert Einstein elsewhere in these pages because his insights lend clarity for lesser intellectuals like me. He lamented,

> **"Older men declare war. But it is youth that must fight and die."**

And back then, it was the older men in Washington who had lost touch with their humanity to impose their immorality, their *stupidity* upon the rest of the country and its youth.

I've now lived long enough to watch history repeat itself more than once. I am staunch in my belief that we Americans are too bloody quick to pull a trigger!

My circle of friends in 1968, both in Rochester and in San Francisco, was *incensed.* We believed that we *must* take action. And if we did, along with so many others, we'd make a difference. As long as we obeyed the law, we did not care about the potential target on our backs, just for exercising our constitutional rights. At least, that is my retrospective as I look back on that brief period of my own history. And as a Minnesotan in 2026, I see history repeating itself yet again.

~

So we had rented that beat-up little shop full of cobwebs and spiders and hope. I forget where exactly, but it was in our neighborhood—*The Haight*. I don't even remember what we called this little venture. We expected someone to shut us down, but they didn't. We flew under the radar as much as possible, as they say. Must've worked. Or nobody cared.

We crafted, copied, and dropped leaflets all over The Haight and a few of the Bay Area's college campuses. We covered City College, San Francisco State U where several peaceful war protests had turned violent at the hands of a few trouble-makers, even UC Berkeley and People's Park way over in Alameda County across the bay.

Then… I received *my* draft notice! The earth quaked beneath my feet. I'd call my parents from a payphone once in a while just to let them know I was okay. I gave them permission to open *the letter*. It said I was to serve two years in the army. The subtext? It was a virtual certainty they'd send me to Vietnam after a period of training where I'd be taught how to efficiently kill other human beings. I was to report to the Minneapolis Recruiting Center within 30 days of the date on the letter. A week had already passed.

I didn't consider myself a conscientious objector where I'd refuse to serve. But my childhood indoctrination into Christianity taught me never to take another person's life—ever—the Sixth Commandment. But I knew if put in the position, that choice may not remain mine. For most of us, survival trumps ethics, sometimes even morals. Well, I knew I still had a choice, a decision to make, based on my conviction —*no* war is holy or just or moral. Period.

Word had spread. More than a few our age, late teens, early twenties—I was nineteen—began sauntering into our little shop. Most scratched their heads, clueless as to what it meant to be drafted into military service, or if it was even compulsory.

Most didn't want to break the law. But some didn't care. They simply failed to show up at their appointed recruiting center by a certain date in response to their draft letter. And a few—those who decided not to leave the country but refused to be gathered up as cannon fodder—wanted to make a clear statement of protest. They knew they'd go to prison. In one instance, we organized a media event, so they'd be hauled off in handcuffs in front of an army of journalists, cameras, and friends with signs of protest. I wasn't in San Francisco all that long, but that was a rainy winter I will *never* forget.

One thing I'd learned hanging out with this group of critical-thinking, action-oriented hippies in the Bay Area? If you get drafted, you're granted the "opportunity" to enlist in a different military service within 30 days. From a draft board perspective, the US Coast Guard was considered a military service even though it reported to the Department of Transportation back then. It now reports to the Department of Defense/*War* (*ugh*)—since September 11, 2001.

So, my parents wired me more money they didn't have via Western Union to fly home and to report to the Minneapolis recruiting center before the deadline. They required me to take and pass a tough test to get into the USCG. I wasn't the only kid to realize this was an option, and getting in had become a competitive affair. I passed muster. Tests and I got along just fine. The only USCG recruits sent *in-country*—to Vietnam—were those who volunteered. I did not. You already know why.

I was just another rebel without a clue. And then something changed.

That decision meant that instead of surviving two years of combat in a Southeast Asia jungle, I'd get to serve twice as long—four years—driving boats and maintaining buoys and foghorns. Plus, I'd be rescuing people instead of killing them. Didn't know at the time, but I'd get shot at occasionally by smugglers or yacht thieves during my four years as a *coastie*. And I almost drowned on more than one occasion as a rescue swimmer, but I never had to shoot anyone.

The more time that passes since that period of my life, the better I feel about my decision. But also for having taken a moral stand against the edicts of immoral politicians on the national stage. I consider my decision to enlist in the USCG another pivotal moment in my life. My *belief* turned *decision* became *actions* that produced *results*. I was involved in saving over fifty souls from likely or certain death, including myself a few times. But more of that story is coming. I just didn't know how frickin' hard it would be.

Chapter 19

Proposed at 19

Despite dire predictions from everyone about our future together, my high school girlfriend Kay and I felt we were destined for each other. We'd make a life together work. Somehow. Even though we couldn't have been more different.

For almost two tempestuous years in high school, she and I had verbally dueled fiercely and loved passionately. We'd argued *daily*, mostly about religion and who was the boss of whom. Yeah, that sounds profoundly silly now. An informal poll by our somewhat homogenous circle of friends at the time voted us least likely to succeed as a couple. After countless break-ups and make-ups, ever the romantic, I'd proposed to Kay over the phone from boot camp in Alameda, California, March 1969. But I shudder to remember that now.

I still hate myself for how clumsily I'd handled that. I was a sorely conflicted 19 years young. She was still an 18-year-old senior in high school with serious morning sickness. In reality, that phone call was yet another moment that changed the direction of my life—and hers. I had not even considered marriage, at least not that soon.

Boot camp was an emotional and physical cyclone. They kept us exhausted and confused in a tempest of physical and emotional exertion. They reshaped us with an iron fist. Some claim Coast Guard basic training is second only in toughness to Marine boot camp. I wasn't sure what that meant. Just something someone told me.

But I became a believer after crawling on my belly, half-naked, through near-icy mud in the gloom before dawn most mornings in the briny Oakland Estuary that swirled around Coast Guard Island. And *high-porting* my dummy-loaded 11.25-pound M1 rifle for ten-mile hikes/runs? Think overhead pushups with a twelve-pound barbell while running. *That* made me want to give up. I had committed a terrible mistake by signing up for this shit-hole job. But *nobody* quit *this* job. The slippery stench of that slimy mud clung to my nostrils for years.

Even though I was in the best shape of my life after weeks of these stupid drills and a pretty grim diet, I wanted to go home. To Mom and Dad, and especially to Kay. I cursed my San Francisco friends—Claire and George and the rest—who were no doubt still partying less than twenty miles west of here. They'd gotten me into this shit. And now, I was only an indentured servant compelled to perform endless fucking drills, mindless and pointless by definition.

THEN THERE WAS that life-changing phone call to Kay. I had just intended to say *hi*. Instead, my heart shot into my throat and struck me speechless when she whispered just two words: "I'm pregnant."

A half-dozen other boots hovered nearby, waiting to use that outdoor public phone on a pedestal at the edge of the goddamn quadrangle. That's where drill instructors hammered us with verbal and physical abuse eighteen hours a day when we weren't slinging mud or hiking the hills. They demanded we perform like trained monkeys. Push-ups, sit-ups, squats, fireman's carries of the idiot next to us. And running endlessly in place, shouting, "Sir, yes, sir!" in response to their every stupid insult and each pointless question barked at us. Like we were little more than disobedient amoebas to be squashed with military discipline.

I got whacked on the back of my head so many times I wondered if I'd go brain-dead. I didn't worry so much about the kicks to my ass or the slugs to my back. Oh, and don't get me started on the *endless* hours of senseless pool drills. I alternated between holding my breath for longer than humanly possible and jumping from a tower that looked to be a hundred feet above the water. All to rescue two-hundred-pound dummies from certain dummy death.

So, I'd responded to sweet Kay's declaration of impending motherhood—*with our child*—with the most insensitive comment in the history of intolerable jerks: "What? I gotta go." Worse, I then followed it up with an even more callous gesture: I softly hung up the phone without uttering another word. I ran like a spoiled crybaby back to my barracks, stuck my head in my half-height locker containing everything I now owned, all government-issued, and bawled like a self-indulgent *child*.

It took me, what? Two days? Three? To call her back and propose? I joke about that now, but back then, how self-centered can one shallow little prick be? And into what emotional purgatory must I have cast that poor sweet girl in her shaken and vulnerable state? I take minor consolation in the fact that I was in a purgatory of my own, whatever that meant. Some feeble excuse, right?

A WEEK or two later into my basic training, another switch flipped inside of me. I transformed from a crybaby to a confident hard-ass who'd shout, *Semper Par*—Always Ready—with immense pride, followed by a snappy salute, almost eagerly anticipating the next hurdle to clear. *Semper Paratus* was the Coast Guard's motto, our equivalent of the Marine's *Semper Fi.* From then on, I not only kept up with the pack, I sometimes led it. Felt damn good.

Now armed with a shit-ton of informative classroom lectures on the critical importance of our jobs after graduating and deploying, we listened and learned how to do them. Then we drilled. Dawn to dusk. Gladly. Because we'd be our victims' only lifeline. We *dared not let them down.* My chest swelled. Was *this* the worthwhile purpose that justified all the chickenshit that I—*we*—had endured the last several weeks? Perhaps *this* rebel had found a clue at last!

And then, yet another unexpected course change intervened. A chief warrant officer—a high-ranking *god* from a raw boot's perspective—came around asking if anyone played a musical instrument. His uniform was the coolest ever. Lots of gold stripes, medals, the works. Even sported a blue ribbon dangling from the right side of his blinding white officer's hat that trailed down onto his right shoulder. Like it announced strength and honor, or... royalty?

He represented the United States Coast Guard Marching Band. Didn't know they—*we*—even had a band. He was one impressive dude. Walked like a panther on the prowl, with every movement planned before executed. But what did I know? He said they were an elite unit that precision-marched in parades and ceremonies all over the West Coast. They performed for dignitaries, community and various other events. They also marched with the USCG Color Guard. Claimed it was a high honor to be asked to join.

My head was full of fantasies at that point. I only vaguely heard the rest of his pitch. But I did hear him say they needed a trumpet player—on a temporary basis. I wanted in. After all, I played the trumpet in high school! And in a band! That marched! My hand shot up. So, he invited me to audition.

They must've liked what they heard because they asked me to join. I'd even take my turn blowing camp reveille near the flagpole to wake up the entire base, and taps at night for lights out. Also, sometimes I'd blow morning and evening colors for hoisting and securing the flag if I wasn't touring with the band. Pomp 'n circumstance, baby! I suddenly transformed from being an ordinary boot in my hundred-recruit company to someone who possessed a unique skill and purpose.

Being a member of the Coast Guard Band came with perks. Instead of pointless marching on field hikes around Coast Guard Island with a forty-pound backpack and slinging an M1 carbine, I practiced with the band in their musical and marching programs. We marched and performed in formation as a tight unit with the honor guard. The coolest thing ever. And that new trumpet they entrusted to me? A two-tone silver and gold work of engraved art. They also taught me how to move. With form, purpose, and deliberation. I became a panther on the prowl, too!

We practiced rousing marches and other inspirational melodies. Without end. We'd either perch in the band room to practice a new number, or march while performing the same tune over and over again until we *nailed it*. We maneuvered and played as a single hive mind. A thrilling experience.

Shortly, I was as ready as any of them. We were *loud, proud, and ready to tour!* The only catch? They expected me to commit to an additional four weeks on Coast Guard Island in Alameda. An easy decision, even though it seemed like an eternity. I'd even discussed it with Kay over the phone.

Two weeks later, we marched in a parade in Sacramento, California's capital. I don't recall the occasion. But I remember buying Kay's engagement *and* wedding rings on an installment plan at a local jeweler during some rare free time before boarding the bus back to Alameda. After all, I received a regular paycheck now! *Free time off base during basic training? Incredible!* I marched and performed with the band at several other venues over the ensuing month.

That all was so... *weird*, a word that kept popping into my vocabulary-starved consciousness back then. My feared maturity happened without my noticing. I was a proud member of an elite military unit for a time and bought a wedding ring for my *fiancée* while rambling around Northern California? Like I said, *weird.*

And then it ended. I graduated from basic training. When I enlisted, I had negotiated to get stationed in the Midwest after basic, as close as possible to my pregnant girlfriend. I remember laying it on pretty thick. It worked. My recruiter had been my advocate. After a quick leave in Minnesota, I was to report to USCG Station Belle Isle in Detroit, Michigan, a little over 800 miles east of Rochester. A doable driving distance! I was on my way. But I had something important to take care of first.

Chapter 20

Married at 19

While on my short leave after boot, our poverty-practical wedding topped a whopping hundred bucks. Total. Most of the cost went for cake and sandwich fixings. The ceremony took place at the old First Baptist Church in downtown Rochester in the spring of 1969.

I remember the billboard-sized green sign on the church's roof that declared, *Jesus Saves!* Some hoodlums had added with black spray paint, *Green Stamps.* Remember trading stamps? Not unlike more modern *rewards* programs, or collecting *points*. A stupid joke.*

Because of an egregious lack of funds, Kay wore a well-used baby blue dress she'd worn for our junior *and* senior high school proms. It sported an *empire waist* (whatever that meant), which she said worked well even though her *baby bump* had not yet begun to show. I remained oblivious. Pastor Bill Pencille said she couldn't wear

* They tore down that old church a few years later. The Mayo Clinic built its Baldwin Community Medicine building on that site. Of course, they did.

white, anyway. I assumed God penalized us for admitting in one of the church's required pre-marriage counseling sessions we'd surrendered our virginity to passion. I guess God frowned on non-virgin brides wearing white wedding gowns.

I remember stifling a persistent snicker or three. Unlike the church's regular minister, as an old family friend, Pastor Bill had agreed to marry us, regardless. But because of my month-long delay leaving basic training, Pastor Bill's prior commitments prevented him from marrying us. Someone else stood in for him. But still no white. Kay didn't have a white dress, anyway.

I donned my new spit-and-polish, heavy wool, formal midnight-blue US Coast Guard uniform, complete with a blinding white ascot at my throat. On my shoulder I sported my new twin Seaman Apprentice stripes, now a source of tremendous pride. Carried my brilliant white dress hat, featuring razor-sharp edges inside my left elbow, per regulation, leaving my right hand free to salute on those rare occasions when required indoors. And my dress shoes gleamed, of course. All of this impressive regalia at no additional charge, on Uncle Sam's dime.

As for the rest of the wedding party, the guys furnished their own suits, too, and the girls their own dresses. They didn't quite match. Kay seemed okay with that. I didn't give a shit. I just wanted Kay to myself, now, with a sense of some urgency. Romantic, right?

I stood at attention during the entire ceremony, even later at the reception. Arched back, clenched fists at my sides, chin in and back, heels together, at full attention... the works. My high school friends told me to relax, as this was now a social affair. That fell on deaf ears. I thought, *What do these* ***children*** *know?*

I HEARD the following pre-wedding conversation after the fact:

"Hey, where did these beautiful flowers come from?" Kay asked her best friend, Debbie Jensen.

"I heard Gene's mom scored them from a funeral they had here at the church yesterday. Something like that."

"Excellent. All I see is more flowers than we could ever afford. She must not hate me as much as I thought."

"*Or,*" Debbie deadpanned, "she does, but loves her baby boy *more* than you thought." They both chuckled. Or so they told me. Long after.

My mom had grown apoplectic that her baby boy intended to "marry a *Catholic, and* a *teenager* to boot." Her words. She remained certain I'd get sucked through the gates of Hell by association. She even attempted to talk me *and* Kay's mom out of that unholy union. My words. She lamented, "You're only 19!" Said she'd never be able to accept this girl into her family, much less with open arms. After all, I was *perfect* until I met this *Catholic child.* She also said that as a Christian, she'd be civil, for her *GG's* sake—her pet name for her perfect son—if she'd only faced reality. Her best offer. Good enough.

Likewise, Kay's mom, Violet—Vi—was not pleased about her daughter marrying into a non-Catholic family, in a ***Protest****ant* church, no less, and she was not afraid to show it. But she understood her daughter's love for a good young man, despite their certain one-way trip to Hell, possibly after a chunk of eternity in Purgatory. Said she'd worry about that later. I was, after all, making an honest woman of her daughter. That's how Kay later relayed their discussion before the wedding. Vi was a wiry old bird, but she loved her daughter, even if their home life had always been hardscrabble at best, and raw survival mode at worst, which was most of the time.

My dad didn't seem to have much of an opinion at all, other than these *crummy kids*—his enduring term of endearment—would at least be together. He said, "a man has to make his own way and you're now a man, son." I think his impression of me had elevated by an order of magnitude after boot, compared to that hapless and clueless hippie before. He grinned and said he thought I did okay. "She sure is a looker, GG, and a darn nice girl to hug."

Daddy loved hugging. Everybody and anybody. He'd say, "Tells a lot about a person by how they hug!" Daddy. Frustrated dreamer. My unsung hero. He bailed me out of trouble more often than I cared to admit, or even to remember. Hmmmm, I'd forgotten about *that* until just now as I write this. Not sure he ever told Mom. Probably did.

Kay's stepdad, the father of the bride, begrudgingly walked her down the aisle. May the lascivious bastard rot in hell. God bless Kay's new firecracker of a mother, though. Amen.

Mr. & Mrs. Eugene Jurrens, April 20, 1969, en route to the "wedding limo."

My friends had decorated the *wedding limo*. Charlie Donney, my best friend from my childhood neighborhood, had borrowed his mom's decrepit-chic '63-ish Mercury *woodie* station wagon and volunteered to drive us. He had fun playing chauffeur and being the lead dog of a 13-car parade. Charlie'd been awarded his driver's license the week before.

He still struggled with stop signs and turns while handling that enormous steering wheel with only one hand. He needed the other to smoke a cigarette, of course. Not because he enjoyed smoking, but because it was essential for his brand-spankin' new persona as a driver.

My new bride and I *necked* all the way to my mom's house, where they served coffee and cake after the church basement reception. Charlie blew through at least two stop signs, and it's possible he side-swiped a neighbor's hedge. But he got us to 227 7th Avenue SE safe and sound.

Carol, one of my two older sisters by almost ten years, had made ham sandwiches and potato salad ahead of time with some of the church ladies. I barely knew Carol back then, as she was so much older and long-married. I've since rejoined the lives of both my sisters after remaining estranged from most of my family for my few decades as a practicing alcoholic. Lovely ladies, Carol and Yvonne.

Carol survived two husbands. Yvonne, my oldest sister, outlasted one husband. As I write this, Carol just passed away peacefully, bless her heart. Her hard farm wife mileage finally caught up with her. Yvonne is 87 and is still performing at a high-energy level in a mid-size manufacturing company in Ohio. She walks several miles a day and still soars high in the corporate world without compromising her morals. Both have always persisted in demonstrating kindness, consistently overwhelm all who know them with their humanity, and will always be my heroes!

Speaking of my older siblings, the eldest of our gang of five? Like Daddy, my brother Stan was a dreamer, but better equipped to apply his creativity. And he wasn't too proud to ask for help. He worked for IBM as a machinist and had a good head for business, but struggled with math. I remember helping him with algebra when I was 16. He was 30. His heavy foot killed him in a high-speed traffic accident just seven months earlier. But that's another story.

And Rod, my younger brother by three years, evolved into a brilliant professional musician. I admired his talent and flamboyant lifestyle as a drummer, vocalist, and later as a bass guitar player. He'd held other jobs, but always came back to music. Unlike me, he also returned to the family faith.

Except for Stan, they all attended our wedding on April 20, 1969.

We spent our first night as a married couple at the Kahler Hotel in downtown Rochester, where Kay had worked for a while not so long ago. It took our friends forever to leave our in-room party. Kay's best friend, Karen, passed out spread-eagle on our bed! I stayed up to polish my shoes until two am. The power of basic training.

In retrospect, our wedding, and reception were both intimate *and* grand. Virtually everyone thought this unlikely couple would last a year at the most. Except my mother. For all her bluster, she knew her boy and the traditional values she'd instilled in him—you don't get divorced. Ever. You make it work. No excuses. Love takes work, she'd say.

I had just turned 19, been drafted, and was fresh out of twelve weeks of hellacious but fulfilling basic training. Kay was still 18 and had been suffering from severe morning sickness. Plus, we were moving away from our families and friends for several years. She'd join me after graduating. The odds were indeed stacked against us. *We did not care.* Such was the devotion and spirited rebellion driving our precocious passion for one another.

~

Yeah, I was growing up, but not in the direction neither I nor my high school sweetheart envisioned. When I'd rebelled against the religion of my youth, I pulverized my devout parents' hearts. I truly regret that, but I had to follow my own heart. I'd later read a letter of apology over their gravestones.

I'd graduated from high school with mediocre grades, but with stellar marks for engaging in and surviving violent vehicular encounters. I'd been drafted at the height of the Vietnam War. No wonder my parents worried about me dying *over there* like so many others. Had they been worried I'd be reckless and fearless in combat, too? I'm profoundly grateful neither they nor I ever had to find out.

The memory of discussing this with my parents before I enlisted? It had not gone well. "Look, it's not like I have a choice, you guys. I've been *drafted*." They weren't clear on that concept, hoping for some exception to save their baby from the war. I didn't bother reminding them I'd let my student exemption lapse due to lack of interest in college. I just wasn't ready to take higher education seriously.

Their tortured spirits hovered millimeters above Dante's seventh circle of Hell, not that they believed in such a Satanic literary reference. Why? Because it didn't exist in the King James version of the Holy Bible, the *only* book they believed worth reading and trusting.

To set their minds at ease for having enlisted, I said, "The really good news here is that I won't spend two years carrying the Army's guns into combat. Instead, I'll spend four years driving a boat in the Coast Guard. That's good news, right?" After all, my older brother Stan had survived a stint in the peacetime Air Force.

I reminded them in a muted conversation after the wedding that I was no coward, nor was I a killer. Besides, the idea of being a heroic seagoing rescuer appealed to my egocentric sensibilities, though I didn't yet even know how to *spell*

b-o-a-t

before I'd enlisted. I was learning. That seemed to resonate with my dear parents.

Chapter 21

Extraordinary Becomes Ordinary

Many duties and experiences became commonplace during my four years in the USCG, even those things most folks would find extraordinary. We considered those events just part of the job, perhaps not unlike law enforcement officers, firefighters, or healthcare workers.

We'd recover people's bodies—sometimes bloated or split-open corpses—of adults, or worse, the broken bodies of drowned children. We'd navigate ferocious seas to maneuver dangerously close to a disabled boat, sometimes after a 20- or 25-hour search in the most atrocious conditions imaginable. Sometimes, we'd dive into a maelstrom to swim toward a victim in the water. Or to a vessel in distress hauling a messenger line in order to bring over a heavier tow line once aboard, often while dealing with hysterical victims.

You know, normal SAR (search and rescue) stuff.

But one memory still haunts me to this day. I will never remember that sunny afternoon as *ordinary*. A small open boat capsized with six obese adults and a baby aboard as soon as they left the protected waters of the Saginaw River and hit the big water of the wide-open bay. No life jackets. Nearby boats radioed us even as this drama unfolded.

The mission horn blew at the station. We ran for the 20-ton, steel-hull 40-footer, got her underway in less than two minutes. Nearby recreational boaters had picked up five of the six adults—floundering, but alive—in the bay's steep chop. Once on the scene in less than five minutes, we spotted a woman and an infant still in the rough water who were not floundering, both floating face down, not moving.

I will never forget that tiny infant's body we lifted from the water, too late to save her. We then pulled aboard the drowned mother.

When a person drowns, they sink until internal gases build up because of decomposition. Within 24 hours, they pop back to the surface, bloated by these gases. That's when we'd most often find them, usually after a lengthy search. But the fat content was high enough in both this obese woman and her well-nourished baby that they didn't sink right away.

I was still a seaman, and "Andy" Anderson was my cox'n. His engineer (mechanic) and I used a boat hook to coax the baby's body close enough to the 40's port gunwale (pronounced *GUN'el,* the boat's low railing aft) to retrieve it once Andy had expertly maneuvered close enough in the rough chop. We *had* to treat these body recoveries with objectivity, or it'd tear our hearts out. Still, nightmares plagued me for weeks after that day. I still visualize... the entire scene... 55 years later. It's a part of me. Forever.

Once we'd retrieved the baby's little body—no bigger than a chubby puppy—which only took a couple of minutes, we focused on the woman. Same procedure. But she was *really* heavy. Like three-hundred-pounds heavy. It took all three of us to hoist her body aboard. When we got her atop the gunwale, we lost control, and she flopped onto our boat's aft deck. She fell less than two feet and landed face-down with a mighty *thump* on the steel deck, which featured several bolted-down access hatches.

We rolled over her body, and it emitted a huge *AAAHHHH!* Sometimes that happens when corpses *off-gas.* It was SOP (Standard Operating Procedure) to check for a pulse—always. *And we found one!* Weak and thready. She was *alive!* But she now sported a definitive bolt-shaped indentation right in the middle of her forehead. We rolled her onto her side to the *rescue position* so she could more easily expel water from her lungs. She choked and vomited, and blinked her eyes open!

This woman, the mother of the deceased baby girl, we later learned, miraculously recovered, even though she'd been face-down in the water for several minutes. We figured the thump when she fell onto the deck was an accidental but effective *precordial thump.* This is a medical procedure where a firm strike delivered to the chest can restart the heart during certain types of cardiac arrest. It's effective, but can be dangerous if not performed correctly. Yeah, we got lucky.

This poor woman had lost her little baby girl, but she, herself, came back from the dead. She visited our station several weeks later, complete with the visible bolt-shaped impression still evident in her forehead. With tears aplenty, she thanked us for saving her life and for recovering her baby's body. She even brought us a pan of muffins as a token. How cool is that?

Chapter 22

Almost Sinking My New Command

Some time later, they promoted me to Petty Office Second Class Boatswain's Mate (pronounced *BO-s'ns mate*). I commanded my own vessel and crew less than a year into my hitch. We entered the early phase of one SAR mission to rescue a family aboard a dis-masted sailboat during a raging gale.

We often joked that our 40-foot steel-hull patrol boat seldom got underway in decent weather. She wouldn't know how to behave herself if we weren't pounding through crashing waves, dense fog, or racing at high speed toward some unfolding seagoing catastrophe!

One memorable night, I remember unintentionally piloting my 40 *way* too close to an unseen 32-foot tall, nine-ton lighted bell buoy. The Big Red Monster was marked with the number two its designator below it—9x32LBR. It was the outer marker of the Saginaw River Channel in Saginaw Bay, 11 nautical miles to seaward from the river's mouth. We called it Big Red Monster for a reason. The damn thing was a small floating island unto itself, anchored with a huge 50-foot anchor chain to a 10-ton block of steel and concrete buried in the bottom.

Amidst that night's zero-visibility storm because of a heavy horizontal rain, I helplessly watched that buoy scrape down our port side six feet from where I stood at my helm. We never even heard the glancing contact over the wind screaming at the seas all around us. I remember we'd crested a breaking wave that damn-near stood our 40 on end before we slammed down the other side at twice our speed from moments earlier.

I don't recall if I feared for the lives of myself and my crew, or if we truly believed in our oblivious invincibility and simply enjoyed the ride. I regret not remembering that moment. It would have made for an even more astounding memory.

After an overnight search, armed with only our ship's compass and binoculars (no GPS back then, nor were we rigged with radar), we found the distressed vessel, the object of our search. She floundered some 20 miles offshore.

I'd put my seaman in the water to tow over a messenger line. He then hauled over the heavier tow line connected to it after boarding the distressed vessel, and secured the vessel to ours. Everyone aboard survived with minor injuries. We then towed the disabled boat into the first harbor inside the protected mouth of the Saginaw River.

The crew and I spent the next week's odd moments repainting the white 40's scarred port side, as well as her orange, blue, and white diagonal stripe near the bow. Nothing to do for the dents, other than to paint them, along with their numerous predecessors from her rough duty. No holes, thankfully.

Had I veered my command less than six feet to port in that maelstrom as we headed out of the channel? It's likely we'd have holed the hull by slamming head-on at speed coming down off a steep wave atop the Big Red Monster's nine-foot-wide steel deck. Would we have sunk? Who knows? Injuries or fatalities to the crew? Equipment damage? It certainly would have been far worse than a few scrapes and dents on the old 40's stubborn torso. She took the hit, alright.

Since then, I've also asked myself what might have happened to that family aboard the boat we'd never have reached to rescue. Yet another key moment.

Chapter 23

Transcendental Meditation

Fast-forward another year. Halfway through my four-year stint in the Coast Guard circa 1971, my shipmates and I risked our lives on a weekly, sometimes daily basis, still convinced of my invincibility. Some might suggest I remained in serious denial. We'd save the boating public from themselves on Lake Huron, the second largest of the five Great Lakes. Some call these lakes inland seas for good reason.

For example, Huron spans more than 23,000 square miles of open water. Huron and the other Great Lakes are not only gigantic, but their hydrology and intense weather patterns often subject mariners to vicious seas—a unique cycloidal wave shape that breaks the backs of ships.

My job as a small boat captain was to challenge Lake Huron's 1,143-square-mile Saginaw Bay on 700+ SAR missions each year. Yep, that meant at least four missions per day on average in the summer, and far fewer in the winter. We ran ourselves ragged—physically and emotionally.

We'd also get called out to support the Bay County Marine Sheriff's deputies for any in-progress or suspected maritime crimes like stolen boats or suspected international smuggling operations. The deepwater ports-of-call on the Saginaw River included several international terminals. Plus, we'd assist with patrols during ecological disaster recovery operations like oil spills. I found this job fulfilling, but stressful. The idea of peaceful meditation appealed to me for that and *so* many other reasons.

I BECAME enamored of spiritual concepts native to Eastern philosophies like Hinduism and Buddhism, especially after my late-teen disillusionment with Western religions.

In the early '70s, the Beatles were the most popular rock band on the planet. A Hindu guru from India, Maharishi Mahesh Yogi, launched into international fame because he taught the Beatles how to meditate. Maharishi taught a technique called *Transcendental Meditation*, or *TM*. It captured my imagination. This led to another event that changed the fundamental direction of my life yet again.

ONE OF MY senior shipmates at the Saginaw River Lifeboat Station, Tom List, sensed my interest. He mentioned he practiced TM twice a day, part of the same ancient Vedic tradition from which yoga developed. He explained the technique was as simple and subtle as it was powerful. Back then TM was *only* taught by teachers trained by Maharishi himself. Fascinating.

Tom directed me to a teacher who traveled through our area occasionally. Kay and I learned together.* However, learning TM cost what seemed like a king's ransom. Tom explained that a financial

---

* As a sidebar, after they honorably discharged my friend Tom from the USCG, he and his wife would spend time with Maharishi and to become TM teachers at Maharishi International University, later called the Maharishi University of Management. They later relocated the MUM campus from California to the small town of Fairfield, Iowa, of all places.

commitment to the practice filtered out those not serious about it and reflected the immense intrinsic value of the technique. Our investment also helped sustain full-time TM teachers. We struggled to convince ourselves that this was not a scam.

It took us months to save up the $150. I will share with you that my income in 1971 was $231 *per month*, and half of that went to pay for off-base rent. Plus, I had to chip in $35 each month for food at our small Coast Guard station. Yeah, a different sort of *commune*. That left only $86 per month *for all other expenses.* Our daughter Michelle was not yet two years old, and Kay was pregnant with Adam. Plus, I still owed $15 per month for Kay's rings to the jeweler in Sacramento.

We rinsed dirty cloth diapers in our apartment's only toilet and subsisted on boxed Mac 'n Cheese meals. At the end of each month, we'd decide whether to splurge on a candy bar to share *or* for about the same price, a TV Guide (remember those?). Imagine what it took to commit $150 to a complete unknown adventure like TM!

The day came. When asked at the interview, we vowed we had smoked no marijuana nor drunk any alcohol for a month, as that would affect our ability to learn this subtle technique. We had no idea what we were getting into. It looked an awful lot like a Hindu religious ritual at first, complete with candles and incense and a statue. Almost like an altar. I shudder to think what my dear parents would have imagined!

I wasn't sure how I felt about that, my hippie background notwithstanding. Our teacher, Mark, resembled a Jehovah's Witness in *earth shoes* with their wide toe boxes and heels the lowest part of their soles. He said TM's history *was* rooted in Hindu philosophy and religion to which they paid homage.

But the technique itself was simply a way to achieve a profound level of rest which would remove deeply rooted stress from our nervous systems. TM promised to do so more effectively in the lives of busy people—our lives—more effectively than any other known practice. *And* there was a body of serious science to back it up. That sounded good to us.

And guess what? Learning this technique delivered. Through various life changes, some traumatic, over the subsequent decades, we have practiced this technique for twenty minutes twice a day, off and on, for more than half a century. TM also opened my eyes to wisdom beyond what most Americans accept as reasonable or possible, even to this day.

~

THOUGH MUCH OF the literature surrounding TM has always been swathed in hyperbole—seemingly grandiose language—this is because the technique and its effects *transcend* mere words. Verbal and written language only allow a limited level of understanding of the physical world, by a lot. One fundamental principle TM taught me?

> *Keep an open mind, and take* ***nothing*** *for granted, even if it exists outside my current ability to comprehend. Rather, I allowed my* ***experience*** *to speak for itself versus being blindly bound to previously held beliefs when presented with new information.*

While there is a substantial body of peer-reviewed scientific research referenced in the TM literature, there is still *much* to be explained, in *non-transcendental* terms, of its effects. Especially those that extend beyond the individual. One such claim, backed by several large-scale anecdotal studies, is called *the Maharishi Effect*: how to achieve world peace via the critical mass of at least 1% of the population concurrently practicing the technique. The skeptic in me thought, *Yeah, right.* While it is crucial to question statistics, it is *also* truly foolish to deny the veracity of *supportable* statistics, certainly where correlation statistically supports causation. There *is* plenty to support the science behind TM.

How ridiculous did Einstein's *Theory of Relativity* sound when he first proposed such "nonsense?" Or *String Theory* and *Quantum Mechanics*?

The closed mind prevents intellectual growth!

And yes, I enjoy the practice 20 minutes twice a day because I appreciate its practical benefits. I am also astounded at experiencing a state of consciousness that differs from waking, dreaming, or sleeping, which offers me an escape from time itself, not to mention from my physical body. And that yields better results than a two-hour power nap. Sounds crazy, right?

Even in simple physical terms, any technique that allows me to decrease my heart rate, respiration rate, blood pressure, *and* produces beneficial alpha waves in my brain? At will? Hundreds of prestigious studies since the 1970s from the likes of Harvard Medical School verify these capabilities.

Yet much remains to be articulated. *Because words fail.* Take from this, from my *experience*, what you will, and leave behind whatever is beyond the boundaries of your current beliefs. It's okay.

Chapter 24

Cap'n Curmudgeon

Cap'n Brownie, a 40-year harbor tugboat skipper on the Saginaw River, was a crusty old barnacle I'd known for two years. I hung out with that curmudgeon now and then. Not sure if we were friends or if he merely tolerated a coastie now and then. We didn't talk much, but it seemed he'd taken me under his wing. The boathouse where he kept equipment reminded me of some other structures that perched on pilings over the south shore of the Saginaw River that had no right to still be standing.

The entire commercial area where his building still stood had seen better days decades earlier. I chose my every step with care between heaps of old gear as I picked my way through Brownie's decrepit boathouse. I feared falling between the irregular and loose floorboards. Looking down, in muted sunlight and dappled shadows, I saw and heard the river's waves lapping against the rotting pilings that kept the old boathouse from falling into the Saginaw.

Brownie had remained a solitary soul his entire life. "Got no time for the frivolities 'a them skirts." An actual complete sentence he'd uttered to me once between drags on his hand-rolled cigarette held between the yellow-stained thumb and forefinger of his left hand.

The only part of the old sea dog's anatomy more yellow than his tobacco-tainted fingers was his mouth full of too many crooked teeth —more brown that yellow, truth be told. But that's not why everyone called him *Brownie*.

The old crust was a warm soul, simply satisfied plying his trade. He'd employed the same two local mariners for many years. They were as old and crotchety as he. I can't recall either of them ever speaking a word out loud. But those three boatmen regularly wrestled 700-foot freighters around the ports of the half-mile-wide Saginaw River like they were pushing puzzle pieces around a tabletop. Brownie's 38-foot, 3,800-horsepower diesel harbor tug made light work of such gargantuan tasks.

I'D SEEN them in operation one Sunday morning when we were called to prevent a runaway 110-foot-long, 40-foot-wide barge from crashing into the Lafayette Street Bridge. We'd successfully stopped the barge's headway toward the bridge by throwing a couple of lines on it and applying every foot-pound of torque our 40-footer's two big 671-cubic-inch diesels could deliver with its paltry 360 horses. They built our boat more for speed than for power. Even the simple task of killing the barge's forward motion took us several minutes of WOT, or wide-open throttle.

Brownie and his crew arrived on the scene minutes later after having been hailed. While we held the barge's position just upstream from the bridge, we watched him deftly maneuver alongside the monster in the river's swift current. Without uttering a word, his crew secured the barge alongside the tug with huge-diameter fore, aft, and crisscrossed spring lines in a matter of a minute or two.

No sooner secured, Brownie dumped gallons of fuel into the throats of his mammoth engines, and away they went. They were a well-oiled machine with plenty of horsepower at their command! Fortunately for us, that barge was not fully loaded, or we'd not have been able to save the bridge before Brownie's arrival.

. . .

Brownie knew I loved marlinspike seamanship, an ancient nautical art form. It included the use, maintenance, and repair of rope, including tying knots, splicing, and securing lines involving both practical techniques as well as decorative rope work. He'd allowed me to practice my coxcombing—decorative knot work wrapped around a railing—on his tug. He'd then have his crew paint it. Looked darn good and created an effective non-slip surface to grab in "lumpy" weather. But it took time and nimble fingers which neither Brownie nor his seasoned crew possessed.

Coxcombing makes for both beautiful and easy-to-grip railings on a vessel when in less-than-ideal conditions.

One day I hung around his boathouse while on liberty—off duty—waiting to see if he'd toss me a paying gig. Yes, we were allowed to moonlight. Brownie's clap-trap boathouse was also where the old mariner lived when not sleeping in the pilothouse of his powerful tug tied alongside.

He put me to work today. He needed an old, hundred-foot pile of scrap mooring line called a *hawser* hauled away. I told him I'd get my chief's permission to use the CG's Dodge Power Wagon to take it off his hands. That pile was the size of a Volkswagen Beetle.

I had plans for that huge-diameter rope. Figured I'd un-lay it after I hung it from the top of the lighthouse tower at Saginaw River Station. I'd then weave the three separate strands into a rope fender—a boat bumper—that I'd sell back to Brownie. He said he liked that idea. But I had my work cut out for me.

That pile of weathered hemp rope, as big around as my thigh, stressed the load limit of our station's *one-ton pickup!* Took over two hours just to feed it onto the truck's bed. Felt like I played tug-o-war with the planet herself. That shit was *heavy.* I didn't have enough energy to unload it at the station until the next day. Never occurred to me to ask for help. Anyway, this was a solo project.

Each of us coasties needed something to do during downtime between calls at the station while on port-and-starboard liberty. We'd be on duty for one day (24 hours), and off the next in the summer. Or two days on (48 hours), with two days off in the winter. Boredom was our fiercest adversary when there were no SAR calls, practice drills, or other duties. So, I spent a few weeks of idle on-duty time on this project one autumn when nothing else required my attention.

US Coast Guard Saginaw River Station, circa 1970.

First, I rigged a block and tackle system (pulleys and rope) from the railing surrounding the light's house at the top of the tower. The square brick tower stood 55+ feet (six stories) above the veranda that surrounded the tower at the edge of the canal where we moored our boats. Then, I hoisted one end of the line up as high as possible using that tackle. Took some grunt, even with a 6:1 purchase (mechanical advantage).

I grabbed a hacksaw from the shop to cut the hawser three feet short of the veranda's deck at the base of the tower. An old ten-foot chunk of 2" x 12" plank served as an anchor point for the 3 strands as I separated them. I used a hole saw to cut three equidistant 2-inch holes along that board's length. I unraveled a few feet of the old 3-lay hawser and passed one strand through each of the holes. Bound each end as tight as I was able with waxed twine. I then drove a marlin-spike—a slender, wooden-handled steel spike that resembled a curved ice pick—through each bitter end. That kept 'em from coming out of their holes.

Now, with some 50 feet of that heavy old line dangling from the lighthouse tower, I slowly un-lay (un-twisted) the line by rotating that plank. It resisted, of course, as I was coaxing it out of its native twist of a few decades. This grueling task took an entire day. But I was on a mission, and like firefighters, we'd wait and train and eat and sleep and work on pet projects between SAR calls. I now possessed a purpose!

As I convinced the three parts of the rope to stay separated, I'd run inside the station every fifteen minutes or so. I'd cross through the radio room and scurry up the five-story spiral staircase to the top of the tower to lower the entire hawser by a few feet. Then I'd run back down and outside to un-lay a couple more feet. Rinse 'n repeat.

Once I finished unlaying its entire length, I dealt with the trio of huge piles. Each of these "smaller" lines was the diameter of my wrist. It took all of my strength and a ton of time to weave these three ropes into a curved cylindrical pattern around a smaller fender—a cylindrical boat bumper. I'd woven that core fender of smaller line the week before I scored the hawser from Brownie.

This project took several more weeks, with permission from Chief Kirkpatrick, the station's officer-in-charge. But only between SAR calls, law enforcement support calls, and my other regular duties. Every time Chief came out of the station to smoke a Lucky Strike, he'd hoist one boot up on the veranda railing's middle rung. He'd gaze up at the dangling rope over his shoulder, at me slaving away, and chuckle. One day he said, "Listen, Jurrens, I get that you're advancing your marlinspike skills 'n all, but what're you going to do with that monster once you finish it? Ain't goin' in the ready room." He already knew it wasn't.

"It's gonna stand proud on the bow of Cap'n Brownie's tug to protect his beloved workhorse. Said he'd pay me a hundred bucks for it. And I'm making it with the hawser he paid *me* to haul *away*!"

"Huh. That right? How many hours you gonna have in that big bitch when you're done?"

I smiled. "Doesn't matter, Chief. It's fun, and I'm learning a bunch. See?"

I felt like a kid imploring his mom to "Look-it! Look-it!"

Chief hoisted a critical eye and drew in a huge lungful from his cigarette before responding in a voice thickened by the smoke. "Got your crew roster updated?"

I grinned. I hadn't come out to work on this thing until my duties were ship-shape. And he knew it. He was gruff and another man of few words, but Chief was a good shit. This was his way of delivering an *attaboy* without resorting to saying so. "A hundred percent, Chief. And Pate assured me he'll complete his annuals on the 40's 671s by end-of-day. We're ready to rock whenever the next horn blows."

Rick Pate was my EM2—Engineman Second Class—and he was due to complete an exhaustive maintenance diagnostic checklist on the 40-footer's diesel engines. He didn't need me on his back. Pate knew his job. But it made Chief feel good that his skippers stayed on top of every aspect of keeping their vessels—*his* vessels—safe, properly equipped, and ready to respond when the horn blew.

Two weeks later, I delivered a curved cylindrical rope fender that was 38 inches in diameter and damn near seven feet long to Cap'n Brownie. I got some help at the station to load it up. No idea how heavy it was. Grunt-worthy, for sure! His crew unloaded it from the truck at his boathouse. He nodded with a little grin and slantwise glance—of admiration? Slapped a crumpled hundred-dollar bill into my palm and shook my other hand with his gnarled paw.

He spat a spent cheekful of chaw onto the pier by his boathouse before he limped away with a grunt. Not word one. A man of few words, alright. I grinned too as I looked down at the grease-stained C-note. Kay would be thrilled!

See the circled bow fender on this tug for an example of a curved bow fender on a work boat.

Chapter 25

Ice Ops Prep

I learned a half-dozen valuable lessons during my four years of active government service:

1. How to work within a team as if lives depended on it. They often did.
2. How to lead that same team.
3. With nothing but a compass, a nautical chart, a little science, and a powerful boat under my feet, finding lost souls at sea was my major stock in trade. Yeah, I could make any boat dance to any tune, or no tune at all, even in the harshest conditions, for a truly admirable purpose.
4. I learned a lot about maintaining and fixing major aids to navigation: range lights; lighted bell buoys; channel markers; and other boring stuff.
5. Each of us became experts at chipping old paint off rusted surfaces, as well as how to properly paint with, clean and maintain paint brushes. Now, how valuable are *those* skills in the job market?

6. Also, government service did not pay well. I'd not be a lifer; that is, I made the financial decision not to extend my service to 20 years to earn a pension. Not if I wanted to make a decent living! I convinced myself I could do better, both financially and intellectually.

But I remember one mission where the first and second skills saved a lot of lives, including my own, and made #6 above a more difficult decision.

During my sometimes boring, often adventurous years in the Coast Guard, I served most of my time on the huge Saginaw Bay, a part of Lake Huron, as mentioned earlier.

You also already know we responded to over 700 SAR (search and rescue) calls each year. I could publish another complete volume to regale you with delicious and horrific tales from those thousands of sorties (missions). But one mission stands out in my memory more than most.

This anecdote is based on an actual SAR case. While the details may have shifted in my not-so-great memory, I've made every attempt to faithfully reproduce the spirit of that night's seismic events. Seismic for me, anyway. A night that changed me forever.

On February 26, 1972, relentless winds shrieked and shifted across the frozen 25-mile-wide, 45-mile-long Saginaw Bay. Sudden changes in temperature and a howling southerly wind drove the softened ice pack away from the bay's southern shore. A colorless sunset —a blurry gray specter—crept closer to our historic lighthouse and attached duty station.

After a century of often-brutal lake winds battering her stone and brick carcass, the weathered caulk around her old windows still arrested most of the howling wind.

The solitary watch stander, Ron Mayfield, had succumbed to profound boredom. The phone rang. Startled, then relieved at the prospect of rare human contact during a winter watch, Ron snatched up the receiver.

"Coast Guard Saginaw River Station, Seaman Ron Mayfield. How may I help you?"

"This is Martha Diggins, Ron. I believe I might have some business for you boys."

"Afternoon, Mrs. Diggins. It's nice to hear from you again. Can you tell me a little more about your concern today?" Ron was always so *very* polite. His nickname was *Pooh*.

Mrs. Diggins, a widow of twenty years, lived just six miles overland from the station, north of Bayshore Drive near the mouth of the Kawkawlin River that fed into the bay. Through knee-to-ceiling waterfront windows, she enjoyed a spectacular view of the bay.

"Ron, I watched a bunch a darn fool fishermen drive their cars and trucks out onto the ice quite a few hours ago. They've done this before and they always come back this way long before sunset. Now I see a crack has opened up all along the shore out a ways. I got some good binoculars the captain left me, you know." Her deceased husband commanded a laker—a freighter built for the rigors of plying the Great Lakes—for many years. "Those boys are now officially in deep trouble, Ron. Thought you should know. I just don't see how they're gonna get home without help from you boys."

Over the years, the Saginaw River Station received numerous calls from Martha Diggins. She was one of our favorite and most reliable civilian spotters.

HANGING UP AFTER THANKING MARTHA, Ron initiated a *Mayday* search-and-rescue mission. A SAR call of this type suggests the potential for loss of life. While the number of incoming SAR calls average four or more per day during the summer months, they were a rare winter occurrence. Thus, the station maintained only a skeleton crew during the winter months.

The Teletype chattered. A ribbon of yellow paper tape with holes punched in it curled toward the floor, recording what was received. Blizzard warnings for the Lake Huron and Saginaw Bay area predicted a severe winter storm that was indeed worsening by the minute.

Only one other person was on duty. Ron hollered at the non-watch stander, Bos'n's Mate Third Class Gene Jurrens—that's me—to ready the necessary equipment for the on-call crew of four prior to their arrival. Ron executed the emergency recall procedure for that crew. "Hey Geno! We got business out on the bay!" I turned off the TV in the adjacent room. Ron briefed me on the case. That really wasn't necessary, since I'd heard the call come in on the speaker-phone and the recall orders going out.

I SAID, "I'M ON IT!" A sense of quiet professionalism held back a flood of adrenaline. I hated ice ops, but loved the break in the boredom. Had to be there for the next 48 hours anyway.

Blowing snow had already drifted in, now driven by blistering gale-force winds. The ice pack's separation from the shore would not be our only challenge. The station's four-wheel-drive Dodge Power Wagon pickup, complete with a snow plow, would need to clear a path to our optimal launch point at the shore, out by Martha Diggins' beach.

Once our crew gained the frozen beach, we'd launch the station's dented old fourteen-foot, three-hundred-pound aluminum skiff, loaded with a two hundred pound ice operations box. Would limited visibility escalate into a white-out? We always planned for the worst while hoping....

At the tender age of twenty-one, I *remained* invincible. Threw on a parka, boots, and gloves. The wind slammed the ready room's already warped door flat against the outside wall. I wedged the door away from the wall and leaned into the worsening gale while simultaneously struggling to close the door. After a minute, I got it latched.

Made my way to the Power Wagon sitting in the snow beside the equipment shed. I dragged the 300-pound plow on its round skid plates across the already obscured asphalt to the front of the Power Wagon and prepared to connect it. This would save mission-critical minutes later while the rest of the off-shift crew made their way to the station.

I threw myself onto my back and slid under the truck's front bumper, pushing newly drifted snow in front of me. I shimmied under the bumper three feet above me. The plow's blade rested on the ground in front of the truck. After lifting the plow's heavy steel frame flush to the truck's undercarriage, I grunted while holding it up in my left hand at the end of my outstretched arm. The blood vessels in my temples threatened to burst with the effort. Used my right hand to slip the first of two lock bolts and pins into place. It resisted, but I forced it. I had successfully secured the plow's frame to the bottom of the truck. And that is the precise moment that my life changed forever. *Again.*

"AW, CRAP!"

A ripping, white-hot sensation radiated from my lower back, but I couldn't allow that to commandeer my attention. The urgency required at that moment sent gallons of adrenaline coursing through my veins. There would be plenty of time for discomfort later.

"Ron, this is Gene," I said over the intercom. "Plow secured. Truck is rigged. Send the crew directly to the ready room the second they arrive. We need to assume the victims' onset of hypothermia." After prolonged exposure, the body's temperature drops dangerously low, drawing blood flow away from extremities and toward vital organs—the beginning of the end. They still had time *if* they weren't already in the icy water. Even partial submersion in freezing water causes certain death in less than a minute or two.

"Roger. Standing by."

THEN FOUR CARS skidded into the parking lot, almost as one. A heavy snow pummeled the crew as they made their way to the station, leaning into the ferocious wind. The snow would get drier and icier as the temps continued to plummet.

THE SMALL READY room smelled like a locker room despite our best intentions. Radiated heat from the lighthouse's boiler eight feet away defeated the incoming draft invading the poorly sealed entrance door that led in from beneath the veranda's overhang.

I cursed the intense pain now radiating in searing waves from my lower back. After stripping to my skivvies, I dusted my now-sweaty legs, arms, and feet with baby powder to ease wedging into my stretchy quarter-inch-thick neoprene wetsuit.

While the skin-tight foam rubber bodysuit was a fight to slide into, this would be my last line of defense against paralyzing ice water that we hoped we'd avoid. I then donned a set of fur-lined Arctic-rated bibs and parka over the wetsuit to further combat the biting winds sweeping across the frozen 25-mile-wide bay.

Seconds ticked away as my anxiety level escalated. This was to be my sortie, my mission to lead. The thought of people dying while I waited was intolerable. As my body responded to escalating back pain with mild shock symptoms, I noticed a cold sweat beading up on my forehead with the onset of lightheadedness. *Sonofabitch, this is not good. No time for this!*

Not a religious guy, I still whispered the same prayer before every mission: *Oh Lord, please don't let us screw this up!* I'd heard that from somebody famous, maybe an astronaut, and adopted it as my own.

Ron's voice sounded thin 'n tinny but loud over the intercom's loudspeaker. Jerked me back from my mental meanderings as spasms continued to clutch at my back and sides. "Hey Geno. I've reported a Mayday to Group Detroit. By the way, officer-in-charge is en route."

"Roger. Assume operations channel 22 primary for the duration, secondary on 24." These would be the mission's two VHF radio channels, which were among those reserved exclusively for Coast Guard use.

The ready room door burst open. The four snow-laden on-call crew barged in with snow swirling around them. Tall and lanky Marty "Jack" Jackson was the first to complete donning his own gear. He met me at the rear of the jacked-up truck. I'd already dragged over the skiff and the massive ice ops box from the nearby storage shed. The fresh snow eased those tasks. The box contained assorted gear we might need.

Jack said, "Geno, you hurting, man? You look like hell!"

"I'm okay. Just pulled something in my back. Let's do this." I turned away from Jack so he wouldn't see the agony in my eyes. The howling wind masked my grunts of pain as we worked.

With considerable effort, we hoisted the painted plywood ice ops box, the size of a short double-wide coffin, into the skiff. I winced, ignoring the starbursts at the periphery of my vision and pressed on. *Oh Lord....* When the rest of the crew arrived from the ready room, all four hoisted the skiff containing the box up almost five feet into the bed of the huge pickup.

Since I was the ranking on-scene petty officer, I grabbed the wheel as Jack wedged into the passenger seat. I hated driving in full ice ops gear. The other three hunkered in the truck's bed around the box and skiff. We prepared for a rough ride at a speed as fast as blowing snow would allow through fender-high drifts. Off-road Dodge Power Wagons were most definitely *not* known for their smooth ride.

The trip to the shore where Mrs. Diggins saw the fisherman head out burned thirty precious minutes. Locked in low-range four-wheel-drive, progress was slow. But without that plow and generous ground clearance under that ridiculous-looking truck, we would not have made it.

Chapter 26

Onto the Ice Pack

At the shore, with the skiff unloaded from the truck but still containing the box, our crew of five strapped ice cleats over our wetsuit boots. Regulations required that the bulk of our bodies remain inboard of the skiff's gunwales, along with the box. This safety protocol allowed one leg outside the skiff, biting into and pushing on the ice. This was in case the entire affair crashed through the rimy—soft and slushy—ice into the deadly water below.

Now, an hour after sunset, with lousy near-zero visibility only made worse by our portable spotlights reflecting off the wind-driven snow, we set off using the vector provided by Mrs. Diggins. Barely made out her silhouette through her window. Might have been waving to us. I radio'd Ron on 22.

Pushing and sliding that five-hundred-pound boat/sled with another half ton of humanity aboard made for slow skidding. After five torturous minutes of this, there it was, the crack—cold obsidian water—that Mrs. Diggins had spotted before sunset. With the crew in the skiff, Jack pushed from behind before jumping in himself as the boat slid into the cold water.

. . .

Two of the crew pulling on the now-deployed oars propelled us across the thirty-foot span of open water in no time. Then it was a matter of shipping—storing—the oars, transferring the crew, and once again pulling the boat up onto the offshore ice pack. We continued skidding it from inside, one foot pushing on the ice with our cleats biting in. Like a gang of five boys on one scooter.

Compounding the torment from my back, my thighs burned and chafed against the coarse seams inside my wetsuit. After only a quarter mile and just thirty minutes of desperate effort, I learned to hate that rubber wrapper that night. Nobody complained, though. We were *on mission.* Cramped thighs, shoulders, and backs begged for relief. There could be none. For how long we did not know.

Through gritted teeth, I said, "C'mon, guys. Time's a wastin'."

Over an hour later, when fatigue slowed us to a crawl, we barely spotted the headlights of a cluster of vehicles perhaps a hundred feet to our northwest.

Jack shouted over the shrieking wind, "Hey Geno, over there!" Upon sighting our mission objective, fatigue evaporated. We corrected course to our left, and approached the motley bunch of victims we referred to as *vics*—one syllable versus two. Five minutes later, we reached a second crack in the ice. It lay between us and the twenty-five men, eight women, six pickups and four sedans, including a brand new Cadillac De Ville. We could see the Caddy still sported a dealer sticker in the rear driver-side window.

I scanned the frazzled group of victims on the other side of the crack with my powerful handheld spotlight, now just a couple dozen feet away. "Look at that, Jack. None of 'em took shelter in their vehicles. I bet they're afraid of getting trapped inside if the ice breaks. If they only knew it wouldn't make any difference if that happened."

Jack hollered, "Think they're happy to see us, dude?" We thought so based on their waving and shouting. Not that we heard much over the wind, but we imagined they were shouting based on their expansive body language. Sheltering the handheld VHF radio from the wind, I updated Ron. "Saginaw River, be advised 33 vics, several vehicles."

Their lights also now revealed disappearing tracks behind the vehicles on the snow-covered ice. They'd driven back toward shore when this crack in the ice had stopped them. Already five feet across, it now widened by the moment, and none of us was sure of the stability of their large ice floe.

"Guys, this crack isn't much wider than the beam of the skiff right now, so drop her in the water and stabilize her from both sides of the break." I directed the victims to line up single file on the far side with an up-and-down motion of my arm, the pain of now doing so notwithstanding. One by one, the first few stepped into the skiff, using it as a bridge to cross the crack.

Another crew member, Boo Baxter, warned everyone that the gap had widened further. Nobody needed to mention that this far from shore, shelter, and dry clothes, one misstep meant certain death.

I said, "Jack, un-ship the oars and ferry four across at a time. Take Boo with you to help. This break will now get a lot wider fast, so let's get it done safely. Remember our training."

"Roger." Jack knew his job. He also knew it helped me to remind him. Jack was up for promotion and would soon lead his own sorties.

During the next ten minutes, the crack expanded to at least 20 feet across. Jack rowed the skiff toward the remaining anglers. Boo hollered, "Folks, there's no hurry, so wait until Jack and I help you aboard *one at a time*, okay? We do *not* want to capsize this little boat. We have time." He accompanied his every verbal direction with hand signals. The wind shrieked.

The skiff's port side now lay against the sea side of the crack. Boo kneeled on the ice with a firm grasp on the skiff's gunwale. They saw no visible panic in the group. The fishermen remained in single file and had even kept the women who had not yet been ferried across at the head of the line. *Huh. Chivalry lives.*

Jack made eye contact with each woman as they approached the edge of the ice, repeating loudly, also using hand signals. "Hi. I'm Jack. This is Boo. Okay, I need one of you at a time to *slowly* board the boat with Boo's help. *Stay low*, and carefully make your way toward the bow of the boat—that's the front. Here we go. Ma'am, you first. Start forward into the boat now."

Wide-eyed and trembling, the first woman tripped as she struggled to gain control of her feet. Despite the cold, he saw a ring of sweat around the neck of her sweatshirt, underneath her parka. She did not panic despite her obvious fear and stiff joints from exposure.

With four vics aboard, Boo pushed off and Jack rowed the now-heavily laden craft. Once back to the shore side of the crack, I held the skiff while each vic crawled up onto the ice.

Jack repeated this process until only three fishermen and all the vehicles remained. The crack's choppy maw now yawned at least 50 feet across and continued to widen at an accelerating rate. The offshore wind howled louder than ever, and had sunk its teeth into the ice pack, driving it farther north. And the temperature continued to plummet.

Boo relieved Jack, who was now obviously exhausted. Rowing a loaded skiff against a strong wind had sapped his remaining strength. I accompanied Boo to assist the last of the vics. Standard crew rotation.

The rest of the crew kept the shore-side vics in a tight group. Two handheld spotlights tried to illuminate portions of the scene. A vortex of snow and wind made conversation impossible. Visibility now approached zero—a white-out. Choppy water made controlling the skiff difficult. Upon arriving back at the seaward side of the break, it was clear enough to read the unmitigated fear swelling in the first man's eyes.

"Don't leave us here!" the first man shouted. His voice broke. Wasn't sure what he said. His eyes screamed his fear.

I crawled out of the gyrating skiff onto the ice down on all fours.

The now-steep wind-driven chop threatened to hole her thin aluminum skin on the floe's jagged edge.

I put my covered mouth to his covered ear and screamed until my throat hurt. "Okay, sir, we're gonna get you into the boat now. You know the drill. Move slowly, stay low, *crawl* forward. But first, you'll need to take a big step. Are you ready?"

He screamed in my ear. "Please don't let me fall in!" The smell of fear oozed from this guy's every pore, now that it was his turn.

Boo gripped the boat, balancing the need to keep it close to the ice but pushing off hard enough against the wind doing its best to crush it into the ice's jagged edge. We now kept as low as possible in the heart of this menacing maelstrom. Wincing in pain at the effort, fighting off those stars again, I helped the fisherman into the skiff, who then crawled forward. On the verge of capitulating to his fear, the poor fellow hugged the skiff's forward bench in a white-knuckled embrace.

The next guy seemed composed and seated himself next to his terror-stricken friend in seconds to console him with pats on the back and a brotherly hug.

The last man, however, stood back and waved me over.

He shouted into my ear over the gale, "Hey, man, I ain't leavin' my Caddy!" I didn't hear him. He repeated his declaration.

"Sir, you have no choice. We gotta go before it becomes impossible to row against that wind."

"Son, that car is brand-frickin' new!"

In a single fluid motion, I shoved into the man's face a standard liability release and a pen extracted from a waterproof envelope, using my body as a windscreen. SOP. The guy looked shocked as pen and paper seemed to magically appear, with the wind trying its best to shred it or snatch it away. I had had it tucked inside an inner pocket of my parka. We always carry liability releases.

"Sir, I need you to sign this form, please. Here, use my back to write on, but please hurry."

"The hell is *this*?"

"After you're dead, nobody gets sued. You will be gone by dawn if you stay with your brand new car. Your signature on this document prevents your surviving heirs from suing Uncle Sam. Otherwise, I suggest you get into the boat. Like RIGHT *NOW!*"

There were those stars confusing my vision again. The stress didn't help. *Oh, Lord....*

Chapter 27

Nobody Died

With everyone safely on the shore-side of the break at last, the tattered group began our mile-plus trek toward shore into the teeth of the unrelenting gale. We didn't really know how far it was. We had a compass, nothing more. Protocol mandated the same push-and-slide routine, but with so many of us now, that was no longer practical.

With visibility measured in feet, we connected everyone to the skiff with a hundred feet of stout but small-diameter double-braided nylon line retrieved from the ice ops box. Two of our crew remained in the skiff to push-and-slide. The other three pushed from its rear. Everyone leaned into the wind, heads down, and I imagined more than a few of us were uttering prayers.

If anyone got lost in the maelstrom now, they would not survive. Strung out behind us, the party trudged along in single file, like soaps-on-a-rope out for a hike. This also distributed our collective weight over a larger surface area on the increasingly fragile ice pack. We didn't say any of this out loud, but if anyone plunged to a now-certain death, at least we'd have their body tethered to the skiff for easier recovery of their corpse, assuming we didn't all perish.

Jack and I determined the shoreward course from within the boat. We guided the group on the reciprocal course of our original path out. Survival without that handheld compass that night was improbable. Too easy to imagine a straight line to oblivion. We both knew that from experience on the boats in a dense summertime fog. The mind plays tricks. And like wave-tossed water, there were no tracks to follow.

Heading into the wind was an indicator, but if the wind shifted, or we missed the location of our truck by any distance? We already suffered from fatigue, and many from exposure, especially the vics. No, without that compass, well, do the math.

By the time our ragged human chain arrived at the next crack, it had widened to reveal seventy-five feet of wind-savaged chop. Nothing is harder to cross in a small craft than vicious cycloidal waves, common in rough water less than 30 or 40 feet in depth. Once again, the crew rowed like madmen *against* the wind one way, carrying four vics at a time, and wildly skidding empty *with* the wind the other.

We'd long ago spent our adrenaline, now replaced with the shakes. Raw determination and commitment born of training and desperation drove us now. And for me, acute pain. Exhaustion created waves of nausea for some. At least once, I veered to the side of our path to puke on the ice with the wind at my back. Then, back to work. Nobody noticed.

Moving the skiff across the expanse of open water became dangerous as it disappeared in the blowing snow. Even though that gap was too rough to safely navigate, we had no choice. We reduced the load to three vics for each crossing instead of four. Then two. Somehow, an hour later, thirty-three victims and five crew walked ashore less than a hundred yards from our truck. We were all the worse for wear, but alive. I updated Ron on channel 22. He advised medical transport would be standing by at the terminus of Bayshore Drive.

. . .

By this time, several of the group suffered from severe hypothermia, like discolored noses, fingers, and lethargy. General shock symptoms made it difficult for some to walk the last few steps. Especially once we encountered the up-slope of the snow-drifted beach. Our stiff semi-able-bodied crew or their fellow anglers half-carried those worst off.

"Please, let me lie down for five minutes. I can't...." cried one young man before his voice died in the gale; although the winds here were partially blocked by beach house and trees.

"We're almost there, partner," Jack hollered as he threw the man's arm around his own neck and continued trudging through drifting snow.

Six hours into the mission, victims, and rescuers required medical attention. From his post at the station, Ron had indeed arranged for a train of ambulances from two counties to stand by near the end of Bayshore Drive. Six brief trips to and from the beach with the Power Wagon delivered the entire party to transport and treatment.

The slogan of the US Coast Guard is *Semper Paratus—Always Ready*. But in the cab of that rusty old Power Wagon that night, I whispered a rather different slogan: "Nobody died, man." By now, non-stop convulsive muscle spasms wracked my back and muddled my brain. I knew that even pressing the truck's stiff clutch to shift gears was now beyond my ability. So, I just crawled up into the passenger seat.

"Hey Geno," Jack looked to his right once we were both in the dimly lit cab, "Are you *cryin'*, man?"

"Naw, the frickin' wind, ya know?"

Euphoria at completing this mission trumped the near-debilitating pain. At least for now. This had been a good night.

Meanwhile, the trio of 18- to 20-year-old crew members in the truck's bed hunkered low against the wind's brutality. They all fell sound asleep despite the old Power Wagon's best effort to buck them out.

Eight weeks later, the USCG delivered an official *hazard to navigation citation* to the owner of the Cadillac. After the ice melted that spring, he was obligated by maritime law to remove that *hazard to navigation* four miles off the southern shore of Saginaw Bay in shallow water. It would cost him at least ten-thousand dollars. Sea salvage never came cheap. The water was less than twenty feet deep, or it would have cost much more. They issued citations to the others, too, but *this* one felt good to me. Moral? No moral. The guy was alive, along with the rest of 'em. Good enough.

Chronic lower-back muscle spasms and two ruptured discs forced me to undergo intensive physical therapy at the VA Hospital in Detroit. While I completed the last year of my service commitment before my honorable discharge with distinction, this would be the genesis of my lifelong battle with acute or chronic back pain. I'd put off surgery for another 35 years before the pain grew so intense that my mobility, even with a walker, became my biggest challenge.

I'll remember this mission for the rest of my life. A small-town reporter had later asked me about that night. I just said, "I'm grateful for the opportunity to serve as a member of a US Coast Guard Search and Rescue teams right here in America. Many of my high school friends have no choice but to *take* human lives in Vietnam. I'm honored to have helped *save* a lot of lives in my four years with the teams. I will forever be grateful for that. Will always feel good. And I thank my brothers and sisters who got their jobs done in combat, too. Just not right for me." Ever the messenger of a socially conscious message, I am!

But to myself, I thought, *Why did I have to rip the shit out of my back for that arrogant Cadillac owner who wasn't the least bit grateful?* In that instant, I saw myself just as arrogant as that asshole. We'd done something really good, and here I was wallowing in a self-pity party. I was ashamed. More *trouble with thinking.*

Looking back on that night now, I *know* if we hadn't *believed* we'd finish that mission, fortified by knowing those people had only us to depend on, we likely would have perished along with them. The conditions were that abominable. But... nobody died.

Chapter 28

Pain Management with Attitude

Boot camp had indeed been a painful growth experience for me—rough *and* rewarding. They had said the same about the rigors of frenzied duty on the Coast Guard Search and Rescue teams. But I found SAR duty *profoundly* fulfilling. My Navy buddies joked about us coasties in the *shallow-water Navy*. But most possessed an abiding respect for how many different jobs a single coastie filled compared to a Navy billet, and how we accomplished so much with so little.

After all, compared to the well-funded Navy, we often joked that the USCG held itself together with bubble gum and bailing wire. But we also relied on the can-do attitude of every coastie with diverse skills working as part of a tight team.

Those four years cost me most of the foolishness of my youth, *and* a painful spinal injury that remained a lifelong badge of honor, a useful reminder. The Coast Guard taught me how to shut up, show up, take command, and fix problems.

. . .

After four proud years of service, however, I spent much of my twenties in a dusky haze of cigarette and marijuana smoke. I offered no excuses or explanations, other than perhaps *pain management with attitude.* During periods of clarity after the first few years, TM really helped. Yes, I was now a disabled veteran, a hard pill to swallow. And I hated pills. But this was now part of my trip.

Clearly, complete maturity still eluded me, but I felt much better about myself. Now, I needed to find the grace to treat those around me with more respect. Starting with my bride of almost five years by then, and the mother of our two children—daughter Michelle, and son Adam. I had transitioned directly from a full-time *coastie* to a professional student. Seems I had at last developed a yearning for learning. Everything. But it would take several more decades to learn the most important lesson of all—the universe did not revolve around me. Like it or not, my life was no longer a command-and-control situation.

Soon after my discharge, we bought our first house. Kay recently reminded me that was only possible because, once again, my dear parents had come to the rescue in their latter years with little or no acknowledgment from me. God, I was so self-centered. They'd cashed in a whole-life insurance policy they'd carried on me forever to help us with a down-payment. We paid a whopping $16,000 for that rather humble abode late in 1973, and I think we only paid 10% down. Still a bloody fortune. I marvel that we recently paid more than twice the cost of that first house for a used car.

Chapter 29

Professional Student

I WORKED A FEW SHORT-TERM JOBS AFTER RECEIVING MY honorable discharge from the Coast Guard in February 1973. These included night manager of a hotel, spinning records at an FM radio station, and I even sold advertising for a short time. I realized none of these were fulfilling. Besides, these filler jobs weren't paying the bills, even though Kay worked two jobs as a waitress *and* as a hotel switchboard operator. I decided the need for higher education had come due. Besides, now the G.I. Bill—Uncle Sam—would help pay my tuition.

But I saw no reason to jump headlong into a curriculum that'd probably earn me a paycheck just yet. Even though I was now a family man with a wife and two kids, I still lacked usable commercial wisdom. So, I followed my heart, as I was prone to do. Still am. I studied liberal arts: the humanities, including philosophy; art appreciation; sculpture; comparative religions; and a few other such courses. You know, intellectual masturbation. Yep, I dove into a course of study that, outside of academia, possessed little commercial value. That wore on for a couple of years.

~

Then, Kay delivered an ultimatum, of sorts. "Gene, I know you love learning and thinking creatively, but when are you gonna take some classes that will earn us an actual living?"

Upon introspection, I thought, *Jeez, she's right. Besides, it's time to learn something new anyway.* Since men earned so much higher salaries than women for comparable jobs, we'd made the mutual decision to put our meager funds into getting the man of the house educated. And now, it was time I put on my big-boy pants. So I informed my college guidance counselor at the Rochester Community College of my intention to switch from Liberal Arts to Electronics Engineering Technology—the next day.

The befuddled woman failed to prevent her incredulous surprise from reaching her face. She blurted, "*What?!*"

But I was resolute. Kay was right. As usual. She always has been, and still is, my voice of logic and reason. Probably how Mom operated with Daddy, now that I think about it. I was okay that my voice of reason came from her mouth. Always struck me how quickly she could retrieve a gazillion salient facts, but just never had the advantage of much higher education. Yeah, I needed to get serious about earning an adequate paycheck. That meant a real job. And to me, that meant the right college degree. And once I get set on a course of action, *jump back!*

After all, I had been out of the service for almost three years and had no sheepskin to show for it. My 27th birthday had come and gone, for cryin' out loud. Yeah, Kay was right. You'll notice it never occurred to me to abandon my higher education altogether. Not since the age of 19, when my head was still firmly embedded in my punk ass.

~

I FOUND the next year-and-a-half exhilarating. A new passion captivated me—electronics! Brought back memories of my pre-teen years (before I became *cool*) when smoke curling up from a soldering iron loaded with flux and melting solder conjured fantasies of over-the-air communication from a kit I built. I'd forgotten how much I enjoyed a visit to the hobby store with Dad (I no longer called him *Daddy*). I was thirteen. I bought, then built a crystal radio set. And the subsequent thrill of hearing it receive music and voice out of thin air? None of my friends got it. Dad did. A dreamer. Like me.

So, RCC trained me to be an effective electronics research and development lab technician. I even thought about pursuing a four-year electronics engineering degree. But when within a quarter of achieving my two-year Associate's degree in EET, the time came to cast a wide net by sending out resumes. First, locally. And failing a satisfactory result, I'd made a gazillion paper copies. I sent them to any company in the electronics industry nationwide. Email wasn't a thing yet.

My guidance counselor helped me assemble a list. As I recall, my GPA was excellent. A pleasant surprise to everyone, including me. Not 4.0 of 4.0, but close to it. I had a knack for this electronics stuff: theory of circuitry, logic, computer-aided design, and diligently documenting the results of lab experiments. But who'd hire an aging adult student? After all, I'd be pushing 30 in a couple of years. Not a spring chicken anymore.

IF YOU WERE FROM ROCHESTER, Minnesota, possessed ambition, and were career-oriented, two major employers instantly sprang to mind: Mayo and IBM. I held a computer operator job in the ECG lab at the Mayo Clinic for a couple of semesters while at school. Later, I applied for an entry position at IBM. After all, I *imagined* I was ambitious, and Kay wanted a career for me. For us.

She worked at the front desk of one of the two local Holiday Inns.

This was where the Rochester IBM midrange computer systems research, development, and manufacturing facility, comprising almost 8,000 employees, boarded its out-of-town recruits. So, when job applicants came to town for an interview, IBM put them up at the second-nicest hotel in town—the Holiday Inn Downtown. The Kahler Hotel was for Middle Eastern oil sheiks and visiting politicians who were patients at the Mayo Clinic. And where Kay and I had spent our two-night honeymoon nine years earlier.

While working the hotel's front desk, Kay got to know one of the IBM HR guys who screened job applicants. I forget his name. Let's call him Ray. She noticed my name on one of Ray's potential recruit's folders as she made small talk with him at the hotel's front desk. "Hey, that's my husband, Ray! Take a serious look at him. He's sharp and ambitious. Plus, since he's local, no need to move him to Rochester as we already live here."

Now, I do not know how much that influenced Ray, but three days later I got a call. Would I come in for an interview? *Hell, yeah.* A month later, three months before graduating from RCC, I started an entry-level job as a lab technician supporting hardcore development engineers responsible for large-scale integration. Think *complex computer chip design.* They told me I needed to learn a lot of new stuff about computer-aided microchip design. I chuckled and thought, *Bring it on!*

Both Kay and I sailed higher than a kite that February in 1977, *four years to the day* after my discharge from the service. The pay was decent, although our bills were not. I started as an hourly employee, but possessed some latitude in deciding how much time-and-a-half overtime to work. There was no shortage of work.

Kay advised me precisely how many overtime hours I needed to work to pay the bills each pay period. But not so much that we'd get thrown into a higher tax bracket. She's a genius with money and budgets. Always has been. One smart girl.

I reveled in how readily I absorbed any technical task thrown at me and took pride in excelling at it. My managers valued my contributions. They consistently rated me a *one-performer.* IBM's merit-based pay-for-performance system rated each employee annually from top performance as a *one-performer* to substandard as a *four-performer.* If anyone got appraised a *four* more than once, they'd be on their way out the door. But I'd found my niche. Thankfully, I had listened to Kay about changing my course of study to something with a payout!

But it wouldn't be long before life threw another wild twist of fate at us.

Chapter 30

Flood of the Century

A little more than a year later, in early July of 1978, merciless gods pummeled Rochester with 5.5 inches of rain within a few hours. This became the genesis of yet another life-changing event for me and for my little family.

We had returned from visiting Kay's relatives in Chicago earlier that day. She and I had taken the kids to a movie: "The Cheap Detective" starring Peter Falk. The theater lost power. The manager announced that they were refunding the cost of our tickets and that we needed to evacuate the theater immediately. We headed for the parking lot that night to retrieve our old 1967 flat-nosed Dodge van. We each carried one of our young kids and *waded* to the van in ankle-deep water.

We slow-slogged the three miles home to find the pancake-flat lot around our house under at least four inches of standing water. Once we'd carried Michelle and Adam into the house, which was only three steps up from the sidewalk to the main floor, we put them to bed upstairs in their story-and-a-half bedrooms.

. . .

Thunder rolled through the Rochester valley non-stop. I worried about all that water. Lightning lit up the sky outside. I stumbled down the basement stairs of our ancient house to inspect the foundation. I was still stiff from the seven-hour drive in our old van earlier that day. The walls of our foundation were little more than stacked limestone blocks with no mortar between them, but covered with a veneer of cement. The entire Rube Goldberg affair extended about two feet under the outside perimeter of the house.

Water *shot* in several horizontal streams six feet into the basement's interior. I kneeled down at the base of the stairs to inspect one crack in the concrete through which water invaded my beloved man cave. That basement was little more than a hole in the ground. Its floor was so uneven that it presented numerous tripping hazards, like a real cave, but that was where I tinkered with my electronics experiments. That was also my place of refuge, even though I couldn't stand up straight except between the ragged old wooden beams holding the house up above me.

Then the wall phone near the top of the stairs rang. Kay answered and hollered down to me, "Gene, it's Meek. Wants to talk!"

I hustled up the creaky steps, worrying about the pressure behind all that water that, so far, was just swirling down the floor drain. "Hey, Meek, what's up?" Meek was one of my dope-smoking buddies after I got out of the service during my foolish hiatus from TM. He was also a year behind me at RCC. A smart guy, but like me, lacked what Kay called common sense. And he didn't have Kay.

"Geno, how're you liking your gig at Big Blue?"

"It's good, man. Really good. Pay is decent, and I'm actually using some of the stuff I learned at RCC. I'm helping some engineers with circuit design, and not just that analog op-amp stuff from school. Real transistor-to-transistor digital logic. Micro shit. That's the future. Why?"

I heard Meek's noisy mental wheels grinding and spinning. After a brief silence, he said, "They called me up. Offered me an interview."

"That's awesome, dude. So what's the problem?"

"Well, I'm just one quarter from graduating with my two-year degree. Think I'll make more after I that." This was to be one of Meek's pivotal moments; he'd realize that years later.

"You're not thinking about declining—"

"Not sure. You never finished your two-year degree. You regret that?"

"Look, man, I'll tell you what Kay told me. 'You're going to school to get a job.' You're likely to get an offer after that interview. And I'm guessing they'll only call ya once. Do the math, old buddy."

"I hear ya, but—" And the entire house shook as if it were being crunched down under a giant's boot heel. Earthquake? In Minnesota? Probably not. Meek said, "What the hell was *that*?" He'd heard me gasp and maybe heard the *bang*, too.

"Gotta go." I slammed down the wall phone's receiver.

At first, we thought maybe a car had crashed into the house. I looked out the small kitchen window, then the big one in the living room. In the darkness, lightning still blazed non-stop. I saw water still standing on the grass outside by lightning's light, although it now looked like it was... *moving*? Then, remembering the water spraying into the basement, I opened the door, peered down the steps, and saw... more lightning! And horizontal rain... *in a basement with no windows?*

As I crept down the stairs to figure out what had happened, there was a pile of rubble that had crushed the bottom few steps. Right above where I'd been kneeling less than a minute earlier. *Oh, shit!* Did Meek's call just save my life? Most of the foundation on the west side of our house, more than half its length, had caved in onto the basement floor. I'd learn the next day over 30 feet of collapsed foundation took out our entire electrical panel. Yup, that explained the immediate power outage.

We also lost our ancient gravity furnace, all our family picture albums in boxes down there, and most of my experiments. I'd imagined some of those might produce substantive results. Yeah, along with our old basement, *I* was crushed. We all were. We feared the entire house would now collapse into the basement.

First things first. Staying in a hotel wasn't an affordable option, even for one night, much less indefinitely. But we trundled the kids and our two dogs into our old windowless van through about six inches of standing water now in our gravel driveway and went... somewhere. I don't remember where. At least we were all safe. We might have even slept in the back of the van. I'd done so before in the Coast Guard. She already sported a mattress and a bucket. All the essentials. We envisioned her as a camper.

Most of the next year proved to be both chaotic and transforming. For months, all four of us experienced terrible nightmares about thunderstorms, houses collapsing, and becoming homeless. IBM threw a thousand dollars at us, which was a godsend. That was a lot of money in 1978. They helped us hire a contractor and to apply for a low-interest disaster relief loan. Many people in Rochester, particularly on the east side of town, were in the same boat (bad pun intended).

IBM also gave me as much time off as I needed to get our personal situation settled. I truly believed their motto after that: *Our people are our most important asset.* That belief would capture my absolute loyalty for the next 30 years!

Fortunately, we had not yet accumulated a lot of debt. We leased an apartment across town. The kids were still preschool age, so school wasn't yet an issue. But our two dogs were. They spent the first few nights with us in our van, I think. Had we splurged and rented a hotel room? Or had we indeed hunkered down in our beloved teal-green "hippie van"? Another memory lost in the fog of time-worn tragedy.

. . .

The water in our neighborhood subsided in less than 24 hours. Once we recovered from the initial shock of losing our home, we decided to keep our two huge Irish wolfhounds, our gentle giants, in the house's fenced-in backyard. They weren't allowed in the apartment we rented. If you're not aware, Irish wolfhounds are the tallest dogs in the world.

Even though Brogan and Heather were mostly inside dogs (I know, I know), I built a backyard shelter from bales of hay topped with a 4-by-8-foot sheet of plywood. With summer temperatures, they were in no danger of freezing. We'd cross town to visit them twice a day to feed and play with them. This was long before someone popularized the concept of emotional support animals, but we later realized that's precisely what they'd become to all four of us.

Chapter 31

Flood Recovery

Contracting a house-moving company proved to be yet another adventure, even though we only needed to move it up. Human Resources (Personnel) at IBM helped us locate such a contractor. It was a miracle the house hadn't caved in to the basement, they said.

But with no electricity or water, the place was an unlivable mess anyway. I shoveled mud for weeks. We indeed lost all of our family picture albums and everything else stored down there. My manager, Bob Braaten, even showed up in rubber boots to help shovel mud and to hand Kay a check. I'll never forget *that.* Thanks again, IBM, and Bob, wherever you are.

Over the next few months, we salvaged what little was possible from that muddy hole that now also stunk like a sewer-fed swamp. But we saw progress as the movers raised the entire house over six feet, a few inches at a time. They'd punched holes in the foundation opposite the cave-in, and hoisted huge wooden beams under the house through those holes. They then blocked up the entire structure from both outside and inside the hole under each beam-end.

Quite an impressive engineering feat. They positioned dozens of hydraulic barrel jacks under their beams, pumped 'em each up a few inches, and wedged in more timbers. Then, they'd repeat the process until they'd achieved the desired elevation of the entire structure.

Once they'd raised the house and secured it, a crew dug out the hole six feet larger than the house's perimeter. First, the rubble got trucked away after a great deal of hand-shoveling. Later, a skilled operator drove a skid-loader with a small hydraulic bucket down a short earthen ramp into the hole beneath the house to haul out more dirt and rubble to a waiting dump truck.

Over a quiet weekend, I tried my hand at driving that skid loader. Yeah, that was not one of my skills, nor one of my finer moments. I tipped the whole damn rig into the hole. The contractor had to rescue it from my handiwork on Monday. Boy, was he pissed! But I'd learned my lesson. I was a desk jockey and an electronics nerd. I'd stick to my skill set after that.

Rain continued to plague the area for several weeks. The house mover's concern? The rain-saturated dirt walls of his fresh hole kept peeling off and tumbling into the hole, threatening the bracing that held up the entire house.

I DON'T REMEMBER how long it took to complete the clean-out, to pour the footings, and to lay up 13 courses (layers) of steel-rebar-reinforced concrete block. We then installed drain "tile"—4-inch-diameter perforated plastic pipe—around the base of the new foundation and slapped a heavy layer of tar and plastic sheeting around the foundation's exterior. I think I did a lot of this myself. The drain tile tied into a sump basket recessed in the basement floor, where we'd install a pump if needed. We never found the need.

The contractor also built up the dirt all around the house to create a drainage slope away from our new foundation. They poured the concrete for a new driveway, interior floor, installed a new furnace, and electrical panel. As I recall, we moved back in after several months, before the winter of 1978-1979. Much remained in-progress or unfinished. We didn't care.

Later, someone in the media labeled this 1978 "water event" the *hundred-year flood.* Folks who lived in the Rochester valley at the time still call it that. This progressive city spent millions on flood control projects after that. We've not seen damage of that magnitude since. Of course, it's *only* been a *half*-century.

Once this old house sat atop its new foundation, however, none of the doors or windows worked. The new foundation was dead-nuts level and square. Obviously, the old house on top of it was none of the above. They'd warned us about this probability. New stresses pinched every opening, and not in a way that was window- or door- or cabinet-friendly.

It took much of the next decade to correct the plethora of problems created by bending our house to the will of this foreign foundation. Why so long? We needed time, motivation, energy, *and* money *concurrently* to keep the endless list of projects moving forward.

We spent those years in a somewhat dysfunctional but livable house. We continued to remodel it from the new basement floor all the way up to the shingles atop this story-and-a-half relic. An electrical engineer friend and fellow nerd I worked with at IBM, John Schmidt, spent a lot of time with me overthinking solutions to every little or big problem. Solving problems is what engineers do. Thanks, old friend. Our creative solutions provided an ongoing therapeutic distraction. For me, at least.

For example, no ordinary steep set of stairs like the ones we had would work, anymore. The house now perched almost six feet higher. A much longer set of stairs would take too much space. So we decided that a three-quarter-turn *spiral* staircase made better design sense. Plus, that would be a lot *cooler* (that word stuck to me like a big dog on a short leash back then).

We acquired 2-inch-thick rough-sawn white-oak lumber from a nearby small-town lumber mill and hauled it in an old Ford pickup I got a deal on—that's how I talked back then, ending sentences with prepositions, and all. The wood was still wet; that is, it wasn't cured and was likely to warp a lot, since we bought it fresh and cheap right off the sawmill's blades.

We engineered the staircase so that as that wet wood cured, it only got stronger and straighter. This project became a functional work of art. We notched the hollow square center pole and the walls on two sides of the staircase to receive each step's open tread and assembled the entire 12-foot-tall *sculpture* without using a single bolt or screw. We'd add that hardware once we'd proven the concept, but only as a backup.

Then Kay slapped us with a rude splash of reality. She said, "So, boys, how are we gonna get furniture down this contraption?" No mistaking her condescending down-nod toward what she called *the hole*.

"Oh, shit," I said.

But then John's brilliant engineering brain kicked in. "No problem. We'll build an outside entrance, like the slanted steel doors to a tornado shelter. Use that space to store and haul in firewood, too. It'll be great!"

I don't recall if Kay rolled her eyes at that point, but I gotta believe she did. John had helped us so much already. She gave us the green light. At least, this is how *I* remember it.

Next challenge. Those slanted doors would be set on a cinder block extension to the new foundation underneath our new rear deck, which was about five feet above ground level. The steps were oak slats to be removed when we'd use that that pit to store firewood, which was most of the time. Remember, we'd raised the entire house. Hard to move furniture underneath that deck, though. So *naturally,* John and I built a drawbridge over those doors! Perfect sense, right?

Well, this would be a raisable five-foot-wide section of deck, eight feet long, and hinged to a header bolted the house's new concrete block foundation. We'd hoist it high enough above those exterior doors with draw ropes or cables to provide adequate clearance above the *tornado doors.* We then conjured a cool idea to raise that 200+ pound section of deck with a series of cables and pulleys. Power it with a garage door opener motor bolted high to the rear wall of the house. But that's where Kay put her foot down. Oh, well.

Instead, we'd lift it manually and prop it up on the rare occasions when we'd need to move furniture in or out. When we removed the steps so that the pit underneath received a pickup load of firewood once a week, there was no need to raise the drawbridge.

A pickup load of firewood weekly? Yeah, that's because we'd installed a freestanding wood-burning stove in our new *lower-level* family room. It was no longer just a *basement*! That stove was our Plan B for providing heat during frigid Minnesota winters. That stove heated the entire house when necessary because the spiral staircase conducted heat upward to the kitchen and even to the small second story like a giant chimney flue.

We further increased the efficiency of that flue effect with a ceiling fan above the spiral's center pole. Shades of Rube Goldberg, or what? One winter the temps plummeted to a minus 90-degree windchill, and we were mighty glad we had that stove! So was our new furnace that tried unsuccessfully to keep up.

After purchasing a chainsaw, I spent a good deal of time finding sources of wood to cut, split, and burn. That became a therapeutic avocation for me for the years we owned that needy house. While not at work, I nurtured a network of farmers and landowners who needed small areas of tillable land or *gray ghosts* (long-dead trees) cleared. I'd offer my services for free. Talk about the frontier spirit! At least, that's what it felt like. A white-collar guy by day, and a lumberjack nights and weekends!

Chapter 32

Fired Up!

Then, the delectable madness escalated even further, or so judged level-headed Kay. Blame my hippie heritage. I discovered this amazing new magazine, *Mother Earth News.* That rag was becoming all the rage back then, especially with the hippies who never entirely escaped the '60s. From its pages, I implemented a *wood-fired hot tub.*

Such contraptions—hot tubs—weren't much of a thing in the late '70s. I believe I was one of the first to build and own one in Rochester, maybe in Minnesota! Maybe not. Though it's fun to imagine that now.

Recall the new deck we'd built on the back of the house was five feet above grade. So, I built up a six-by-six-foot square comprising five layers of cinder block atop a 4-inch-thick concrete slab, all inset into the deck. Pouring that slab *under* the deck taught me yet another new set of rudimentary skills. Remember, I was a desk jockey who struggled to understand the basics of any trade other than computer research and development.

Altogether, this created a five-foot cube, open at the top and flush with the deck's surface, that I'd fill with water. Holes punched through the block at various points provided a way to pump water into that tub. I'd actually had the foresight to put a drain in the slab at the bottom before framing and pouring it, for water to exit this fanciful cube. Yes, I'd almost forgotten that detail during my giddy design phase.

On a smaller slab *behind* the deck and next to the tub sat my boiler. I crafted this affair from an old 50-gallon steel water heater carcass I salvaged somewhere. Yes, I haunted junkyards in those heady days. This was a cylindrical enclosure not quite five feet high. Merle, a neighbor of mine with a welder, cut a firebox door in its side and added a chimney to the top.

Inside its upper half, I coiled 50 feet of soft copper tubing. That became my heat exchanger. I circulated water through this coil with a small pump. This drew water from the bottom of the tub, through the coiled tube in the upper portion of the firebox, and back into the tub's walls. They comprised the tub's *jets*. Plus, the blow side of an old shop-vac provided bubbles via separate incursions through the tub's walls. Hey, it worked!

So, every Saturday morning, I'd stoke the fire in the firebox for a few hours. The small pump wired to a breaker in the basement circulated water non-stop into and out of the tub through that copper tubing inside the boiler just above the wood fire's flames. Then, on Saturday afternoon Kay and I enjoyed *divine soaking*—as the article in *Mother Earth News* called it. Or we'd supervise the kids playing in there. *Or* we'd have a few close friends over for a *pool party*. Later, we added a lid and privacy fence when our "neighbor to the north" complained about us *damn hippies*. Peace, BurDICK!

The whole thing wasn't fancy, but we had an absolute blast, even though it could be a challenge getting out of that monster tub recessed into our new elevated deck. After all, we *were* quite agile in those days.

Our tight circle of friends in the late 1970s enjoyed pool parties, whodunnit murder mystery parties, and just hanging out together. Our kids and sometimes their friends joined the party!

Yes, we lived the high life... on a budget. Nothing has ever felt more luxurious and opulent than that old concrete hot tub, *still* on the wrong side of town. Perspective!

Chapter 33

On a Slow Roll

I've suggested we often skewer, staple, and mutilate memories with time's abrasive passage. But I still remember the day I floated toward heaven, assuming that's where it is. I held a fragile memory in my hand—my Student Pilot Certificate and its Medical Certificate Third Class.

I stared at that yellowed slip of white paper dated November 14, 1983. Can it have been that long? This was just a year after my mother passed, and three years since Dad died. But strangely, their passing did not change the direction of my life. Seemed... natural. They were at peace at last.

So why, then, do I consider *this* memory another key moment to be remembered and celebrated, or lamented? Because on one fateful Saturday a year later, I almost died, taking at least a hundred other souls with me. I often wonder how that day might have turned out differently, or how I'd have been remembered. As a mass murderer? Or a victim of fate? What would I have missed by perishing at the ripe-old age of 35? What might my family have had to endure in the aftermath of ***The Jurrens Massacre?***

Here's what I remember about that day.

1984 WAS ABOUT to become 1985 in a month. CJ, my flight instructor, brought to mind Jessica Biel, an actor who played a tough fighter pilot in the movie "Stealth." As in the movie, CJ was a pilot. But unlike that flick, she was a likable pit bull with one mission in life —to teach student pilots like me how not to screw up, to survive. She was high-speed, low-drag, and generated a helluva lot of lift.

Throughout ground school and flight training with several other student pilots, I eagerly absorbed every nugget of aviation wisdom possible, daring not to miss a thing. Why? Well, CJ threatened the probability of instant death if I didn't pay attention to her every sacred syllable. Her words turned out to be prophetic. "Your life depends on learning this, to make this stuff automatic," she'd say upon offering yet another pearl of wisdom. I believed her.

When the two of us climbed into the cockpit together, I'd fear forgetting some critical factoid. Even back then at the tender age of 34. Flying was a lot like learning how to drive a car, but in three dimensions instead of two. That meant a lot more variables. And no center stripes or dotted lines *up there. So* many things to forget. And every one of them potentially meant auguring into the dirt at 100+ knots. Or into somebody's living room. That was the purpose of an array of checklists on laminated cards. There existed checklists for everything.

My fast-track career at IBM exploded in the '80s. I had little time for punching recreational holes in the sky *every* Saturday morning. But I'd manage an hour or two of flight training with CJ whenever possible. She kept warning, "You gotta take this stuff seriously, Gene. Gotta stay in the moment." That was a polite way to say, "Lousy or poorly exercised memory will cause you to forget something important, and that might get us both dead. Gotta show up more often."

See how my mind works? And hers? I thought she was just selling lessons. Boy, was I wrong!

For a year I meandered through the maze of a student pilot's medical exam, ground training classes, studying FARs—Federal Aviation Regulations—and making too-infrequent training flights. With CJ forever in the right seat.

She kept her aircraft at the Rochester International Airport, the second-busiest in Minnesota. We sat on the service ramp in CJ's single-engine, high-wing Cessna 152. She said, "Let's go."

It was November 30th. We clamped headphones over our ears. Their attached microphones perched in front of our faces. By pushing the intercom button on the yokes—our twin steering wheels—we conversed without shouting over the noise and vibration that bombarded the cockpit once we started the engine.

I completed the departure checklist. We received approval to taxi onto runway one-three near its northern end. As we sat there, it occurred to me that the southern end of that runway disappeared over the curvature of the Earth. They'd built this strip long enough to accommodate any aircraft made—except the space shuttle.

I began my roll by cramming the throttle knob forward into the dash. We accelerated. At fifty-five knots, I slowly pulled my yoke toward me with both hands. The Cessna's nose rose. Then we were airborne. Always magical. The little four-banger power plant corralled its hundred horses up toward the prescribed pattern altitude of 2,300 feet. Yup, there it was—that quivering sensation that drew my stomach tighter to my sphincter.

A typical training day comprised three take-offs, some in-flight maneuvering, and three landings. CJ customarily chattered non-stop—instructing me on the finer points of flight. I'd dwell on her every word while concentrating on bending the little plane to my will.

We took off. Routine. Or so I thought.

But that particular Saturday morning was different. As soon as we were airborne, she said, "Okay, fly the pattern, land, and taxi back to position one on the service ramp." Beyond that, the woman remained silent as a tomb. Yup, she had committed to a decision. This could not be good, right?

While I worried about having forgotten some important bit of protocol, I muttered into the boom microphone that hovered close to my mouth. The foam-encased nodule smelled like the last student's breath. Garlic? Onion? Worse? I said, "Something wrong?"

A dead-eye stare back at me broadcast, *Shut up and do what you've been told.*

CJ's hands rested in her lap. During each previous flight, she'd occasionally tickle her yoke with one or more fingertips. Or she'd touch her penny loafers to one or both of the rudder pedals. I'd only feel the results in the aircraft's reaction as the center console blocked my view of her feet. I knew she'd tickle the controls only as she deemed necessary, which influenced my yoke and pedals in tandem.

But she did it in such a way that I never quite knew how much or how little *she* flew the aircraft versus *me*. I found that both comforting *and* disconcerting. Otherwise, she'd be all business, instructing verbally as we hurtled through the southeastern Minnesota sky. I always got my money's worth.

That day, though, she offered no words of encouragement *or* instruction. She remained silent. *Uh-oh.* I thought I knew CJ well enough to read her. Boy, was I wrong. *Is she mad at me?* I landed hard enough to make the tricycle landing gear squat before bouncing back. With a no-nonsense voice and only peering straight ahead, CJ re-confirmed, "Taxi to position one."

That meant I was to roll the aircraft at slow speed and park close to the front of—and parallel to—the small general aviation terminal. I aimed our little bird for a few hundred yards northwest of the passenger terminal en route to position one.

Both of my feet mashed the brakes. As soon as the wheels stopped turning, we sat still, amidst the din. The engine idled. I asked, "Is everything okay? The aircraft seems fine. Did I do something wrong?"

I worried. That's what I do. Her dead-eye stare transformed into a subtle smile. Like always, her voice sounded thin and scratchy through the intercom. She turned her head to face me full-on and said, "You solo today, Gene. I want three good take-offs and three good landings through the pattern. Try not to flatten my landing gear. Just remember your training, your radio protocol, and trust your muscle memory." All business, no banter.

Through the pattern meant to fly in a big rectangle. I was to take off from the day's active runway as designated by the tower, the one we'd just used. Make two left turns to fly back parallel to that runway at a prescribed altitude for this airport. And then make two more lefts. After that, I'd land on the same runway from which I'd taken off. Easy. A big rectangle. I'd practiced that dozens of times. But only with the petite CJ filling the seat next to me, her slender shoulder inches from mine, her confidence boosting my own, her little hands never far from the controls.

She opened her door to get out. But before she did, she swiveled her hips in her bucket seat to peer at me face-on once more, still speaking to me through her boom mic and listening on her headphones. Even at idle, the cockpit still buzzed with noise and vibration. She placed her left hand on my right knee. She said, "You've got this." Must have felt that was necessary as a nod to my vacant stare with one cheek hoisted in an open-mouth gape of incredulity.

Chapter 34

On to Disaster

I THOUGHT, *WAIT, WHAT? I'M NOT READY FOR THIS, AM I?*

But I *said*, "You really think I'm ready." Not a question. "Or you wouldn't be getting out with the engine still running."

"I'll be standing by on all frequencies." She tossed a nod toward the small terminal's direction, a hundred feet off to my left. "Just execute like we practiced, and you'll be fine. Now go."

With that, she squeezed my knee and stripped off her headphones with both hands. Planted them on their hook outboard of her yoke. Swung to her right, dropped her left foot down onto the starboard wing strut's step, and hopped down to the tarmac. She swiveled back to shut and latch the door behind her without uttering another word. But her eyes now just above the bottom of that door's window, spoke volumes.

I sat there. Alone. Watched her amble toward the plane's tail. The engine idled, awaiting my command. I smelled the hot fumes and allowed myself to notice the little aircraft shaking my already quivering buns in the thinly padded seat, as if to urge me into action. The prop spun, along with my head.

. . .

Oh, *crap! Okay, this is it.* I sucked in a deep breath and referred to a laminated card with the airport's *God's eye diagram.* It portrayed its intersecting runways and a few other bits of info printed around its periphery. "Ground Control, this is student pilot in November-49452 on the service ramp. Request clearance to taxi runway one-three via alpha-one-zero."

It gratified me to remember precisely what to say. I spoke "pilot-ese," like a secret code only for aviation insiders. And it came to me effortlessly. Muscle memory. My mouth was apparently a muscle, too.

"Roger, November-49452, taxi to runway one-three."

"Roger." As I eased my feet off the pedals that served as both brakes on the ground and rudder controls in the air, I nudged the throttle knob forward. The plane rolled forward in obedience. My stomach lurched. Doubt overwhelmed me. At that moment, I considered quitting. *I don't need this. Why am I even* ***doing*** *this?*

Upon arriving at the hold-short line at the edge of runway one-three's northern end, I stood on the brakes. Pressed and held the PTT—push-to-talk—button on the left side of the yoke, my steering wheel.

"Ground, this is student pilot in November-49452. Holding short on one-three at alpha-one-zero."

I heard Ground Control's tinny response in my headphones. "November-49452, ground, roger. Contact tower."

"Roger."

I switched to one-eighteen-point-three, the radio frequency for this airport's tower, and requested to stay in the pattern for touch and goes—repetitive takeoffs and landings. Once granted permission, with both feet still on the brakes, I exercised and eyeballed all the control surfaces—they enabled maneuvering the little plane. They included the rudder on the vertical tail controlled by the pedals under my feet, and the yoke, as it controlled the ailerons—the movable trailing edges of both wings, but they always moved in opposite directions. When one angled up, the other went down, and vice versa. I repeated to myself the mantra, *Rudder under my feet turns me left or right, so neat. Yoke to ailerons under my hands banks the craft, and that's the plan.*

I remained at the edge of the same runway used by the big rigs. Just to be sure, I alternated pressure on the foot pedals and saw in my mirror the vertical rudder on the rear of the tail respond. I turned my yoke back and forth and watched the ailerons waggle up and down in response. Yup, all still working. CJ's unattended yoke mimicked my own. But she wasn't there. Nobody sat there. The seat remained empty, but I imagined her benevolent spirit guiding me.

Stomped both of my feet on both brakes harder. Shoved the throttle knob all the way forward hard into the dash with the heel of my sweaty right hand, hungering for the thrill of the *run-up*. In blind obedience, the engine *roared* as it wound up to its maximum 2,300 RPM. The entire airframe bucked in place like a pissed-off bull raging against his gate, bellowing to be let loose. The tiny plane reeked of power and anticipation. And of hot aviation fuel exhaust through the open window at my left shoulder.

The plane tried to roll forward; the brakes squealed. I stomped even harder on the twin pedals. The squealing stopped. Made a mental note. Then I pulled the throttle back to relative quiet again—to idle. A successful run-up. Everything sounded good and everything worked as I remembered from previous training flights. Everything worked, on the ground, anyway.

I closed and latched my small cockpit window, per the checklist. Eased the pressure on the pedals to release the brakes and nudged the throttle again. Coaxed my yoke to line up the tiny plane with the centerline of that vast field of concrete—runway one-three. Where the real magic was about to happen. I was a mosquito with bloodlust, about to take to the air.

That moment reminded me of my first skydive, the last step before exiting the plane, the instant my commitment became irrevocable, irreversible, and... irresponsible? A delicious dilemma.

This was it. I shoved the throttle all the way into the dash again and the plane charged toward the horizon, a hundred horses champing at the bit, accelerating more rapidly than I had any reason to expect. A pleasant surprise every time. But now, was the little craft even quicker and more nimble without CJ aboard? Of course it was.

Seconds later, at fifty-five knots, or about sixty-three miles-per-hour, I drew the yoke a little closer to my chest, toward my pounding heart, just like I'd done many times before, but this felt different. The horizon disappeared as I rotated my mosquito's nose skyward. That simple response caused my stomach to lurch again. I now had no choice but to land this plane... or die.

Chapter 35

Idiot or Hero?

WHAT AM I ***DOING****?* ***WHY*** *AM I DOING THIS? WHO AM I KIDDING? I love this! At least, I love the* ***idea*** *of it.*

My heart pounded in my chest, more so than the blood throbbing in my temples. "Tower, this is student pilot November-49452, upwind, straight-out departure pattern on one-three. Climbing through one-thousand feet. Request turn onto *crosswind* leg of the pattern."

"Roger, student pilot November-49452, *crosswind* approved at eighteen-hundred feet. But you do not need approval for turns in the pattern unless directed otherwise, captain."

Oops. "Roger." *Captain?* I grinned big.

Once at eighteen-hundred feet AGL—above ground level—less than a minute later, I made the ninety-degree left turn, just as I had so often practiced with CJ. After glancing at her lonely yoke, still mimicking mine, I concentrated on easing mine to the left. Added a touch of left pedal to help the turn. Tugged back a bit on the yoke to keep from losing altitude during the turn. No problem. It was already time to turn onto the *downwind* leg of the airport's traffic pattern, parallel to "my" runway, but on a reciprocal course from takeoff.

After turning downwind, the tower said, "November-49452, I will call your *base*."

"Roger." In other words, they'd inform me when to make my next left turn in the pattern. Then, it would be just one turn away from coming around on *final*, when I'd be lined up for my next momentary landing, my first *touch-and-go*. I remember thinking, *Final... such a ring of...* ***finality***.

As I'd completed that second ninety-degree turn to port—to my left—I noticed my airspeed had increased flying *downwind*. Did that mean I was losing altitude? Nope—a glance at the altimeter showed me in level flight. I maintained the prescribed altitude of 2,300 feet for this airport's pattern. Ah, too much power now that I was no longer climbing, and now that I had leveled off *and* was flying *downwind*. Duh! Nudged the throttle back by pulling that knob between my right index and middle fingers.

The runway and terminal buildings scrolled past below my left cockpit window. I was doing this—alone. Cruising at just under a hundred miles-per-hour in the pattern, I waited for the tower's instruction to turn onto the pattern's *base* course. This would turn me perpendicular to the end of the runway from which I had departed. But... nothing. Radio silence. I waited some more. Had the radio died? Had the tower forgotten about this thirsty little mosquito in the pattern?

This is ***not*** *how I practiced with CJ. At all. I* ***always*** *automatically turned onto base when the end of the runway was forty-five degrees aft of my left shoulder! Are they testing me?*

The airport was located over seven miles *south* of downtown Rochester, out in the country. I still headed *north*. And I now looked down at the world-famous Mayo Clinic below me... *in downtown Rochester!* My *downwind* course continued to carry me north. My turn onto my *base* course in the pattern should have been seven hundred *yards* from the north end of the runway, definitely not seven *miles*. Something was terribly wrong.

Even though the tower said they'd call me, I called them and said,

"Rochester tower, this is student pilot November-49452, uh, in the... ah, pattern? When should I turn onto *base* and *final* for one-three? Please advise."

A momentary delay. Then, "November-49452. Confirm your position."

"Tower, November-49452. Right now, at twenty-three-hundred feet above the Mayo Clinic, downtown Rochester."

Silence. Then.... "November-49452, turn onto *base* and *final* at will for runway one-three." The guy in the tower sounded... flustered?

I reversed course per my dash compass and banked back toward the airport. But every practice flight, including my rate of descent, was predicated on practicing *within* the pattern. This was, well, way different. No big deal for an experienced pilot, but... I had a lot on my overloaded little mind at that moment. This was above my pay grade, as they say. I worried about screwing up now more than ever.

When the end of the runway came back into view a minute later, a slight course correction headed the no-longer-thirsty mosquito's nose straight for it. Then, the pre-landing checklist. *Switch to approach control (radio) frequency of one-nineteen-eight. Reduce speed. Flaps at ten degrees. Slow further. Twenty degree flaps.* The flaps kept my airspeed constant as I descended. *Push the yoke forward a little at a time to ease her nose down. Now past the threshold—the end of the runway, and then....*

The runway rose up to smash me and my frail little mosquito. That was my sense. *It's rushing up at me, right up into my face.* I was still two-hundred feet up, but the aircraft refused to descend further. The plane was fine. I wasn't. Net: the little mosquito flew *over* a major portion of that seven-thousand-foot runway that Saturday morning instead of descending *onto* it.

Then I realized this was stupid. So I pushed her nose down by pushing the yoke forward despite my shaky hands. A bead of sweat threatened to drip into my right eye, right there in that chilly little coffin with mosquito wings.

While I had memorized the airport's runway diagram, including the intersecting runways and their orientation to one another at almost right angles, I failed to remember the distance to their point of intersection. Not that it mattered. I pushed her nose down farther, against my will. One hundred feet. That's when a frantic voice squawked on the approach frequency.

"November-49452, Go around! Repeat, *go around!* **You are *not* cleared to land. *Respond!***"

Oh, crap! Okay, muscle memory. Throttle up! Flaps up! Nose up! WHAT ELSE?

The frantic voice continued to squawk. Too busy to answer, I climbed low over the almost right-angle intersecting runway with one-three. A commercial flight—a Northwest Airlines 727—landed at some speed on runway two-zero... ***under me? Holy almost-bloody enchilada!***

As I climbed and accelerated, I had changed from the approach frequency to the tower frequency. Muscle memory. The next voice I heard on the tower frequency was CJ's. My petite pit bull flight instructor.

CJ sounded as calm as the eye of a Category 5 hurricane. "Gene, this is CJ. Are you okay?"

Wanting to sound cool about nearly dying *and* taking out a hundred or more hapless souls who, no doubt, remained in ignorant bliss, I said with the slightest quiver, "This is November-49452. Roger that, CJ." My right eye twitched, having given birth to a mind of its own. I had shaken off that damn drop of sweat. Had I peed a little in my jeans, too? Or was that just crotch sweat? I lamented a sopping wet back, even though it was winter on the frozen tundra and darn chilly inside this mosquito's belly.

"November-49452, I'm in the tower. Now, I want three good landings and two more takeoffs, okay, Gene?"

Really? Okay. I must not have screwed up the go-around thingy. Yeah, it's called the balked-landing procedure. Stupid name.

"This is student pilot November-49452, uh, yeah, sure thing. I mean, roger."

Twenty minutes later, mission accomplished. No sweat. Yeah, right. I taxied across the service ramp to the general aviation terminal. To position one. Again. CJ stood there, pacing. I secured the aircraft using yet another checklist on yet another laminated card. All fell quiet. My ears still buzzed, and blood pulsed a heavy, syncopated drumbeat in both temples. And in both sides of my neck. *That's new,* I thought. Even my eyeballs banged against their sockets. Noise hangover. And something else. Adrenaline bleed-off? I'd experienced this in the Coast Guard. Hung up the headphones. Collected my thoughts with a vacant gaze. My ears rang in the deafening silence.

I HEARD CJ pop the right-side door. I didn't even look. Startled me in the quiet. Hoisted her petite, one-hundred-fifteen-pound frame—a decent guess—into the aircraft and plopped into the right seat. The aircraft quivered. Wind on the wings? Or CJ's little butt plopping down in the light airframe? *Who cares?*

I glanced over at last. Curly and frizzy on any other day, her hair lay flat, pasted to her forehead. The rest hung like damp ropes around her neck, as if she'd just crawled out of the shower, *or* recently finished a blood-curdling shouting marathon with the tower supervisor. Did that happen? She said nothing, but fluffed her hair. It defied fluffing.

A full two minutes passed. Like we both needed that. We did. We stared in silence at the upper blade of the now-stationary propeller at the plane's nose. When CJ spoke, her voice quivered and croaked. The words came out a half-octave lower than before.

"Great job recovering from that clustercluck, Gene."

"I didn't screw up?"

"The tower should *never* have cleared a commercial heavy to land on an intersecting runway with a student in the pattern, though there is some dispute over that. Remember from studying the regulations what an FAA *Incident* is?"

Took a beat. Then, "That's a really big deal, right?"

"A huge deal. Somebody's in trouble over this. Hopefully not me. You averted a major disaster today, Gene."

"Yeah, after almost causing one."

"Chalk that up to a lack of experience. The guys in the tower, however, have no excuse. Neither do I."

I said, "You? Well, nobody died." I remembered uttering that same *bon mot* after that CG ice op where I injured my back helping to save those ice fishermen more than a decade earlier. Somehow, this time, it sounded less noble. I continued, "Anyway, I'll be too busy flying commercially on business for a while."

CJ looked too tired to be disappointed, but smiled.

I needed a shower.

And coffee.

And clean shorts. It wasn't just crotch sweat, after all.

Chapter 36

Fast-Tracker

Time passed with the languid swiftness of a seductive whisper. I traveled several-hundred-thousand commercial air miles each year on business. That—or a crisis of confidence—dampened my enthusiasm to saddle and ride thirsty mosquitos for the time being.

Before I knew it, my little family and I found ourselves planted nearby a couple of decades later. We'd moved to a fancy four-bedroom, four-level home in northwest Rochester—on the *right side of town.* Both kids were grown and gone. Kay worked at various restaurant, hotel, data processing, and secretarial jobs over the years.

I had dedicated myself to my career. Yeah, I was all in, but doing it for the family. At least, that's the convincing lie that became my mantra. Kay raised our kids like a single parent in my frequent emotional and physical absence. In fact, I was gone so much that Michelle and Adam became strangers to me, and I to them. I can't shake loose that profound regret, one of the few that just won't let go.

I scored raises, promotions, bonuses, and stock options regularly. But the bitterness at the back of my throat refused to be washed away, even when treated regularly with one stout martini after another.

This confused and conflicted me. More *trouble with thinking*. I flashed back to that road trip to Denver with my old traveling buddies, Rafe and Sebastian. I recalled Rafe worrying that a witch had cursed us. That ridiculous thought recurred more than once. Was I somehow the victim of a curse of some kind? Was I venturing too far from where I was meant to be? Here's what I mean....

My career didn't start out with these silly doubts. As an entry-level electronics engineering technician, and later as a systems programmer who too-quickly became a front-line manager, life in the ever-faster lane grew exhilarating. I found it intoxicating, almost like an(other) addiction. *Almost?* Someone identified me as a *fast-tracker,* what they called an *executive resource* in IBM-speak.

It's not clear whether I sought one mentor after another, or whether they pursued me. I learned about the right jobs to take, and the best mentor-mentee relationships to develop, and frankly, which asses to kiss. I'd let it be known I was hungry.

That was the game, but not the real score. I clearly excelled at leading people far better than designing circuits or programming and testing code—software. And yeah, I worked my ass off at all of it.

One of my well-connected work friends, Glenn, an influential director in the lab, suggested I apply for a managerial position and I got it. Before long, I excelled at it. Then Glenn thought I'd benefit from the experience of becoming his executive assistant. He was right. I better understood the middle management machine after that. From there, someone poached me for a second-line job—a manager of managers, along with responsibility for their individual departments.

Most everyone realized that a decent manager advanced through the ranks and got raises faster than programmers of average talent—that was me. Early on, with two small children at home, no college degree under my belt, and no shortage of bills to pay meant I *was* doing all of this for my family. Certainly not just because of my desire to be respected by my professional peers, most of whom had earned college-degrees from damn fine schools before starting with the business.

Were my modest roots now driving me more than holding me back? Or was I denying my humble past when convenient by becoming one of... *them?*

Before long, it felt *really* good to be recognized for my latent managerial talent. Seems I had a knack. Yeah, damn it, I *would* do this job better than anyone! And that fire-spitting spirit sustained my progress on the track—the fast-track. Gene Jurrens: executive resource. Damn right, skippy.

As I MENTIONED, in the early '90s, we had moved from southeast Rochester to a new northwest neighborhood in a house more suitable for entertaining. That's where IBMers lived. I had arrived. Oh, and my wife came too, almost as an afterthought, I now shamefully confess. Now adults, the kids had already flown the coop.

God, I was *such* an ambitious and thoughtless prick. But I was blind to that. No excuse. I *still* maintained my climbing the corporate ladder was a selfless act to provide for my family better than our parents did for us. Financially, anyway.

Since I was now a hot commodity, IBM offered to pay for my college degree if I would earn it with even more sweat equity than before—an unspoken but well-understood assumption. I jumped at the chance, knowing that the lack of a degree would eventually limit my continued growth through the managerial ranks.

So, back when I was still managing just one department of 15 programmers, IBM offered me a full ride toward my bachelor's degree—from the University of Minnesota, no less, a damn fine school. At night as an *adult student*. I had finally left the local community college in my academic dust.

A local doctor's wife, Robin Cherry, and I commuted together to the U of M's Minneapolis campus a hundred miles north for night classes. We used my car, but shared the gas expenses. Sometimes Kay rode along if she was available.

I'll never forget the grind of working during the day and driving to a few classes at a time. Or traveling to study groups in *the cities* (Minneapolis and St. Paul) at night, several nights each week. It took me until 1989 to complete my BS degree in business.

I graduated with little fanfare. Kay was ready to breathe a sigh of relief, hoping to retrieve her husband and the father of her children. But alas, duty called once again. Yeah, duty. That's what I called it.

Chapter 37

Wined and Dined in Spain

After a few more promotions, one of my mentors advocated my nomination into a prestigious program reserved for sustained fast-trackers like me in 1993. Being selected would be a great honor, he said. Well, I was all about recognition at that point in my life. Come to think of it, when have I ever *not* been all about recognition?

Kay was *such* a trooper. She wanted me to realize my dreams. I remember that, and the stories I'd tell her about my dad never realizing his. What I don't remember? How much did I encourage her to realize *her* dreams, if *at all?* What a schmuck!

They selected me to participate in a prestigious Master of Science program called *Management of Technology*. This was an MBA / IT hybrid program modeled after one at either Wharton or Harvard called their *executive format*. One other candidate, Drew Flaada, and I represented IBM Rochester's population of 8,000 in this program from 1994 to 1996. Yeah, baby!

Drew and I drove to classes in the cities on the U campus in IBM-leased cars. But not at night, like before—just *one entire day* each week. This format offered a generous accommodation to our already hectic schedules. By then, each of us managed a half-dozen first-line managers, who each managed a few dozen programmers and engineers, plus responsibility for all their missions and budgets, and schedules.

The two of us attended classes on campus all day Friday, one week, and all day Saturday the next week. Plus, we'd travel to two or three optional study group meetings in the cities each week at night on our own. We'd complete 32 graduate credits in 21 months, plus a 3-week international residency—an aggressive load for two hungry young executive wannabes. That represented a full-time job, and then some, *in addition to our day jobs*.

Twenty-six of us from several top-tier Minnesota companies completed the entire two-year program together. Quite an honor, countless wonderful networking opportunities with other middle managers from other top companies, and a hell of a lot of challenges juggling school and work. Yes, those were heady days. There was no pretense now. We'd internalized that we were headed for "greatness," having now set aside *all* humility that might have once cast a shadow of doubt on our motives or diligence.

Two events served as capstones for this MOT (Management of Technology) program. First, we'd each author and verbally defend a comprehensive thesis based on the Harvard Business Review case study format. Mine focused on the *Efficacy of Remote Leadership, and Candidate Selection for Working Remotely* before much of today's enabling technology existed and popularity of the concept.

Second, we'd complete a multi-week international residency serving as business and operational process consultants to a select group of fast-growing high-tech international firms. After studying their business and operational models, as well as their financials, we visited and advised these varied companies onsite. They were located in Taipei, Taiwan, Hong Kong while still under the British crown, and Beijing in the People's Republic of China. These companies revered us. After all, we were young "turks" from America whose opinions and recommendations were to be respected like no other. As

I look back, dear God, what monumental egos marinated within each of us!

For two years, though, each of us forfeited *any* opportunity for a personal or social life. Kay and I owned a 30-foot sailboat in Lake City, 34 miles distant on a wide spot of the Mississippi River. We loved that boat but sold it since we'd have *zero* time available to use it. For the foreseeable future, no more pleasant weekends sailing or anchoring overnight out on the lake. Another hard pill to swallow.

But I harbored no doubts about engaging in this lunacy. Kay was a saint. She understood this would take my career to the next level and went along. Again, I don't recall how she truly felt about this. Maybe I never bothered to find out other than a cursory discussion from which I assumed a foregone conclusion.

My dear Miss Kay accompanied me to my graduation ceremony on the university campus in the spring of 1996. She'd earned it as much as I. Comparing my flowing gown, cap, and tassel to the even cooler apparel of the PhD candidates, I was in awe. They marched down the aisle *first* in the huge auditorium—the U of M is a mammoth institution. I whispered to Kay in wide-eyed wonder, "Hey, I wonder what it'd be like to get my doctorate?"

Without missing a beat, she hissed, "Be sure to have your next wife let me know."

Alrighty, then! At that point, I guessed she felt I'd taken enough classes to earn us a living! I graduated Magna Cum Laude, and I think I even delivered some sort of commencement address among our small band of graduates.

With this pivotal moment behind us, my boss and my mentor at the time soon asked me to accept a high-level staff assignment for two years at an IBM headquarters location in New York. As a little fish in a bigger pond, I was still tracking.

Two assignments while at IBM HQ stand out in my mind and likely defined another important aspect of my future self. Though exactly how, I'm still not sure. Maybe I developed a sense of great confidence in being asked to accomplish big things and then unexpectedly made them happen with a sense of... wonder?

First, the president of Spain registered an official diplomatic complaint to the senior IBM executive in that country via the US State Department. We—IBM—had created a balance of payments problem with the country *el presidente* ruled. We exported more money out of his country than we were investing in it. So IBM's CEO charged my boss, a Senior Vice President, to address the issue. He asked two other staffers and me to investigate possible and profitable remedies to this issue and to recommend a solution. A goodwill measure, I suspect.

After several weeks of research, the three of us surmised that one rapid solution would be to invest in the growth of an existing IBM software development center in Barcelona on the southern seacoast of Spain—*el Costa Del Sol*. Our bosses then tasked us with implementing that plan to the tune of an additional $100 million annual investment in that center. *If* we thought they could profitably leverage that additional capital.

So, we traveled to Barcelona to interview their senior management team, to tour their facility, and to suggest any changes. Their wining and dining of us for a week seemed excessive, but we did hold the key to a $100 million annual purse. After a week of meetings to review and analyze their plans for the additional funding, we recommended the investment. Mischief managed.

Chapter 38

Comrades in Russia

A SECOND QUASI-DIPLOMATIC PROJECT SIGNIFICANT TO THE corporation also holds a special place in my memory. This trip found five of us in Moscow, Russia. The Iron Curtain had recently collapsed, and Mikhail Gorbachev snatched the reins to what remained of the USSR when that union ceased to exist at the end of 1991. It seemed the Cold War had ended. Gorbachev drove his new confederation of states toward social democracy.

Under Gorbachev's regime, the Russian government realized it was leaving countless millions of rubles on the table every year by not efficiently collecting the equivalent of our US Social Security. We were tasked with convincing the leader of the Russian Pension Fund (RPF) of the value of automating their collection of such funds.

We'd recommend enabling that with the RPF's purchase, deployment, and training in the use of 3,000 networked IBM computers, along with sundry peripheral equipment, across their 12 time zones. Yeah, that's half the circumference of the planet. Russia is a big country.

Again, we were wined and dined. Actually, we drank no wine, but consumed countless *buckets* of the finest Russian vodka! A bucket comprised a fat and tall shot glass equivalent to 3 or 4 traditional shots. The expectation? We'd down each in a single "manly gulp." Their vodka was *so* smooth and *so* easy to enjoy. I blamed that Moscow trip for nurturing my already alcoholic mind. In this way, I painlessly abdicated all personal responsibility for nurturing my DNA's alcoholic gene (sarcastic pun intended).

We thought we'd closed the deal when the politically influential chairman of the RPF suggested they pay IBM with... *freighters of grain?* The chairman's influence was equivalent to an American presidential cabinet position. He reported directly to Gorbachev who was Chairman of the Presidium of the Supreme Soviet (think "president" if you're American).

With diplomatic patience, we explained that we were a company, not a country. We did not close that deal, but a team comprising senior IBM executives and US State Department representatives, did. They used the compelling groundwork we'd laid for them.

As a sidebar, the British president of IBM Russia tried to recruit me as one of his in-country technical marketing support reps. He said, "Your territory would span all of Russia, and I will send you home a wealthy man in two years, Gene. Besides, there's almost no chance you'd be kidnapped or assassinated, old chap." Nope. Hard pass. Thanks, but no thanks. Although I *was* tempted.

I'll never forget that trip. Less than 30 years later, however, the RPF dissolved in 2022. And to think I was part of Russian history during their brief flirtation with social democracy. That experience also reminded me that democracy is fragile. There is no guarantee it will last. Anywhere.

Less than two years later, now a bigger fish in a smaller pond once more, I returned to Rochester. I received another promotion with significantly broader responsibilities, and the years continued to roll past. I made more money, we bought a much bigger boat named

Sojourn, and spent lovely weekends on her in Lake City. She was the biggest sailboat in the huge Lake City Marina back then. I s*till* clearly believed *size mattered.* She measured 51 feet in overall length with a beam (width) of 18 feet, and a mast height of 55 feet. I think you'll find my next story of her acquisition from a world-class spy intriguing.

Chapter 39

Sojourn

I NOW OFFER YOU A FACTUAL EXCERPT FROM MY NOVEL, ***Dangerous Dreams***. I've included this passage on these pages because this boat-buying episode, who we purchased it from, and our years aboard this marvelous little ship became another defining period in our lives starting not long after I graduated from the U of M. And it all started with the fairy tale experience I share with you next, right out of a Vince Flynn novel.

IT WAS October of 1995 in Baltimore, Maryland. The East Coast sweltered that fall. Kay made the money work like she always did. The 13-year-old boat—a classic pilothouse motorsailer—was ours. It was time to transport her 20-ton splendor by truck to Lake City, Minnesota. The marina there, the largest on the entire length of the Mississippi River, perched on the shore of a twenty-mile-long wide spot on the Mississippi River called Lake Pepin. The lake nestled between bluffs on both the Wisconsin and Minnesota shores, two to four miles apart. Most importantly, when we chose to take our new boat to big water, the river system connected to the Gulf of Mexico and beyond.

I took some rare vacation days. I flew solo from Minneapolis to Baltimore-Washington International Airport. I'd packed enough socks and underwear for a week's stay aboard *Sojourn* in Baltimore's dubious waterfront district—Inner Harbor. Situated across the harbor from the famous Camden Yards Stadium, home of the Baltimore Orioles Major League Baseball team. Also, I was within walking distance from a number of eclectic ethnic neighborhood restaurants.

I'd contracted for the use of Tidewater Yacht Service's lift and crane to haul our new boat from the water and onto the bed of a semi-truck's low-boy trailer at the end of my visit. They'd remove the boat's substantial sailing rig for shipping. Her 55-foot mast, boom, tackle, and nine sets of heavy stainless cables and turnbuckles that held it all in place needed to be laid down, coiled, and get shrink-wrapped. All would be road-ready before I preceded her back to Minnesota to await her arrival.

Annie—I suspected that was not her given name—from Annapolis Yacht Brokers, had connected Kay and me with Dale from Tidewater Yacht Services in Baltimore. That's where we had discovered the boat after a protracted search. I procured the services of a truck broker, who arranged hiring the appropriate truck and driver, as well as securing various permits for carefully selected transportation routes. Definitely an oversized load. While *Sojourn* still sat in the water, and while I prepared her for haul-out and shipment, I intended to learn as much as possible about this magnificent old vessel and her many systems while I packed away the small stuff aboard.

Dale from Tidewater stopped by with an offer I couldn't refuse. That's when everything became a great deal more interesting. "Mr. Jurrens, congratulations again on your amazing acquisition. I can't believe Dr. Thompson accepted your offer. He seemed pleased by your respectful promise to give his vessel a loving new home, despite your somewhat lowball offer."

"Thanks, Dale. I'm feeling blessed. What's up?" I refused to engage in that lowball discussion again with this guy. But Dale had not yet let it go. I guess he felt cheated out of a few commission bucks.

"Well, I dropped by to see if you need anything. I also came to ask if you'd like to meet Dr. Thompson. He's offered to spend tomorrow afternoon with you on the boat if you're so inclined."

I didn't even need to think about it. "Are you kidding? Yes! I have so many questions!"

Chapter 40

Took the Hit

Late the next morning, *Sojourn* and I bobbed gently in the harbor's mild chop. She was moored stern to the pier.

As I stowed the canvas Bimini that protected the cockpit from weather, I spotted a rail-thin gentleman sauntering in my direction down the long concrete pier. This stranger stopped at *Sojourn's* transom—her broad hind-end. The old man appeared so ordinary, he seemed nearly invisible. I met his analytical gaze for a couple of beats.

"Howdy!" came the mellifluous drawl of a Southern gentleman. A frumpy sailor's hat cast his eyes in deep shadow. The sun had bleached it almost white, and a ragged fringe surrounded the brim. As he raised his head, I could see his eyes twinkled behind a pair of old-fashioned round spectacles with tinted lenses. The wrinkled *crow's feet* outboard of those eyes either came from age, or from decades of smiling, or frowning, or likely all of the above. He continued, "I'm Joe, and you are Gene. Mighty fine to meet you, sir. I am pleased to see you're getting acquainted with my best girl. Permission to come aboard, captain?"

"Hello, Joe. A real pleasure. Yes, please, sir. I can't tell you how much—"

"Of course, of course. Would you object to my smuggling a few handcrafted micro-brews aboard? To lubricate the launch of our relationship, captain?" It was at that precise moment that a twelve-pack of local Union Craft beers appeared in his left hand, as if by magic. I couldn't tell whether this genteel patrician's demeanor was sincere or contrived. No matter. He pulled it off with aplomb.

"Say no more. Please join me in the shade and comfort of *our* pilothouse."

"You're too kind; however, she's all yours now, sir." It came out all Texas, as in *how-evah,* and *suh.* Or was it Georgia? After twisting the caps off two bottles and handing one to me, we sat in the warm glow of the pilothouse, the boat's living room we called her main salon.

A view of the pilothouse looking aft, as observed from the galley one level down.

The old gentleman swelled with pride. Joe immediately asked about my impressions of the little ship. He wanted to learn of her new home port and any long-range cruising plans. Did we have pets? Would we be living aboard full-time? An inquisitive old gent. He watched my eyes rove over the generous proportions of *our* best girl. I responded with unbridled enthusiasm. The ease with which we conversed seemed preternatural.

Our brilliant but cool afternoon evaporated, as did several bottles of that excellent beer. The two of us puttered around the engine room and generator spaces, bilges, and cockpit lockers. We both comfortably eased into the chilly crimson evening. The two of us spent some time in the hold—a voluminous cargo space beneath the cockpit. We sat cross-legged, knee-to-knee on its epoxy-painted wood floor, engaged in congenial banter. Later, we reconvened to the far more comfortable and spacious pilothouse with Joe's complaint of stiff knees. I lit two traditional oil lamps hanging from the beamed ceiling.

As the evening wore on, I smiled at the sight of all the empties we'd accumulated down in the galley's waste bin. I cracked open the third of three massive, four-inch-thick binders. These books contained the ship's detailed documentation and service records for its various systems. I remained eager to ask more questions. "So, Sam, you were with the NSA?"

Time stopped dead. Steely blue eyes bored into mine. Leaning forward, palms face-down on his knees, elbows braced outward, now way too close to my face, Joe's voice transformed to echo his aggressive posture. The convivial country gentleman had disappeared in a Dallas nanosecond. His next words became coarse gravel grating into a once-bloody wound that had just about healed. "And how is it... you... are aware of... that... *Gene*?"

Those eyes! My mind reeled in shock. I trembled. "Ah, um, your name was, ah, on a sheet of NSA letterhead with, um, this, ah, sketch of an electrical diagram for the lower helm's wiring!" I had blurted this out louder than I intended, waving a crude hand-drawn diagram on a five-by-eight-inch sheet of notepad paper I'd extracted from the binder in its plastic sheet-saver. I stuttered while fluttering my arms as if I might soar above the dense cloud of visceral fear that threatened to smother me in that instant.

Silence.

And then....

Joe flipped the switch back to his genteel demeanor, as if the previous twenty seconds were nothing more than a remote anecdote. His smile returned. A little apologetically, he said, "Sorry. Mine is a rough business. I was Director of Medical Services for the Agency. Job damned near killed me. Now that I'm retired, I'm privileged to serve as Chief of Surgery at Walter Reed in Bethesda just down the road. Still keeping busy even though it's mostly an honorary position."

. . .

While reticent to discuss specifics, I did unearth a few more nuggets about Joe and his wife, Mary. Our budding friendship continued to blossom, and the beers continued to evaporate. "Joe, I only know one other guy who was once affiliated with the US intelligence community, an old friend, Kevin. But the two of you couldn't be more different. You'd like him. He was in air transport."

"Ah, yes, I've worked with a few of those boys over the years. Maybe we'll get a chance to chat one day."

And that was that. A rather abrupt end to a fascinating day. I later learned Joe's rank—full-bird colonel—perched one promotion below brigadier general. If Joe's rank wasn't impressive enough, his job was. I can't remember how I'd discovered Medical Services Director was NSA-speak for Chief Worldwide Interrogator. In retrospect, if even for a few brief but psychologically uncomfortable moments, I had been interrogated by the best!

Too many beers. And a lot of trust born of a common infatuation —*our* best girl. A side note: Colonel N. Joe Thompson served as a consultant on my first novel, ***Dangerous Dreams.*** He chided I needed him to keep me from saying something... awkward.

Our early years with *Sojourn* in Minnesota were enjoyable. But Kay and I also mutually advanced our progressive disease of alcoholism during that time. It had snuck up on us. Another story I further unravel in ***Dangerous Dreams***.

Then, one afternoon in May 1997 in the Lake City Marina, our beloved little ship suffered significant damage while tied alongside her dock. Nobody was aboard. Jim Springer, the harbormaster, called me at my office at IBM in Rochester. "Gene, are you sitting down? The great news is that *Sojourn* is still floating."

"*What?* Jim, what are you talking about, and this had better not be a joke."

"No joke, Gene. A drunken pilot at the helm of an Army Corps of Engineers tug lashed to a work barge lost control in last night's storm. He took shelter in the sailboat harbor. Came in hot due to strong cross-winds when he lost his steering. Leaked over a hundred gallons of hydraulic fluid into my harbor. This, ah, incident destroyed the ends of a couple of my floating docks out there. Twisted 'em like soggy pretzels. Then, that heavy tug chewed pretty hard on your boat's port quarter at her tie-along at the end of the 800 dock. It appears to be cosmetic damage only, but she took several pretty hard hits. That's one stout vessel, Gene."

"Son of a bitch! Okay, I'll be down. I'll spend the night on her... sleep down in the engine room to watch for leaks, I guess. Thanks, Jim."

"You have my home number. If she takes on water, we'll line up the lift. Call anytime, skipper. Not a happy day, but coulda been a lot worse."

I learned later that the tug's crew took a full twenty minutes to secure their barge. It had run aground on the rocks in front of it. During that time, the starboard side of that rusty steel tug bounced around in the harbor's storm chop while she lay right up against *Sojourn's* port side. After chewing on her left rear corner for almost a half-hour, the crew finally pried that rust bucket off. They drew her away with lines secured to the jetty on her far side 50 feet distant.

Sojourn did indeed suffer cosmetic damage only. Unfortunately, the repairs would cost twenty-two thousand dollars. That was a king's ransom in '97. I assumed a simple arrangement between perpetrator and victim could be arranged, but I was mistaken. The Corps would not take responsibility for the incident, citing *The Public Vessels Act*.

I assumed they were trying to prevent yet another citizen from fleecing the government. Uncle Sam self-insures, they said. After months of runarounds and double-talk, our insurance company also grew frustrated. So I appealed to the good Doctor Joe, *Sojourn's* previous owner, for help.

"Sons-a-bitches won't accept responsibility, Joe. Ideas?"

After a half-dozen thoughtful beats, in his patent drawl, Joe said, "Gene, we need to yank on a few tactical levers. I'll email you the draft of a letter this afternoon. It'll contain the names to whom y'all will send it, along with a list of copy and blind-copy names. I want you to leave the blind-copied recipients visible on all copies you send. These mid-level weasels won't tolerate the kind a Hell we're gonna rain down on 'em. No worries, old son. You'll have a check within two weeks. Guaranteed. But now, you say our girl took the hit and just snickered? Yessir. *Yessir!*"

One day shy of two weeks later, I held in my hand a check for twenty-two thousand dollars signed by a contrite Uncle Sam. I endorsed it and sent it to the repair facility. Paid in full.

*Who **are** you, Joe?*

~

Pleasant memories.

Enough nautical daydreaming with you for one day.

Back to business.

Chapter 41

Twenty Percent?

ANOTHER KEY TURNING POINT FOR ME OCCURRED ALMOST TEN years later, circa 2006. I now offer you yet another excerpt from my novel, ***Dangerous Dreams***, which is largely factual and seems appropriate to share with you here. I've changed names to protect the guilty or the easily offended. I've also taken some artistic license in relaying to you an event that occurred late in my career as a low-level tech executive at IBM. This company had treated me well for over a quarter-century. But the times and the players, they were a-changin'. I became compelled to either change with them, or *by* them.

YES, you already know I'd grown up rather poor with humble surroundings in a small Midwestern town. I was okay with that. Sometimes that history even came in handy during my career as an ambitious corporate climber over the years. My modest background illustrated how far I'd come despite what Ivy Leaguers and other high-flyers around me dismissed as... adversity. To them, it was. To me, it was just... home.

You've also already heard me utter the bon mot that I'd *grown up on the wrong side of the tracks*. That's the euphemism I often invoked to characterize my childhood to anyone who mattered, but only when it was to my advantage, of course. Today, this would not be just another euphemism. It would come home to roost as a rock-hard reality. I had gotten in over my head.

I'D CRAWLED out of bed at 4:30 am as usual. But on this day, I left a small suite at the Grand Marquis in midtown Manhattan. The brisk walk to my 9 am helped. I stopped at the cafeteria in the massive lobby of 590 Madison for a cup of arguably the best and strongest coffee anywhere. A stout twenty-ounce French Roast—black, of course—in a tall styrofoam to-go cup, bolstered my courage.

Even as the smoky and delightfully bitter brew slid across my tongue, my 57-year-old stomach grumbled in protest. Should have eaten something, but I knew what was coming, or thought I did. Wouldn't do to puke in my big bad boss's office, maybe even all over his desk.

The private elevator in the lobby reeked of oiled mahogany. It whisked me to an opulent fortieth-floor executive suite. Yeah, I expected an ugly encounter. At the same time, I felt the tingling thrill of being so close to the top of the company's hierarchy. That proximity always bore a price. Always.

Palmer Xavier rarely summoned me to his office in the city. No, this could not be good. It was usually a rare phone call from one of his minions, like the irascible Vinnie Lassaro. Patchouli, one of the COO's three willowy executive assistants, greeted me. These beautiful women were quick to remind anyone who cared that they were *not secretaries*.

Did Palmer's people interview only stunning runway models for his EAs? But up here, they *had* to be more than eye candy to survive. After a luminous smile of blinding white and blood red, I took a seat as Patchouli requested.

The voluminous space appeared spartan. I knew this was part of Palmer's facade of austerity that seemed so contrived. Paradoxically, millions in abstract art stared back at me from the walls in front of me and to my right. I suspected the original oils and vibrant watercolors were little more than decor art to Palmer. And these high-end furnishings reeked of trying too hard to look like he wasn't trying too hard.

The 15-minute wait beyond the appointed time? Blatant power-posturing. Such an obvious old trope. Palmer needed some fresh material, fresh tactics. I listened to the tinkle of contemporary jazz from invisible speakers. As I was being ushered into the inner sanctum at 9:16, before I even sat down, the man blurted, "Gene, I need 20%." Brutal budget challenges had become an annual Fall Plan event, but *this*.... It was as if I should feel honored he was gutting my organization in person instead of via a messenger I could metaphorically shoot.

"What? Palmer, you *do* realize that my budget ends with an *M* and enables revenue that ends with a *B*, right?" I instantly bit into the side of my tongue so hard I tasted blood—an omen. The COO of this global corporation would *not* be swayed by sophomoric excuses.

With faux sincerity, Palmer purred, "Look, Gene, I understand this is tough. You know what I'm going to say next, right? If you can't do it—"

I gaped slack-jawed for a micro-moment as Palmer straightened his already perfect yellow power tie with its tiny navy-blue dots—tiny blue eyes of lost souls? He wasn't even looking me in the eye. Right. Power.

"Yes, okay Palmer, I've got this." I interrupted him, attempting an anemic recovery. I churned mentally, planning how to cut twenty million dollars from my already ravaged budget. Worst case, that meant two hundred jobs, without impacting critical business results, of course.

Somehow.

I continued to tell myself yet another lie—that I'd wield this sword of doom with more compassion than the next ambitious prick. That I was doing this more for my people than for my own myopic ambition. At the end of this *exercise,* people's lives would get screwed up. And I'd be doing the screwing. I took no pleasure in it. *Did I?*

Palmer's heavy-lidded eyes—cold and dead, reflecting nothing but black ice—finally met mine. I wondered how many other foot soldiers must run this gauntlet in the next few hours, the next few days, the next few years under this new regime. "You see, Gene, I have a hundred senior managers reporting to me now, as you know. This provides useful distance, a practical perspective."

The left end of his lip curled upward slightly. Nothing more than a micro-expression. I thought, *This asshole is enjoying this. He **needs** to peer into the anguish reflected in eyes like mine. He **needs** to drink in the bile bubbling in my gut.*

"How many senior managers report to you, Gene? 30? 35? As you drill down, your lower-level managers each have, what, about the same? Down there, it needs to be five times that or more. This is what I'm talking about. There's always fat, Gene. Always."

Now, with a 20% precedent, this would be a recurring catastrophe every year from now on. I reached for better times. I envisioned Kay stretched out on *Sojourn's* foredeck as I ignored the running knife fight with my high school sweetheart, fueled by too many Bombay Sapphire gin martinis. She was also from the wrong side of the tracks in the same small Minnesota town, surrounded by the same cornfields and the same cows. I was out of my freakin' league here at the center of the corporate universe.

Palmer continued his ambush. "Another thing. How many of your employees are in high-cost geographies? The U.S.? Western Europe? Scandinavia? Japan? Singapore? About 80%, am I right? And less than 20% in low cost countries? In two years, you're going to flip that ratio. The future is in low-cost geographies like China, Eastern Europe, Malaysia...."

I didn't mention that India used to be the prime example of a *low-cost geography*. That was just 36 short months ago. Once those kids in Bangalore and Delhi got a taste of the good life, courtesy of our company and others like ours, they'd jump ship. They'd head for the next high-tech firm across the street with their updated resume. *After* we'd trained them for 18 months or more to do *our* jobs. Low cost? *Sure, Palmer. Whatever produces solid short-term financials before the business craters and you've moved on, right?*

The ambush continued. "So I want you to shed your expensive talent. Hire cheaper talent. Increase your span-of-management tenfold. And convince those who we ask to leave the business to stay long enough to train their offshore successors, or they don't get their severance package. Oh, and focus on cutting troops who are closest to collecting a pension. No need to pay them a retirement annuity forever. Can do?"

Palmer possessed a rare attribute. It allowed him to slash jugulars in the afternoon and sleep like a baby at night. Classic high-functioning sociopathic behavior. I knew I did not possess that attribute so important this near the top. Or maybe I did, but to a lesser degree, if I were honest with myself. But certainly less with every turn of the soul-crunching crank. Which is why I'd never be a senior VP. Besides, I held no Ivy League pedigree. I'd always be from the wrong side of town, in the middle of the Bible Belt, no less.

Before I offered my unconditional surrender, Palmer's desk phone chirped. As a reflex, he punched the speakerphone button. Patchouli said, "Mr. Xavier, Mr. Enoch Slattery needs to speak with you. Line three." Before he picked up the phone for privacy, Palmer said, "Gene, I look forward to your plan by next week. Remember, *you're that guy*."

Dismissed.

What an exquisite prick. He <u>is</u> good, but good at what?

Chapter 42

Elevator Pitch

By May 2007, visiting my remaining 600 worldwide employees, down from over a thousand, thanks to achieving Palmer's *challenges,* took a good deal of my time and energy. Even more, now, because I managed plummeting morale, supervising the training of new-hires when we could find them in *low-cost geographies*, which was time-consuming, and massaging business results to keep the wolves at bay.

I'd flown into Laguardia from Minneapolis the previous afternoon after visiting my Rochester team. The rarefied atmosphere at corporate headquarters locations in Westchester County, New York, north of the city, existed in a different world. It was one into which I inserted myself so often these days it seemed second nature.

Riding an elevator at CHQ with a senior executive could be a boon or a bane. It depended. I was not to be ignored. "Yes, Gene, I'm all too aware that division is in the red for a hundred mil a quarter. Product issues, right? By the way, I hear congrats are in order. You made your budget numbers. I remained confident for good reason."

It still astounded me how casually a guy like Palmer—Chief Operations Officer—mentioned a one-hundred-ten-million-dollar loss *per quarter*, for *years*, as if it were merely a minor embarrassment. *And* in the same sentence, he abdicated personal responsibility for the mess *he'd* left behind. He'd been the Operations VP of that division until recently when he'd been promoted to COO. I guess everyone has a blind spot, even this guy.

Palmer's customary modus operandi mandated quick returns—on paper at least—by firing a pant-load of good people ostensibly to reduce costs. Then post stellar earnings, blame the troops, and move on with full deniability. The backfilling swamp was then some other schmuck's problem later. If I were less concerned about my career and possessed a little more intestinal fortitude....

Maybe this guy should run for office!

I RECALLED my *second* recent 20% *negotiation* with Palmer down in the city. Today, he'd obviously descended from his ivory tower—his Madison Avenue digs—to mix it up with mere mortals at CHQ in Armonk, maybe even his boss and mentor, IBM's relatively new CEO.

Coincidentally, he and I rode the same elevator at the same time that day. But we were on very different missions. I'd realize much later that this would become another defining moment that would once again change my life's direction.

It felt good that I had dangled the bait of my pitch to Palmer on his way to an unrelated status meeting before the elevator doors had even closed. All execs worth their salt carried a 30-to-90-second pitch in their hip pocket. I was no exception.

Ready to quick-draw at a moment's notice, *the pitch* lent visibility to one's cause célèbre. An elevator's confines render an otherwise elusive audience captive, without interruptions. But every exec or wannabe knows that when flying close to a flame, like a moth, there is a very real probability of scorching one's wings. The trick was to leave fear on the ground floor. At least that was conventional Exec-101 wisdom.

"May I assume you have a recommendation, Gene?" Palmer kept his dead eyes locked on the illuminated floor indicator on the far side of the door. We both ignored the tinny Muzak from the overhead speaker. It was obvious to both of us that Palmer had no idea how to fix the *product problems.* He wasn't a techie. I was also aware that he still received disappointing and conflicting recommendations from within his old division. I had friends down there in North Carolina.

This guy was an artist in how to efficiently eviscerate a strong technical team to the point of ineffectiveness. *But* he would score his precious financials. In this case, the numbers had launched him from the piney woods of North Carolina to the COO's office in Armonk. Yes, he was clueless on the technical stuff, but he had me here, and I wasn't. So he *was* listening with greedy intent despite the lack of eye contact and an air of aloofness. Time to butter the muffin.

"Palmer, you had great success financially re-engineering that division. Unfortunately, as you know, product issues do indeed remain. That division's middle managers always present a convincing story about how great it's going to be in the future. That's their job. But the future never arrives. They spin ever deeper into the ditch with that pitch, stuck in the mud of the past. Not their fault."

The locomotive picked up steam. I forged ahead. "The flawed nucleus? Their product line is so different from the rest of the corporation's offerings that its infrastructure *must* be unique. They have no choice but to accommodate a flock of ill-behaved third-party software providers. While that stuff put them on the map 20 years ago, it now plagues them with error-prone, wide-open programming interfaces and flawed function. And *that* demands unique and costly quality control measures. Net? That time has passed.

"In contrast, all of our other products are manufactured on mass production lines and run on our own proprietary application program interfaces, our own APIs. This proprietary API model allows more intuitive and cost-effective integration and testing with our hardware in-house. And that's all enabled with a single cross-platform business process infrastructure which commands premium pricing. Conversely, investing in unique production lines and using third party stuff is costly on *so* many fronts.

"That division's PC heritage has always been innovative. It satisfied a market niche but created an outlaw garage-band culture. Think *one-off* where the entire rest of the company is streamlining our own *mass production*. That made sense for the first quarter century of its life. No longer. We need different thinking now as times get tougher. As you well know, our corporation is now in an artillery battle down on Wall Street. These guys are bringing Saturday night specials from Washington Heights."

I thought, *In for a penny...* Now I gotta carry the ball across the goal line with only a few seconds remaining, as I smiled inside. I knew Palmer loved sports similes, distant recollections from his glory days on the gridiron. "Only two choices as I see it, Palmer," as I looked up at this arrogant jerk standing to my left, almost a foot taller. Palmer's eyes stayed locked on the floor numbers at the far side of the door. In a fraction of a second, I observed his perfectly trimmed hair and face of granite. His upturned nose was close to bursting with a gin bloom, *or* chronic use of something else. "Plan B: Corral the product's technical design to be more in line with the rest of the company's offerings. This will be expensive and span years of effort. That's why this is Plan B."

"So what's your proposed Plan A then, Gene?"

Bingo! He ***is*** *listening. Not much time left.* "Divest. Sell it off. At least the PC client side. Desktop computers are messy and no longer have a legitimate slot in our big-iron portfolio. *Contract* for what we need, because *ownership* of this small stuff just costs too much. Decide whether to keep the server side on its own merits. They're more in line with our distinctive competence and mainstream infrastructure.

"Palmer, our payday is big-bucks high-end servers and enterprise systems, along with the stuff that goes with 'em. Ditch the scrap metal, boss. With less than 5% margins on the desktops, we could corral more profit selling heads of lettuce, *if* that were our business."

I spoke even faster now. Almost there. "We brought the personal computer to major markets in 1977—almost three decades ago. I was there. We got the footprints. The time for kudos is long past. It's likely time to lose that costly *tradition* before it drags us down any further. We need a touchdown, Palmer. I recommend an in-depth analysis of a divestment strategy for all or a part of that division. If that becomes the right play, we grab the cash and run. That's the pitch."

My last words gushed out faster than I would have liked, but we'd arrived at Palmer's floor—where the big dogs pissed. After the doors opened three seconds later, Palmer thanked me for an interesting ride with a disinterested nod.

I can't believe I just did that. Immediately, I wished the man forgot this ever happened.

What had I done? The next day, back in my Rochester office, eleven-hundred miles west, I spent some time thinking. I wondered about the pitch to my *big bad boss,* and where that might lead, if anywhere. I'd proposed a bold plan. But had I gored his oxen; that is, had I pissed him off by criticizing his old team? *Screw it. Truth is truth.* I wondered how much trouble I'd just gotten myself into.

At any rate, I'd moved on to considering the delicious logistics of moving aboard *Sojourn* for the summer over in Lake City. Kay and I planned to sell our largish four-bedroom, two-bath house in Northwest Rochester. It seemed superfluous now.

The plan was to spend summers on our good ship *Sojourn*, berthed at the Lake City Marina, less than an hour's drive from my Rochester office. When I wasn't traveling, I'd work from my home office in our Florida condo from October to April until I hung up my spurs. I eagerly anticipated spending the summer on *Sojourn* with Kay.

After the house sold, Sojourn would be our summer home. I felt good about getting out of Dodge, as they say. Especially with a mob of local employees that I'd been compelled to *surplus.* A few had even threatened me. Most understood they weren't victims of a personal vendetta, but of a slashed budget from on high. *Most* of them....

Chapter 43

What Did You Say!

Yeah, I'd drive 30 minutes to my Rochester office each day from the Lake City docks. I drew a deep, cleansing breath at that notion. This promised to be a therapeutic return to Minnesota, and to the lake, at least for the summer. We'd also visit family, maybe even host a few family outings.

I relished going home to Kay on the boat every night. Then, when the temps descended in October, we'd pull our 20-ton home out of the water, drop her onto her cradle, winterize, and cover her for storage. We'd load up the SUV, and aim it south. Snowbirds... like the older folks—real people. We were confident our Rochester home would sell quickly.

Kay had developed rather severe osteoarthritis. The unrelenting Minnesota winters made it painful for her to get around. Prescription? Other than pills? Tropical warmth. She still had the mind of an eighteen-year-old gymnast, but the body? Not so much anymore. Not that I could talk! I remembered those bittersweet days of passion and the battle of emotions during our more active drinking days as I reminisced. *Ah, the memories!* But her 55-year-old body reminded us both of our mortality. Sometimes, pain trumped fanciful visions of the spirit.

My desk phone shrilled. It didn't care that it startled me out of my reverie's warm embrace. A delicious afterglow lingered.

"WHAT ON EARTH did you say to Palmer the other day, Gene?" The caller didn't need to introduce himself. That raspy voice saturated with New York attitude, was unmistakable. I shared a *dotted-line* relationship on the org chart with Vinnie Lassaro, who was on Palmer's staff. Vinnie was my direct boss with whom I seldom had contact. "Hey, Vinnie, nice to hear from you. I'm fine. Kay's fine. Man, we gotta work on your people skills."

"Kiss my ass, Gene. The man's all revved up about something you said to him yesterday. In an elevator? That old gag? That's rich. Nobody still does that, man." Vinnie vented. "He's establishing a war room in Research Triangle Park starting *tomorrow*, for God's sake! He wants you and your fifty best and brightest on a plane. *Tonight*. Folks from a dozen other smaller teams are also now converging on RTP. Son, you got his motor revving in the red on whatever his old Raleigh team has been spoon-feeding him. Seems to trust you more than them. Unbelievable. What the Hell did you *say*? All joking aside, you got to the guy, and now it's time to follow through. Will do?"

All joking aside? Was *that* Vinnie's idea of humor? Neither humor nor people skills were his strong suits, at times. "Uh, wow, yeah Vinnie. I'm on it. Won't all be there at 8 am tomorrow, but we'll start mobilizing the teams. Great, I guess. I've been bitching about that division being held up as our gold standard for a while. Not to the right people, until now, obviously."

"Yeah, quit screwin' around, kid. This is serious stuff. Piss off the wrong people, and... never mind. Look, I'll assume this train has left the station, and you're already on it. Jee-ZEUS, Gene! And 8 am? Think more like 5 am, okay? You're in for a wild ride, m'boy, knowing *the cowboy* and his posse. Not sure who his on-scene guys will be, but it will *not* be a vacation."

He ended the call like he started it, but I *heard* a smile, or smirk, in Vinnie's final words before the click. Vinnie liked people who got things done. *Why do these younger bucks insist on calling me kid, son, or boy?* I smiled. I liked it. I recall spending the first part of my career at Big Blue convincing key folks I was older than I was. Then, at some magic juncture, I wanted them to think I was younger than my years. Yes, I still possessed the staunch stuff bequeathed only to the young. That was the theory.

"Hi, Kay? Guess what, babe?" She knew that tone.

"Aaaah... Geno, how long this time?"

So much for romantic summer sunsets on dusky Lake Pepin, listening to the loons at twilight, although I had yet to actually hear a loon on that lake. Too big. I knew Kay liked the money I was making, but she also wanted me to live long enough to enjoy it *with* her. I also knew this was not doing my marriage any good, but what was I going to say? No? And being out of town for a while might help. The tempestuous ebb and flow in our relationship never quite achieved what either of us wanted. But neither of us could imagine life without the other.

Chapter 44

War Room

Most of my hand-picked team and I converged on RTP within forty-eight hours of Vinnie's panicked call. The logistics drove my staff crazy. "Tough shit, chew harder," I'd chided, but with a smirk that said, "We're in this together! I'm right there with ya."

War room mode was always ugly. This meant taking extraordinary measures to make emergency business changes leveraging the best resources available. ASAFP, of course. Ground zero was a portion of the once-bustling IBM facility within Research Triangle Park—the Personal Computer Division.

RTP was an industrial park that had attracted hundreds of high-tech firms sprawled across seven thousand acres of aromatic pine woods, thanks to generous state and county subsidies. The cities of Raleigh, Durham, and Chapel Hill comprise the triangle's points. Not that the lovely rural setting mattered. The assembled team from across several IBM organizations worked seven days a week, fifteen hours a day, starting well before sunrise each day and not leaving until long after sunset, often not adjourning at all when things deviated from bad to worse.

I gave each of my newly arrived team members a personal orientation to their home away from home for the next few months at one end of the IBM facility. We'd stand within the sprawling IBM lab complex where the war room was set up. The place resembled a high-tech ghost town. Invariably they asked, "What *is* this place? The only thing missing is the digital tumbleweed. Creepy, isn't it?"

"Yeah, but it has all the comforts of home. Except for our families, friends, and our actual homes. Can't beat the tech." The team named this complex the *Ghost Town* for obvious reasons. Quarter-mile-long hallways connected hundreds of empty offices and conference rooms. Broken and stained acoustic tiles in the ceilings hung askew everywhere. Phones sat neglected in corners, on the floor, at the end of long, tangled cords, amidst dust bunnies the size of softballs.

The entire area appeared long-abandoned, as if the *Second Coming* had occurred in the not-so-recent past. No doubt these were artifacts of my elevator buddy Palmer's handiwork when he still ran IBM RTP.

Goddamn cowboys....

I BRIEFED each of my new arrivals. "Eat if you're able. They cater food in—morning, midday, and evening every day. Pretty decent stuff, too. Plus, strong coffee, fresh fruit, and pastries are available twenty-four/seven." I knew from personal experience—the fare was indeed sumptuous, over the top. Most of us were too busy skidding off the rails with the work or too nauseated from stress to care. Or even to eat at all. I lost 20 pounds in the first month. Odors in the nearby restrooms alternated between the stench of vomit and vaporous clouds of industrial disinfectant. Or, more frequently, both.

One of my team members, Gary, a manager from Poughkeepsie, NY, asked the same question that every new arrival asked. "So what's with the cots and blankets in empty offices off *Broadway?*" That was what we called the widest hallway, a hundred feet from *Times Square*. And *that* was where the onsite senior execs directed *The*

Gauntlet to be set up. Offices with cots featured clear glass windows, waist-to-ceiling, on the wall that faced *Broadway*.

"Available for anyone to use, Gar'. A contracted service—bonded, of course—comes in to change the bedding daily. The cots are not assigned. Fair warning, though. It's not cool to be caught napping except between midnight and 4 am."

"Gene, is it me, or is this whole scenario surreal... like an existential Hell in the woods?"

"Yeah, Gar', a lot of pressure, for sure. The message is obvious with those cots, though. Sleep here if you want to save commute time, but only when the senior execs are off-site. Otherwise, somebody will blow you serious shit." And to each new arrival's astounded expression, I'd reply, "I know, I know...."

The summer slow-galloped by in a thunderous cloud of adrenaline and cortisol—the stress hormone. It had already been a long September. Neither I nor my best people from various locations had seen daylight in months. Except during brief interludes in a small open-air courtyard to sneak a smoke or a quick cell call to a loved one. I didn't smoke, but no signal penetrated these walls.

The entire affair reeked of a tacky joke.... *"What happens when you lock a hundred heavily caffeinated geeks up in a dungeon buried in a dark and scary wood with a pack of ravenous corporate wolves prowling around?"* The only punchline that occurred to me was not funny: *emotional carnage.*

Chapter 45

Sanity Prevails

Harsh admonishments and demeaning remarks pelted down on innocent techies who weren't equipped to deal with sociopathic and narcissistic VPs from CHQ who were themselves under unbelievable pressure to produce results. Tears and sobbing and empty rooms with privately administered holes punched in the sheetrock were the norm. Nobody gave a shit about the holes. Therapy?

Behind their backs, we quietly whispered about the two senior execs onsite—the *Brooklyn cowboys,* part of Palmer's personal posse. Yeah, they'd likely never even seen a cow on the hoof, but they were indeed little more than boys. You dared not vent in front of them, or *to* them, even though *they* regularly vented in front of the brilliant techies who produced the results. And at the people responsible for their techies' morale—people like me and other middle managers. Palmer's minions could not have cared any less about people's feelings.

Subject matter experts from several other areas of the business shared the same dismal fate that summer. I did my best to stay in touch with the rest of my global organization, not sequestered in

RTP, those picking up the serious slack for 50 empty chairs. Our war room teams managed six senior executive updates on a standing schedule every day of every week. They started at 6 am and took place every two hours through noon. Each lasted fifteen minutes. Precisely. The last two took place at 4 and 8 pm.

If an issue caused any downstream schedule delay, the guilty party brought a status report with recommendations to rectify it. For these meetings, every project manager dropped everything and headed to the *Gauntlet*. This was the not-so-affectionate term given to the conference room at the heart of *Times Square*.

The *Gauntlet* was a cobbled-together, impromptu video conferencing center. This was where each team's lead updated a half-dozen cross-disciplinary executives in person, including the two cowboys, as well as at least that many more piped in via video and/or audio. Regular bludgeoning was the norm—a full-on blame game whenever a team failed to fulfill wildly unrealistic expectations. Also, the norm.

Between updates, execs yelled into phones in offices surrounding the *Gauntlet*. Or called in project managers for private ass-chewing sessions. This area called *Times Square* hopped with activity every hour of every day, except between midnight and 4 am.

Usual corporate war room stuff.

The RTP Marriott in Durham was my digs when not on site. I'd snuck down the road to the rather pleasant hotel for at least a few hours on non-cot nights over the last four months. I also did my best to make it back to Lake City for a conjugal visit to Kay on the boat once a month. But I'd get jerked back to RTP after fifteen or twenty hours. Every time.

Without exception.

On principle.

Better to ask forgiveness, or better yet, say nothing, and just fucking go.

. . .

KAY COULDN'T CONCEAL her loneliness and disappointment. But she made the best of it. Whenever I managed a quick flight to Minneapolis, she'd pick me up. The forty-five-minute drive to the boat comprised the bulk of our quality time together that summer. More than once she'd muttered, "Hon, I see this project taking more of a toll on you than any of your projects over the last thirty years. I'm worried about you. I also worry about us."

"Look, babe, it's a tough gig. I've missed being with you more than anything. The only thing worse than bickering when we're together is missing you when we're apart."

To me, it seemed like a test. But for whom, and of what?

"Dunno, Geno, every time you come home for a visit, you're called away again within hours."

And every time I left to return to RTP with my overstuffed garment bag over one shoulder, and my laptop bag over the other, I felt her watching me walk the dock toward shore. I'd catch the airport express back to MSP. I'd quiz myself, *How long can this go on?* We'd been fighting less lately. No doubt because we'd been spending so little time together.

Absence makes... what?

ONE MEMORY that lingers to this day involved me and the top *cowboy* on site at RTP one Saturday morning after the 6 am update. Let's call him Jim. He pulled me into one of the many empty conference rooms off *Times Square.* Or had this one been a large office? Jim stood at least six inches taller. With his hands on his hips and one foot tapping from the center of the room, he half-whispered, half-seethed, "Jurrens, where's your client/server architecture project manager? You pitched for him."

"Jim, Randy's wife is studying for her Minnesota state nursing boards. They have two small children. She needed him home for the weekend so she could study. His project is in decent shape as you just heard."

The man now hissed like a snake. He'd kicked his admonition up a notch. "You sent him *home?*"

"My team, my call. This is very important to him and to his family." The man now absolutely radiated waves of... rage? He sniffled, rubbed his nose with the thumb and forefinger side of a loose fist, then threw his arms down to his sides where he clenched and unclenched his hands. The pressure on this 30-something-year-old VP had to be close to unbearable. Maybe more than close. *Is he... coked up?* That did NOT give him license to say what he said next. "You get his ass back here by this afternoon, or else!"

At that, I started to heat up, too. I'd had enough. "Or else, Jim? What does that mean? Exactly."

"It means you losing your job will mean nothing to you. Because I'll kill your wife. Then I'll kill your kids, and then your fucking dog. And after that, Jurrens, I'll come after *you*. Clear enough?" He now gasped like a big bad wolf who'd just finished a hundred-yard dash before huffing and puffing as he glowered down at me.

My jaw dropped... and stayed there. *Yep, he's on somethin'*. This guy had the ear of the COO and probably the CEO, too. I didn't give a flying rat's fart. I took a step closer to him and abruptly brought my left index finger to within a few inches of his nose. He must have thought I was going to punch him. He jerked back. I said, "Look, Jim, I can't imagine the heat coming down on you right now. That does *not* give you the right to talk to me or any of us like this. We're all here doing our goddamn jobs best we can. And this shit?" My finger pointed first at him, then at me and back again, "does not help. I'll get Randy back here tomorrow night. Is *that* clear enough? *Sir?*"

Must have been. After a half dozen more closed-mouth nostril-flaring inhales and exhales and another sniffle accompanied by another swipe across his nose, he stomped out of that ghastly room in silence.

Yeah, memory serves.

Not long after that *discussion*, I reflected how I felt after almost five months of non-stop heart-sputtering stress, most of the time fasting to prevent puking. Some nights, as the clock crept up on midnight, maybe I'd snag a sporadic Crunchwrap Supreme from the Taco Bell's drive-thru between the *Ghost Town* and "my" Marriott. I'd chase down that gut bomb with a twelve-ounce tumbler of gin. How did I feel about the endless pressure to maintain business results with my 48 best programmers and business analysts held hostage here in RTP? Yeah, on the way "home" one night, for one moment, I had indeed considered just ending it all. Thankfully, a moment of sanity prevailed.

AND THEN... two weeks later, as unceremoniously as it had begun, we completed our recommendations to the senior team—the decision-makers in New York. We presented them with detailed technical and business analyses to back them up. The war room concluded. We went home. That was it.

I thought, *Did anyone thank us for a shed-load of kinship, hardship, and chickenshit?*

For that? Memory does not serve.

I considered long and hard whether to report Jim's personal threats. In the end, I decided he needed help.

The COO and the CEO accepted our recommendations to divest the personal computer desktop part of IBM to a Chinese company called Lenovo.

But soon, I'd face another frightening challenge I'll never forget.

Chapter 46

Swan Song

More than a thousand programmers and business people had depended on me to lead them into the future. Then, before, during, and after lighting a fire under the COO's butt with all that PC business in RTP, he'd just cut my organization's budget by 40% in less than 24 months.

These talented people worked for me at several IBM sites in the US and in various countries worldwide. Prior to these cuts, my annual budget hovered around $100 *million.* That sounds like a lot, but my organization was on the critical path of enabling $37 *billion* (USD). That represented almost 40% of the company's entire global revenue stream in 2007.

But competition was increasing, and the pressure piled on. We also expected a global financial crisis the following year, which indeed happened. Even that didn't justify cutting people who provided significantly greater value than many who didn't. But because they had a frickin' target painted on their backs, they had to go.

Was this partially because I humiliated my *big bad boss* into looking hard at the consequences of what *he'd* done gutting his old division at RTP into relative ineffectiveness? This had to be my fault, didn't it? Or did I just suffer from illusions of fictitious grandeur? It's possible I simply needed to wallow in personal guilt for cutting all those people loose.

I WON'T PUNISH you too much with the details of my team's mission. But they updated the massive sales support systems that made possible the ordering and purchase of every major hardware, software, and service offering sold by IBM. These programs empowered sales and marketing representatives to rapidly assemble obscenely complex proposals and orders with unerring technical quality and financial accuracy for huge customer installations or upgrades.

AN AVERAGE ORDER comprised millions of dollars in products and associated services. Without our key part of that fulfillment system, sales just could not happen. It was that simple, and that complex. The days of the paper ordering pad were *long* gone.

Here's the deal. My team updated and tested a massive body of worldwide software used to configure virtually all major quotes and orders with the detailed specifications and dependencies for approximately *600 new computer products and accessories every week.* IBM sold new and existing products to customers in several dozen countries with different languages, currencies, and legal systems. During those massive updates, we tested the entire body of software before releasing it. You'd be amazed how small errors could render much of the system unusable. That *just could not be allowed to happen*.

This means we lived smack-dab in the middle of IBM's road leading to the twin corporate holy grails: profit and shareholder value. The palpable pressure to stay on schedule weighed on the shoulders of my team, but especially on my own. This incredible group of experts knew the critical importance of their jobs, and they excelled at performing them. They were a tough crew who bore monumental stress every hour of every day. But they also demonstrated immense pride in this critical mission. Even when they survived *my* massive cuts and had to pick up the slack for a now-empty chair on either side of their own.

And then number-crunching pricks demanded I fire two out of every five of my superb employees so *they'd* look like heroes? They could not have cared any less about the longer-term impact on the business. They'd worry about that down the road *after* they'd achieved their stellar quarterly financials and attaboys but *before* the business and our customers suffered too much, claiming a mere transitional issue. And the cost in human wreckage of *my* people? Inconsequential.

All of this marinated in my consciousness as I seriously re-evaluated my part in this morass of moral absurdity. Then, one more experience thrust me into yet more *trouble with thinking*. It was no longer just about me, or my employees, or about IBM.

Chapter 47

One Bad Apple

The pain of firing an employee is best described with a factual excerpt from my novel, ***Dangerous Dreams****. I changed the names of others to protect their anonymity.*

At light speed, my job had transformed from technical alchemy into a personal nightmare. One memorable vignette still sticks with me, although this example was unique in both cause and effect. The stressors, however, were not.

The painful process of giving this condemned man time to make his peace became more and more awkward. We'd fired Dent Canfield for just cause. He'd lied on his application for employment, and more recently, exhibited an unrelenting pattern of near-psychotic sexual harassment.

Under supervision, he now emptied his desk drawers with ponderous deliberation, dwelling on every artifact of his eight years with IBM. Every object received long minutes of his attention before placing it in his box of shame. Dent seemed determined to make this process as difficult as possible. Was he relishing our collective discomfort? After 30 minutes of this torture, my abrupt voice was like a gunshot in his silent office, my patience gone. "That's it. Time to go." I felt a dreary blend of pity and disgust, but retained my practiced guise of neutrality.

Dent's managers, Donny and Maxine, both appeared grateful for my intervention. Maxine worked for me, Donny worked for Maxine, and Dent had worked for Donny. At last, the maudlin pity party within which Dent immersed himself came to a merciful end.

Our small group approached an exterior security door that opened onto the sidewalk. The armed IBM Rochester security team followed. Just in case. As we walked out into the crisp Minnesota evening, we trudged through connected pools of garish mercury-vapor light that speared the darkness from above. I didn't have to be here. I felt compelled.

Dent clung to his meager box of memorabilia. He was performing his best don't-give-a-shit act with his awkward swagger, not quite pulling it off. I placed a paternal hand on the side of Dent's upper arm. I leaned in close and, in what I thought was a not unkind voice, whispered, "Dent, please seek professional help. Luck to you." I'd hoped to spare him any more embarrassment in front of the others.

Equally discreet, his mouth to my ear, Dent responded, "Oh, I'll get professional help alright, Jurrens. Say goodbye to Kay."

I shuddered as Dent jerked away, levying his glassy dead-eye glare before turning and strolling toward his car. What remained unspoken behind that malevolent glare? I flashed on the death row movie *The Green Mile* and recalled the iconic phrase, *dead man walking*. But Dent's thinly veiled threat left me wondering who that might be. *Was* ***he*** *looking at* ***me*** *thinking the same?'*

Dried maple leaves crunched underfoot on the sidewalk. Were we merely trampling nature's detritus the color of old blood, or crushing the remains of those whose lives we'd ruined? Virulent malignancy radiated from Dent in white-hot waves as he turned to disappear into the night.

Revulsed, I thought, *So many levels to that sick and suffering soul. Dent isn't the first, and won't be the last.* I lamented, *God in Heaven, forgive me for having become so callous.* My hands trembled as they cowered within the privacy of my pockets.

9:30 pm. A quick end to this drawn-out spectacle couldn't come soon enough for us. After a wrinkled moment with a knitted brow, I turned to Maxine and Donny. I whispered, "Please see Mr. Canfield to his car. Take security." Then, to the security team leader in a quiet voice, "Take no chances." He rewarded me with a purposeful nod, the heel of his right hand resting on the holster of his compact sidearm. *Oh, Lord....*

Fifteen minutes later, my line management and HR teams debriefed in my conference room. They often used this room in my absence during the winter months. Even then, they'd pipe me in via video from our condo in Florida. Or from wherever my travels found me. It was a pleasant enough room from which every one of us could not escape fast enough.

Donny's hands betrayed the bluster in his voice. He hid them under the table. "This poor schmuck is sick, alright. Maybe even dangerous. Why are we just letting him go?" His ragged voice matched his tear-stained grimace. His exit interview with Dent had not gone well. We all trusted Donny's sensitivity. He was a superb people person—an empath. But I also sensed his profound relief now that Dent was gone. This series of events had clearly shaken him. As it had all of us. Each of us sensed this was far from over.

Claire Peterson, the HR manager, responded. "Look, folks, I've seen thousands of troubled souls in my thirty-six years wading through the underbelly of this business. Especially in the last few difficult years. But what has the guy really done?"

As Dent's direct manager, Donny did not like where this conversation seemed to be going. Claire sounded more like a defense attorney than an HR manager; however, the disgust in her voice was clear. "He lied on his application about his military experience and work history. That's not a criminal offense, but it *is* a condition of employment. We fired him for that.

"Next, he jacked off to a picture of a beautiful girl, his team leader, and confronted her in the parking lot, but with words only." Claire was on a roll. "We tossed the guy a lifeline for evaluation and potential treatment. But he threw it back in our faces. He's an adult. He's entitled. One thing we should discuss is a restraining order. An RO might give Ms. Mathers, at least a veneer of legal protection if we have enough to get one. Might she want help with that, Donny?"

Donny shook his head. "She was clear. She wants this to be over and doesn't want to pile on. Thinks it was puppy love, innocent or not. Sounds like she still feels a little sorry for the guy. He was a good team member until.... Look, I don't feel good about what I think right now. I actually liked the guy myself."

"That's it then. We're done. Good job, guys. These are never easy." Claire snapped her folder shut, visibly startling Donny. She placed it on her lap as she deftly spun her wheelchair around. The practiced maneuver was impressive—a swift 180-degree arc. Claire sped out of the room. We knew she needed to feed her cats.

At 10 pm everybody ended this long and hard day, everyone except me. I was the only one who'd heard Dent's ominous threat: *"I'll get professional help, alright. Say goodbye to Kay."* I sat alone in my office for a long time with the lights off. The only ambient light radiated from the mercury vapors in the parking lot through my waist-to-ceiling windows. Kay would already be asleep on the boat. She wouldn't ask me about my day until tomorrow morning. I needed time.

This guy Canfield, differed from the hundreds of others I'd had to let go just because I didn't have the budget to pay them, or failed to place them in another organization that still had budget. It was times like these when I wondered whether my natural style of getting close to my teams was tactically naïve. *Dent knows Kay. He and so many others have been to our house and to our boat for social gatherings. Dear God, am I losing perspective, like Palmer had accused me? Is that* ***all*** *I'm losing?*

Chapter 48

Shotgun

~

A LOADED SHOTGUN WAS A TOOL. I NEVER IMAGINED NEEDING such a tool within corporate America. I hate guns for the latent violence they represent, even though I'd trained with them in the service.

Now, shoulder-to-shoulder across the side-yard fence, I didn't exactly whisper. "Kevin, can I borrow one of your guns and a few rounds to go with it for a couple of weeks? Until we head south anyway? How about a shotgun?"

Living next door to Kevin in Rochester was always exciting and interesting. A bit of the Wild West. The lovable lone-wolf Harley dude never failed to intrigue me. And now I was grateful for our friendship.

"Sure, man. What's going on?"

"Aw, just some BS at work that could follow me home."

"I hear that. Dangerous times. I'll bring it over later. Under the table?" Kevin managed an explosives company and occasionally traveled in rough circles. No stranger to danger.

"Yes, please. What Kay doesn't know...."

"Copy that, brother."

THE FOLLOWING WEEK, I reported to the police a white Cadillac parked down the street across from a house under construction on Hillsboro Drive. I'd spotted it there three nights in a row. Yeah, my head was on a swivel. Dent drove a white Caddy. A cruiser showed up. The Caddy was already gone. Kevin offered to tail him next time, but I didn't think any good could come of that.

I analyzed our situation. The time had come to sell this house in any event. It was already sold, and we'd only been spending time there instead of at the boat to ready all our stuff for the move to Florida.

After work, usually around 9 pm or later, I often enjoyed hanging out for a while with Kevin in his garage next door. The ultimate Minnesota man cave, that garage. A full bar, heat, ribald conversation, and provocative posters of motorcycle babes—little more than soft porn posing as high-octane ads. A relaxed respite from what the IBM pressure cooker had become... for me, at least.

If Kevin's overhead door was open in warm weather, the party was on. And for him, hanging out with a white-collar stiff like me over the years when I was in town was an amusing diversion. He'd said so. Mocked that IBM had sure *diversified* me. I loved Kevin despite his rather monochrome intellect. Maybe because of it.

Life was so simple for him. Hell, Kevin would move to Florida too if he could afford to retire. If *he* wanted to relax, he'd just blow up an old refrigerator in an open field on his company's dime. Even around explosives, Kevin's omnipresent can of beer and smoldering Marlboro cigarette signaled job satisfaction. The simple life.

Time to turn the page, start the next chapter. We'd be heading south in another week for the winter. That would provide some distance between us and this sick madman. I had to wonder, though, just how sick and how mad was Canfield?

I HAD JUST TURNED 58 in late 2007 after almost 32 grand years with an awesome company. I could now retire with a full pension at any time. And that's what I did. Why? Between vicious *surplus* cycles I called "purges," and brutal war room projects, the job was literally killing me. I couldn't sleep without drinking myself into a stupor every night, topped off with an Ambien, a strong sleeping pill. My weight topped 240, and acid reflux became a major health issue for me. My doctor said if I didn't make some major lifestyle changes, like *yesterday,* my survival was questionable.

Severe obstructive sleep apnea found me constantly waking up and gasping for air, even though I was beyond physical and emotional exhaustion. I was flirting with congestive heart failure. The nightmares made matters even worse.

I took a perverse satisfaction in knowing the name of every one of the employees I had had to let go, knowing I'd cratered their careers, or at least changed their life's direction. Avoiding this very feeling was the same reason I had enlisted in the Coast Guard instead of the Army. I wanted to save people's lives, not be responsible for harming them!

Kay, my financial sherpa, said it'd be a challenge with our debt load for a few years, but she understood. It was hard to admit that this was a matter of life or death for me. Especially when I told her what occurred during that grueling war room project that kept me away from home for almost five months.

Fire folks during the day and sleep like a baby at night? All for corporate profit? And now looking over my shoulder? Nope, I was *not* that guy. Not anymore, anyway.

Chapter 49

Adios

Yes, I refused to be complicit in that humanity-tampering chicanery any longer. With my head held high, I did the deed. I walked away from the job I loved with a full pension after almost 32 years of faithful and loyal service. This great company's motto had originally attracted me back in 1977, and I still remember it: *Our people are our most important asset.* That's how I'd managed my people until....

At age 58, it was time for me to shuffle on down the road.

I love IBM for the opportunities it has provided me. I love the people I worked with, almost without exception. And I met wonderful folks from all over the world that I will never forget: IBMers, customers, friends, classmates, and professional adversaries. That includes others I met in meeting rooms, customer conferences, airports, and on the streets of Copenhagen, Denmark; Vienna, Austria; Bratislava, Slovakia; Tokyo, Japan; Singapore; the Republic of Belarus.... And other cities I visited presenting to customers in Los

Angeles, Hamamatsu, Japan; Stuttgart, Germany; and myriad other wonderful venues.

I love where I started—in Rochester, Minnesota. *And* having transacted business with folks of integrity in Armonk, White Plains, Somers, Purchase, and Poughkeepsie, New York; Tucson, Arizona; Boca Raton, Florida; Raleigh, North Carolina; Atlanta, Georgia; Austin, Texas; Rome, Italy; Barcelona, Spain; Paris, France; and so many other fascinating places too numerous to mention, each with their own unique and delightful people and culture.

If any of you wonderful folks read this account, my old IBM acquaintances or customers, I love you all, even if we may have pissed each other off in the past. And if you are among the 422 employees my organization had to let go between 2006 and 2008, *you* are the reason I walked away. Not because of IBM, but because of me. I salute you from *my* post-IBM life, and maybe yours, too. To this day, I still believe people are more important than *making the numbers.* That is why I am not, nor will I ever be, a captain of industry doing what is necessary to survive within late-stage capitalism.

After retiring, three avocations would define Kay and me to our present day:

1. Our boating life,
2. Our motorhome life,
3. My quasi-career as an author, artist, musician, and poet—a now-geriatric hippie re-emerging from his long-dormant cocoon, but with a lot less hair, and a tad more wisdom!

Beyond this trio of activities? To be determined. So let's talk boating....

Chapter 50

Down the River

We'd been boaters since leaving the United States Coast Guard in 1973. Other than car-top dinghy sailboats, however, we owned no serious sailing craft until we bought *Skye*, a lovely 30-foot Catalina sloop, in 1987. *Skye* was a comfortable-enough weekender on inland waters.

But our dream of voyaging crystalized when we acquired *Sojourn* in late 1995—a serious ocean-capable live-aboard vessel. And then Kay and I retired early enough to enjoy *cruising* (living and traveling on a boat) as an active lifestyle.

In late August 2008, less than three months after my early May retirement date, we departed Lake City, Minnesota by water. We went *right to paradise,* finally taking a right turn outside the sailboat basin aboard our beloved little ship, *Sojourn.*

Many Lake City boaters flirted with the dream of *going down the river* over the years, but only a handful of us actually did it. After all, such a voyage was *not* to be taken lightly. Some even started this serious once-in-a-lifetime endeavor, but never completed their dream.

Please realize that *Sojourn's* maximum speed was only eight or nine mph, under sail or power, even though we had a big-ass diesel power plant down in the engine room fed by twin 150-gallon fuel tanks for long-range cruising under power if necessary. It was necessary. *And* we'd not be able to navigate the river at night. Rules of the river road. This limited our rate of progress to a snail's crawl, or as I like to say, *a stately and dignified pace.* Like sailors in centuries past. Yeah, that's it.

Our vessel proved to be both seaworthy and economical to operate. Under sail, we used no fuel. But that wasn't possible much until we reached the Gulf some 1,500 miles downstream. Too busy dodging commercial river traffic and navigating shallows. But *then*, she'd stretch her sea legs under sail. She was built for *that* purpose, not for the river system.

Until then, we burned *1.5 gallons of diesel per hour* on average while under power at ~6 mph. That's because we efficiently cut *through* the water, not on plane; that is, not *on top of* the water. A comparable powerboat or motor yacht on plane will cruise at 20 to 30 mph; some even faster. But they will burn *40 to 60 gallons per hour*, depending on a wide range of variables. What doesn't vary? Speed is spendy!

Once we left the retirement and bon voyage parties behind us, we shoved off, knowing that *Sojourn*, a distinctive fixture in Lake City's marina for 13 years, was never to return. A dozen boats waiting outside the marina on the lake saw us off with a fleet salute of horns. A moving experience. Yeah, another bad pun.

I don't recall what day of the week we left, but I guarantee it was not on a Friday—bad luck, of course. Sailors may not admit it out loud, but we are a superstitious lot. Neither did we want to start our voyage this far north this late in the season. But some last-minute repairs and essential modifications delayed us.

As a couple of examples, we needed a new fridge when the old Norcold (nicknamed *N'er Cold*) failed. We also waited for a new suite of navigation electronics to be installed. They took longer to arrive than expected. Plus, end-to-end voyage planning and research involved far more time and effort than we had anticipated.

We then worried we'd not arrive in hurricane country until well into the storm season. Hey, no risk, no gain! Or so some say. We wanted our ship in the tropics, but she, and we, had to be ship-shape before disembarking!

. . .

After I retired, I confess to struggling with my identity. I had become a dreaded *PIP*—a *previously* important person, at least in my own egoistic mind. My personal identity had become too entangled with my IBM boss-man persona for too damn long. So, for the next few years, I diluted that bitter tincture with alcohol, more than ever. Kay came along for the bumpy ride.

As a result, we found it necessary to enter a survival pact. If we'd anchor on the river at night, which was possible only on the Upper Mississippi, we'd not drink once we'd *dropped the hooks* (anchors). This was in case we needed to move the boat fast because of a too-large or out-of-control tow (tug/barges), or a too-narrow stretch of river.

Unlike us, the tows navigated at night. So we agreed to imbibe only if safely tied to a dock in a marina. And because of *that,* we spent half our time on this trip with symptoms of alcohol withdrawal. Not a great first episode for a dream coming true.

We plodded along for almost 800 miles downstream on the *Mighty Muddy* to Cairo, Illinois, 170 miles south of St. Louis, Missouri. This included traversing some 22 locks on the Upper Mississippi River starting with Lock & Dam No. 4 in Alma, Wisconsin, the first lock downstream from Lake City.

Stress ran high, much because of our own design. Some not. With just the two of us wrestling a 20-ton vessel over 50 feet long into and out of locks, that added to our already elevated stress levels. If you're not familiar with lock operation, they can be adventurous for the recreational inland waterway voyager. Especially if the weather is less than ideal.

For example, if you are competing with huge and heavy commercial barges for a tie-up inside a lock's tight quarters, that can be stressful, if not downright dangerous. Or when entering/exiting the lock with dozens of other pleasure craft, many throw thoughtless wakes. Some produce *enormous* waves as they power up to exit a lock at speed, even in designated no-wake zones.

Farther down the waterway, lock masters prioritize commercial traffic over recreational vessels. Some of us waited *days* for passage through a busy lock!

For you procedural fanatics, the principle of lock operation is simple. For a boat like us aboard *Sojourn* traveling downstream, here's the process:

1. If the water in the chamber is low, we wait while the upstream valve fills the chamber.
2. The lock master then opens the upstream gates and we move in with deliberation. They toss us a couple of mooring lines, usually more appropriate for boats *much* smaller and lighter than ours in these waters. Commercial tows are allowed to use their own much heavier lines. We are not.
3. They close the upstream gates.
4. The downstream valve drains the chamber until the water levels match on the far (downstream) side of the lock. We manually feed out mooring lines as the water level drops. Too often, the lock-supplied mooring lines aren't long enough to feed around a cleat on our boat, which makes for a smooth and controlled descent. That means holding our 20-ton vessel in place with a small line *in only our hands*. Dangerous stuff! Oddly, most lock masters on this stretch of the river just don't understand heavy recreational vessels. Or they do, and gain some perverse pleasure watching fancy boats operated by folks

who have too much time and money on their hands, most of whom display crappy boat-handling skills.

5. The gates downstream then open, and we move out at slow speed by releasing the lock's mooring lines, shoving off, and powering up.

Occasionally, because of the rather unique physics of our vessel's single-screw design; that is, only one propeller, not two like most powerboats our size, we'd end up in the lock facing *upstream.* Normally, we'd face our vessel downstream. We'd often be required to tie up with our port (left) side to the lock wall; that is, to our left, as we enter. However, to stop our considerable forward momentum, since we had no brakes, I *always* needed to apply a serious burst of power in reverse to kill our headway.

Our boat *walked to starboard* (to the right) when in reverse. That meant her butt would invariably swing to the right—*away* from where we needed her butt to be in order to grab the lock's skimpy stern mooring line. Got the picture? Given anything more than a little wind, which was quite often late that summer, I'd frequently anticipate this problem even as I entered the lock. So, what to do?

Instead of obediently approaching the *left* side of the lock chamber to quietly grab the offered mooring lines, I'd head to the *middle* of the chamber, cram my wheel all the way to port, and feed her a *healthy* burst of *forward* power. The bow would obviously swing to *port.* But before making any significant forward progress, I'd then quickly shift into *neutral*, then into reverse, and immediately give her another *serious* burst of power in *reverse.* Her butt would predictably swing to *starboard.* I'd repeat that process a few times in rapid but deliberate succession—never touching the wheel—until I was heading toward the spot where the lock master had originally directed me, but facing the "wrong" direction (upstream). Then, when I approached the lock wall, giving her a small burst of reverse would swing her butt right snug up against the wall, and she'd settle in exactly where the lock master wanted us.

Easy, right? Well, that took some skill and a good deal of experience with this particular boat. And while this *looked* impressive, this swift maneuver with such a large vessel in such a small space usually drove apoplectic lock masters to shouting panicked orders over the radio, or an impressive bout of arm-waving and pointing if he were outside watching this spectacle from the railing atop the wall. We'd not respond until the vessel was secured. I'd radio ahead with my intentions when I knew this would be necessary, but often I didn't know until I entered the lock. The current inside the chamber, which also played havoc with handling, was seldom predictable.

So, why did this maneuver so concern lock masters? Especially the young ones who'd never been exposed to such a maneuver by an experienced captain of an ocean-capable vessel? Well, by swinging our relatively large boat in a swift 180-degree pivot *in place* with precision in a chamber not much wider than our boat's length, they feared I'd get jammed sideways in their lock and block the passage of all river traffic!

I guess they were accustomed to weekend boaters who failed to master their vessels. Kay invariably settled them down, either shouting up to them face-to-face from the foredeck, or over the radio, once we were secured. "Sir, the captain knows his vessel. This is safest under these conditions. He'll swing her about before leaving your chamber. Thank you. Out."

The farther downstream we ventured, however, the river's currents picked up to where we struggled to maintain steerage, starting in southern Illinois. We ducked into a floating marina just upstream from the last lock and dam on the Mississippi. And we were stuck there for three weeks, along with at least a dozen other boats also cruising downstream. Severe flooding on the river drove this circumstance.

Storm season. As we feared.

Chapter 51

Stranded, But Not Alone

While stranded in East Alton, Illinois, Kay and I developed an instant friendship we will never forget, and which would endure for the rest of this voyage. That precious friendship would also end with an emotional earthquake.

Cap'n Larry (not sure we ever learned his last name), an erstwhile Rhode Island lobsterman, drank and smoked too much. He was short, skinny as a compass needle, brash, even vulgar. He didn't mean to be. Larry was just... authentic as Hell. He was the real deal, a crusty little curmudgeon with barnacles on his keel and wrinkles in his rigging from a lifetime at sea. He reminded me of Cap'n Brownie, my tug captain friend from my Coast Guard days.

We'd gotten tied up (pun) in a floating marina in East Alton. Didn't know for how long. It turned out to be a three-week delay. The river had flooded. We blamed feeder bands from Hurricane Ike that fall of 2008. Feeder bands are outlying weather patterns that radiate outward from the storm proper and can affect weather patterns a thousand miles from the eye.

As feared, we'd failed to beat the storm season to our Florida destination, but that was no surprise. There'd be weather hell to pay on the Gulf, too, and that'd now already affected voyaging boaters as far north as southern Illinois.

The Coast Guard shut down the river to all traffic—not optional—because of extreme flooding just north of St. Louis. That meant we were stuck a half-mile upstream from the last lock and dam on the Mississippi. We'd watch 60-foot uprooted trees floating past the marina out on the river in currents running far faster than our boat (or most boats) could have maintained control. We also observed other small-craft-threatening debris, like refrigerators and broken-up boats, carried away by the floodwaters. Not even the most powerful tows were allowed on the river.

One night, the harbor master feared the water had risen so high he'd lose his marina. It was about to float off the top of its thirty-foot-tall pilings. Even the seawall between the marina and the turbulent river was now almost underwater too, which wouldn't stop it. This situation had stressed the giant electrical cables that fed the marina from shore. And *that* started a serious electrical fire.

Before firefighters arrived to quench the blaze, the harbor master issued the alarm to evacuate. The marina crew banged on every boat to wake everyone at 2 am. Kay tried to arouse me. I remained unresponsive. I had chased an Ambien, a serious prescription-strength sleeping pill, with a half-dozen martinis before retiring, like most nights. When she finally slapped me conscious, we grabbed our ditch bag before heading for the safety of the shore.

Not only was the marina in jeopardy, but we'd have lost our boat, like all the other boats moored there. Fortunately, we lost neither that night. But I then knew I had a serious problem. They quelled the fire, and the marina with all its moored boats—including our retirement investment—did not float downstream that night to be chopped to pieces by roaring over the massive Melvin Price Dam.

. . .

DURING THAT TIME in East Alton, we learned that the overnight moorages downstream could handle only three to six boats at a time. They existed only every 50 miles or so along this desolate stretch of the *Mighty Muddy*. And *any* anchoring on the river overnight down there was neither possible nor safe, even after the floodwaters subsided. The shipping channel consumed the entire river's breadth.

So, we joined the Great Loop Cruisers Association. The members of this experienced and well-coordinated boating group's quest was to circumnavigate the eastern US via inland, coastal, and Great Lakes waterways. The river system we were navigating comprised the western portion of *the loop. Loopers* performed a superb service coordinating their member fleet's movement downstream to the Gulf. They were the only group crazy enough to navigate the Mississippi that far down. By the way, we were the only sailboat among a fleet of at least 60 powerboats backed up at Alton and its environs awaiting passage south.

Once the USCG opened up the river again, the GLCA beautifully orchestrated staging the fleet's movement downstream. This ensured no looper vessel was left stranded out on the river overnight by ensuring each member had a reservation for a suitable mooring. This not only made perfect sense; it proved to be a critical safety issue in very practical terms. I shudder to think what dangerous twist fate might have dealt us if we hadn't joined forces with this savvy bunch of inland yachtsmen!

Every evening at 5 pm while stranded at Alton for those three weeks, one designated *looper,* a boat captain, convened a *captain's meeting*. It was often little more than an excuse to inhale boat drinks. Nothing too fancy, mind you, as stores aboard each vessel were limited to essentials. The only non-negotiable? High-proof alcohol.

Chapter 52

Cap'n Larry the Lobsterman

Boaters are like any other social group. Most were kind and considerate people; however, a few cliques existed there, as anywhere. One such clique shunned Cap'n Larry's rough manner, some said crude, especially when he drank or smoked too much, which was more frequent than not. Some ostracized him completely. Well, my dear Kay tolerated none of that chickenshit and said so. I was oblivious. I liked Larry. Real people. And he had stories to tell. As for what others thought, they didn't mess with me.

Like some others hanging out in Alton that autumn, we had rented a sedan to haul our dinghy's outboard motor in the trunk to a local repair shop. Fuel problems. This little motor preferred zero-ethanol gas, but that was hard to find back then down there. Plus, who knew you were supposed to let the gas line run dry when shutting down a small 4-cycle outboard? Lesson learned.

Not surprisingly, Kay invited Larry to go with us everywhere. While we had the car, Kay made grocery runs and invited Larry to join us. She'd drag him along with us to the captains' meetings, too, when nobody else even thought to invite him. Some still shunned the swarthy little drunk with the basso profundo voice—surprisingly deep for such a slip of a man. Larry smelled of booze and stale tobacco and often slurred his speech. We'd frequently invite him aboard *Sojourn* just to talk. He seemed desperate for companionship as he traveled alone and often lamented his estranged relationship with his son. No wife in the picture. He never talked about that.

He'd invite us over to his little 32-foot Nordic Tug, *Adriana,* for *Cap'n Morgan 'n waters*—spiced rum with a splash of water. Ice optional. "Like the pirates!" he'd boom in his startlingly deep voice with what sounded like a flat Bostonian accent to our untrained ears. Reminded me of a less loquacious and more sullen Captain Jack Sparrow from the movie, "Pirates of the Caribbean." If Jack would have been from Beantown or its environs.

Larry watched out for us, too. Others in the fleet made jokes about us as the only *rag-toppers*—sailors—in the fleet. After leaving Alton, we'd trail the rest of the group of faster boats traveling together for the day. The lead *stinkpot*—powerboat—on a day's movement might joke over the radio that they eyeballed the bridge ahead while we chugged along a bend or two in the river behind. Said they feared insufficient clearance for the *rag-topper's* mast. The US Army Corps of Engineers always posted highly visible clearance numbers on each bridge.

We'd hear Larry croak over the radio. "*Sojourn*, *Adriana*. Bridge is fine for you'se. No worries, Admiral K." That's what he called Kay. That or A.K. for short. The tortured little mariner had imprinted on her big-time. He'd also take the lead with his shallow-draft *Adriana* to test the water depth for our much deeper-draft *Sojourn,* especially farther downstream when it was often just *Adriana* and *Sojourn* traveling together. He'd then report to us over his VHF marine radio, the dear little soul. He'd guide us in *before* we ran aground.

Besides, every knowledgeable boater knows an electronic depth sounder, which *Sojourn* had, is worth little more than letting you know *why* you've already run aground. Especially on inland waters where the bottom is always close and usually unpredictable.

Chapter 53

Farther Down-River

Eventually, when the Coast Guard opened the river again, and we were free to leave Alton, we passed through the huge but debris-stuffed Melvin Price Lock. We found it necessary to shove branches and other debris away from our propeller with an extended boat hook. We feared fouling our prop, which would render our engine and steering useless.

From there, with no more dams to slow the river's naturally rapid current, water runs unabated and dangerously fast for recreational craft all the way to New Orleans, even under normal circumstances. Which is why the Lower Mississippi—roughly a thousand miles of *wilderness—far too dangerous* and inhospitable for recreational craft. Besides, down there small craft competed with almost *bumper-to-bumper* commercial traffic. And there is literally nowhere to safely anchor or refuel.

We noticed that the current did indeed pick up speed, and our ability to maneuver diminished, even at WOT (wide-open-throttle). If the water were to remain high from an extended rain, for example, the current on a big watershed like this mammoth river? *That,* my landlubber friends, is mighty hazardous for a slow boat like ours. Makes steering difficult and sometimes impossible.

If the current reached the velocity of our maximum theoretical hull speed of 8 or 9 mph, which it later exceeded 11 mph, we'd have little or no control of the boat! Think about not being able to steer your car on an interstate highway! Only *our* "car" weighed more than a big-rig truck's tractor! Damn dangerous, no matter how you slice fast water. Less of an issue for faster *stinkpots*.

That happened to us twice on this voyage, and it scared the feces right out of our constricted sphincters. Especially since we'd sunk every discretionary penny into this investment. Fortunately, we could get off the river (barely) by turning *upstream* and applying WOT (*full power*) with our autopilot engaged *while still slowly losing headway* before we could ease closer to shore where the current was slightly attenuated before nosing her into a tributary to wait out the fast water.

Net: on a boat, we are *always* subject to the whims of water *and* weather, both inland *and* offshore. I implore you, offshore sailors *and* power boaters, to consider such hazards slower vessels like ours face, particularly when sailing ocean-capable sailboats designed for still water while navigating inland waterways with swift currents.

We then took a huge, hair-raising left turn to travel *upstream* onto the mighty Ohio River for about 60 miles. It enters the Mississippi at Cairo, Illinois, 170 miles downstream from Alton. Cairo (pronounced KAY-ro, *not KY-ro*) was a ghost town by then, at least much of its waterfront. They'd been flooded too many times behind an ineffective dike for which the residents blamed their local politicians.

While our steering control had diminished on the Mississippi, we turned up the Ohio *against* its current without incident where our ability to maneuver improved a lot. That much relieved the ship's captain!

. . .

After uneventfully navigating the Ohio, still with the loopers, we then took a right to travel a short distance on *its* largest tributary, the Tennessee River. We made our way through two locks on the Tennessee through the expansive Kentucky Lake & Pickwick Lake. There, we actually unfurled the sails briefly before entering the first of twelve locks on the Tennessee-Tombigbee Waterway. This was known as the *Tenn-Tom.*

This waterway includes the Black Warrior River, which feeds into the Tombigbee River. Then on to a short length of the Mobile River into Mobile Bay. From there, the approach to the Gulf of Mexico requires passage through and across the huge and tricky Mobile Bay, Alabama. Simple, right? Easy on paper, anyway.

Remember, there are no *lane lines or exit signs* in any of the rivers we navigated. Plus, GPS mapping of these waterways was brand new. We constantly referred to paper *charts*—maps for bodies of water—to ensure our state-of-the-bleeding-edge GPS-based waterway navigation gear wasn't lying to us, and heading us into water too shallow to escape. More than once, the GPS chart showed our boat on dry land. Also, we dodged tows daily—powerful tugboats each pushing up to 42 barges (!) on this section of the waterway.

Keep in mind that a typical 42-barge tow is over 1,200 feet (1/4-mile) long. And at 200 feet wide (2/3 the length of a football field), these vessels cover *over 6 acres* and transport thousands of tons of cargo. Think about that for a moment. More often than I care to remember, they took up the entire river, leaving us, well, either limited or impossible options.

That meant each encounter had better include constant communication with their captains well before each encounter *and* stellar evasive maneuvering on my part. That sometimes included intentionally running aground in shallows not navigable by the gargantuan monsters with whom I jousted.

The captain communicating with the next day's anticipated river traffic and verifying bridge clearances based on water level.

Plus, passing one of those monsters invariably radiated tumultuous wakes—troublesome surface waves *and* turbulent underwater currents—that tossed us around like a cockroach in a flushing toilet. *Sojourn's* keel, her underwater fin, was designed for open water to prevent a boat under sail from sliding sideways, *not* for traffic-congested rivers dominated by turbulence-producing leviathans.

These difficulties surprised our powerboat friends. They really had no idea what we went through in such frequent encounters. Unlike shallower-draft powerboats, our sailboat's deep, full-length, ocean-going keel presented a blunt surface to such boiling currents *and* required us to remain in the 9-foot-deep shipping channel.

That put the best of my boat-handling skills to the test nearly every day. More than once I found myself repeatedly spinning my heavy wooden and spoked *destroyer* steering wheel five-and-a-half turns lock-to-lock, back and forth repeatedly, just to avoid a collision or a hard grounding.

~

Most locks dropped the water level—and us aboard *Sojourn*—10 to 15 feet per lock on the Upper Mississippi, and an average of 30 feet on the Tennessee-Tombigbee Waterway. The Jamie Whitten Lock on the Tenn-Tom, however, dropped us a whopping **84 feet!** Plus, once inside that lock and descending toward its bottom, we watched with trepidation as jets of water sprayed through age-old cracks in the lock's concrete walls that towered several stories above us.

As the level dropped us closer to the Gulf's water table, it reminded me of our first house's precarious basement foundation just before it collapsed in 1978. And the currents inside that lock to move that much water in 10-15 short minutes? We felt like we'd landed in the bottom of a blender jar almost a third of a football field deep after someone pushed *liquefy!*

Just handling the lock's slimy mooring lines and my fender boards suspended horizontally outboard of our fenders (*bumpers*) for such an enormous drop to keep our boat from banging into either the lock wall or other boats? Bloody terrifying! They say *cruising on a sailboat comprises days and weeks of boredom punctuated by moments of sheer terror*. And *this* was one of those terrifying moments.

Here are some of the countless exciting challenges we encountered on the inland waterway leg of this voyage:

- The sheer length of the river trip at such slow speeds tested our patience and endurance,
- Traversed some 39 locks, under 99 bridges, and countless low-hanging high-voltage lines, each of which presented similar and some unique challenges,
- Frequently motored through gear-threatening debris, constantly worrying about fouled steering and propulsion causing loss of control, running aground, or hitting

underwater weir dams (yes, underwater concrete or rock *dams* just outside the channel),

- Double-anchored (bow and stern) outside narrow channels when possible so we wouldn't swing into the path of a mammoth, fast-moving tow. They'd sometimes pass within 30 feet of us in the dead of night at speed. If they'd even skimmed us? Certain death. So I'd deploy a stern anchor. This required:
    - lowering the 600-pound dinghy from its davits (hoists) on our stern;
    - climbing down the five-foot ladder to our swim platform, and transferring to the dinghy a 45-pound stern anchor attached to its anchor line;
    - tow the anchor and line out in the dinghy;
    - dropping the anchor over the dinghy's gunwale into the water,
    - then re-securing the dinghy aft of the mother ship,
    - once back aboard, I'd manually draw that stern anchor line taught and make it off (tie it) to a stern cleat;
    - next morning, retrieve the anchor with the dinghy,
    - transfer it and its line back aboard *Sojourn* (mud and all),
    - rinse the anchor and line with the cockpit's hose and faucet,
    - secure (stow) it and its hundred feet or more of line,
    - manually re-attach and re-hoist the 600-pound dinghy onto its davits using their winches. Nobody promised this was gonna be easy;
- Stayed sober (just) long enough to avoid committing a potentially fatal error, which created painful anxiety between captain and mate.

But the statistic that kept us awake at night the most? A series of

16 fixed-clearance bridges spanning the Tenn-Tom whose charted vertical clearances above the waterway were not high enough. We'd somehow need to clear our overall mast, instruments, and antenna at a height of 55 feet above the water. Their minimum clearance was only 52 feet at *ordinary high water.* This gauntlet, beginning 450 miles upstream from Mobile Bay, tested our nautical mettle most of all.

Only two options presented themselves. The first option? We'd need to:

- Construct a heavy wooden scaffolding upon which the mast would rest (obstructing most of our deck surface and would leave scars on our painted deck),
- Disconnect and lower our 700-pound mast onto that scaffolding with a hired crane and to secure it into place before arriving at these bridges,
- Find and hire an appropriate shipper to ship the mast, two booms, roller furled sails and associated gear; shrouds & stays comprising cables, turnbuckles, myriad pins and bolts,
- Secure all of this on a semi-truck's flatbed trailer,
- Then pay to have the mast re-stepped (raised by yet another crane and lowered vertically back into place by another crew) with all the rigging to then be reattached and re-tensioned.

This would be time-consuming and expensive, not to mention risky. Something would likely be damaged or lost during shipment. Much of this was custom gear, and some of it one of a kind.

Worse, moving the boat through locks with all that scaffolding and gear on deck would make safe operations nearly impossible.

~

THE ONLY *OTHER* OPTION, also risky, was to:

- Leave the mast up,
- Top off the fuel and water tanks she'd ride several inches lower still, and then we'd hope for the best,
- Take all the instruments off the masthead to reduce overall height by a few feet,
- And wait for low water.

Yup, the *sphincter factor* would prevail once more. And this latter option is what we'd decided even before we left Lake City, Minnesota.

AS YOU SAILORS KNOW, touching the underside of an immovable overhead structure like a bridge span, or even passing close to high-voltage power lines with the top of your rig while underway, and worse, while inexorably being carried forward by 20-tons of momentum and being pushed by a swift current, is usually the kiss of death. Very dangerous, potentially fatal, and always bitterly expensive. A little more habañero ghost-pepper cheese in the omelet of life. To leave the rig up while running this particular gauntlet? *Se necesita huevos rancheros grande, mis amigos!* Yeah, that's Spanish gutter slang for *It takes big brass balls, my friends.* Roughly translated.

Oh, and did I mention that the water levels vary *unpredictably* for those last 450 miles by as much as 30 *feet?* Not a nice, regular, and tidy twice-a-day ocean tidal range of a foot or three either, but a genuine weather phenomenon. Much of the southeastern US watershed feeds into the Tenn-Tom. We saw with our own eyes barren banks *at least* 30 feet high from fast-moving-water erosion. They don't render this shit explicitly in the guidebooks, y'all.

. . .

Yes, we opted to leave our rig up, minus all instruments and antennas. We'd then wait to proceed by checking the forecasts and predicted water level *daily* with the Army Corps of Engineers. We then made a run for each leg of the next 450 miles when it seemed we'd clear the next fixed (non-opening) bridge. Yeah, we rolled the dice and we won our bet against steep odds! Our advanced planning, and more than a little blind, dumb luck, were fundamental to this well-timed but questionably conceived success. Yeah, those were the most tense three weeks of our entire inland voyage.

Let there be no doubt, though. If we hadn't benefitted from Kay's extraordinary planning acumen, combined with my boat-handling skills in this big old sailboat, this once-in-a-lifetime voyage would have turned out quite differently, and not for the better.

Do you offshore sailors *still* think zero-sea-room inland boat handling and navigation with hostile shores is child's play? And do you think 1/4-mile-long commercial vessels never far from either side of your own vessel in hellacious currents and unpredictable rig-killers is a piece of cake? Especially when you knowledgeable offshore sailors know *the* most treacherous part of any voyage is landfall; that is, navigating close to land, nautical traffic, and hazards to navigation? Try 1,500 miles and three months of... *that!* Child's play? If you think so, you advertise your own ignorance, mates.

Chapter 54

Table of Knowledge

Once we made Mobile Bay (pronounced MO-BEEL, and definitely *not* MO-b'l), it was all about leveraging critical local experience. We knew from the charts that the 30-mile-long, shallow and shifting shoals of the bay would be a navigational nightmare. Especially for a deep-draft ocean-going vessel like *Sojourn,* once outside the main shipping channel. The bay's water got especially *skinny* whenever the wind blew out of the north.

We'd need to leave the major shipping channel en route to Alabama's Gulf Shores, our next eastward waypoint, since we would not head directly out to the Gulf from there. Too blustery for comfort. Besides, we wanted to spend the night in a small marina next to the restaurant owned by Lulu—Jimmy Buffett's sister—in Gulf Shores. Boat drinks!

No electronic navigation system, not even ours, could by itself provide safe passage in these ever-shifting shallows, combined with a rather unique tidal pattern that's influenced by the bay's briny waters. Only local knowledge of *dead reckoning* would make safe passage possible.

Dead reckoning (DR) meant steering a specific compass course for a prescribed number of minutes and seconds before changing course onto a different heading with a different course and speed for a new duration. Skilled mariners, armed with local knowledge, would repeat this process until clear of obstacles and/or arrive at their destination.

DR was old-school navigation when the only reliable instruments comprised a compass and a chronometer (an accurate clock). I'd had plenty of DR training and experience in the Coast Guard, but not on Mobile Bay!

Fortunately, upon tying up on a tributary called Dog River at a small marina across the bay from our next waypoint, a scrawny mariner sauntered by *Sojourn* not long after I tied along their seawall. I sprayed mud off our ground tackle—anchoring gear—as he hailed me. "Better hurry, skipper. You're gonna be late."

"Afternoon. Late for what?"

"Well, the table a knowledge, a course. At 1600 hours!"

"Oh, ah, roger that. Thanks."

As I recall, Kay had borrowed the tiny marina's loaner car. Many small ports such as this made one available, asking only for a few bucks for gas. I was on my own, and thought, *Another adventure, another story!*

I secured my hose and made my way to a shadowy area underneath the marina office's overhang. There sat one of those kitchen table-and-chair sets with rounded chrome corners and red vinyl seats, half-occupied by people chatting quietly. Same with a nearby couch featuring tufts of escaping stuffing and two broken legs, so it sat at an angle. All open air. I heard, "Welcome, captain. This here's the Table of Knowledge!"

That afternoon, two other transients and I harvested a wealth of local knowledge generously shared about safely transiting Mobile Bay. By whom? The couple who owned the tiny marina, two circumnavigators who'd put down roots in the neighborhood, a couple of local commercial fishermen (one might have been a woman) sharing coffee from an old green Thermos, and a sociable commercial salvor. Pure gold!

How many minor miracles had conspired to get us this far safely? This was but one more.

So AFTER TRANSITING the entire 1,500-mile river system from Minnesota to the Gulf, and having made our way across Mobile Bay, we successfully navigated *the ditch,* too. Otherwise known as the Gulf Intracoastal Waterway, or GICW. Much narrower than rivers, almost no-current, salty water, transient-friendly as hell, and best of all, no tows to dodge!

Once we'd transited the bay and passed into a waterfront community called Gulf Shores, Alabama, we did indeed make moorage at the small dozen-or-so-slip marina next to Lulu's restaurant. Lucy Anne Buffett, also known by her childhood nickname LuLu, and the official *Crazy Sista* of the Buffett clan, is a self-proclaimed gypsy rebel, having come from a long line of sailors, salesmen, storytellers, and generation after generation of staunch, Southern matriarchs who were stellar cooks. So says her bio, anyway. We didn't meet her, but the food and ambience *were* darn good. Although once again skinny water in that little marina allowed us to polish the bottom paint off our keel. Oh, well. Ain't nothin' for nothin', I guess.

The GICW transported us from the eastern shore of Mobile Bay, Alabama, to Carrabelle, Florida, another 250 miles to the east. Another glitch, however: some too-low fixed bridges spanning the ditch were okay for power boats and motor yachts, but not for us and our mast. These forced us *outside* onto the angry autumn Gulf through a couple of passes—openings to the sea—more than we had planned. In one case, we doubled back on the ditch, which was no small feat, based on obsolete bridge height information on the charts. So we slipped outside to go around. Oh well.

Chapter 55

On the Gulf

For our first lengthy offshore experience on the Gulf with *Sojourn*, we crossed the *big bend.* There was no following close to shore on an easterly course next to Northwestern Florida's east-west *panhandle* and then transitioning to the Florida north-south *peninsula* on a southerly course. Instead, we crossed the northeastern Gulf of Mexico from Carrabelle on Florida's panhandle directly to Clearwater, down on the peninsula, or about a 165-mile overnight passage.

We had no choice. Closer to shore, that part of the Gulf was too shallow for *Sojourn's* six-foot draft. We still bumped the bottom while at anchor a few miles offshore in a serious chop while waiting for daybreak before entering Clearwater Pass.

Just so you know, *bumping bottom* sounds innocuous enough, doesn't it? But that's serious business in a heavy boat. Damaging a boat's hull with 20 tons of momentum dropping several feet onto a firm or hard bottom because of a serious surface chop? Especially on open water, where conditions are often unpredictable? That can be expensive and potentially hazardous to vessel and crew.

We were okay, though. At least we'd assume so unless we developed leaks in the engine room from one or more cracks in the hull around the hull/keel seam. After we made Clearwater for an overnight stay, we saw no leaks in the bilges. That did not mean we didn't worry until then.

FROM CLEARWATER, we then traveled *inside* on the ditch past Tampa, Sarasota, and Venice, on our way to our own beautiful Charlotte Harbor farther south. We'd made this leg of the journey before—as crew—on our dear friends' boat. Doug and Marti Olson aboard *Tara* had already shared some of their favorite stops with us we wished to revisit.

We ducked outside again to the open water of the Gulf between Venice and Charlotte Harbor, and entered the ten-mile-wide harbor through Boca Grande Pass. Why not stay outside for the entire passage? We were retired, with nothing but time. And to be blunt, unlike those who find sailing offshore enjoyable, we found the lack of scenery offshore disappointing. Not to mention an unnecessarily bumpy ride this time of year. The Gulf's shallow water wave action reminded me of similar potentially vicious wave action I'd experienced in the Coast Guard on Lake Huron. Discretion being the better part of valor, and all that....

AFTER AN EVENTFUL THREE-MONTH passage from Minnesota, we celebrated by touching off our very loud 120-dB air horns after we passed through Boca Grande Pass. That opening between the Gulf and more protected waters was the gateway to our new home waters for sailing, kayaking, and fishing—the 10-mile-wide, 20-mile-long Charlotte Harbor.

That harbor had become a popular eco-tour destination offering interaction with a rich variety of wildlife, a lush shoreline that's fun to explore via kayak, and other protected recreational boating. It had been *discovered* at last, but the towns on its shore, like Punta Gorda and Port Charlotte, remained relatively quaint. Unlike Tampa Bay, this harbor's absence of huge urban areas and commercial shipping traffic further increased its appeal.

Getting *Sojourn* here had been our long-term dream. Now we lived that dream, voyaging adventures notwithstanding. Only ten nautical miles remained. We put *Sojourn* under full sail and headed her due east into Burnt Store Marina, her new home port. BSM is the largest privately owned deep-water marina on the Gulf Coast. A 2,000-door rural village nestled around 525 boat slips in two large basins, between Punta Gorda and Cape Coral. Our little piece of paradise.

Then, repairing and repainting the boat after its rugged journey became essential before pursuing any further cruising plans. And now that we'd arrived in BSM, she did indeed need some sprucing up. But we were in no hurry.

Once we'd arrived at our condo in BSM, our Florida winter home of seven years by that time, and now *Sojourn's* new home port, we took some time to *get our feet dry,* as cruising sailors say.

Cap'n Larry, our little drinking and smoking buddy from Rhode Island, had not departed Carrabelle with us for the crossing as planned. He'd had too many *Cap'n Morgan 'n waters* the previous night, forgotten to take his potassium pills, and consequently suffered from severe leg cramps the morning we were to depart together. He always stood at his tug's helm whenever underway. His legs did not allow that on our departure day.

Larry called us and said he'd be arriving at BSM three days

hence. We looked forward to his visit, eager to show him our little Florida hideaway. Of course, once he'd secured his tug at the BSM guest dock not a hundred yards from us, he walked over to the condo we'd owned since 2001. This was a lovely property to which we flew down from Minnesota or New York when we had the chance. Sometimes we drove.

No sooner had he arrived at Happy Hour—*it was five o'clock somewhere*—than we started slamming cocktails to celebrate our reunion. After midnight, I walked him back to his boat. Both of us came close to falling off the dock a half-dozen times before reaching *Adriana*. We claimed that the well-lit dock was too dark to navigate without mishap and without some essential circuitous navigation!

Not one to stay in one port too long, two nights and two days later, Larry departed on *Adriana* for the Florida Keys. While this was less than a hundred nautical miles, slow displacement vessels like *Adriana* (and *Sojourn*) would make a few stops en route at overnight anchorages. He planned for three leisurely days. Nasty weather turned it into five, we learned.

He said he was headed for Islamorada on the Atlantic side. He'd cross from the Florida Bay to the Atlantic using Moser Channel under the Seven Mile Bridge south of Marathon in the Middle Keys. And then he'd cruise north in the Hawk Channel, a well-marked coastal route, to Islamorada.

No sooner had Larry departed than Kay started planning to visit him in a week by car. We had truly missed Larry. But we canceled our plans a week later when we heard he had drowned in the Islamorada anchorage. They found his body near his boat, with his dinghy adrift. This news crushed Kay. Killed by lethal *Cap'n Morgan 'n waters*, no doubt. Lots of 'em. Maybe he wasn't meant to cruise without Admiral K watching out for him....

Soon thereafter, Jason, Larry's estranged son, contacted us. Larry'd written Jason during our trip down the river system to tell him he missed him, and mentioned cruising with *Admiral Kay and her mate*. After Larry's death, we met with Jason, who felt his father had been ashamed of his own troubled past. We assured him Larry was anything *but* ashamed. We told Jason that Larry could not stop talking about how proud he was of his son.

I assembled a few hundred pictures of Larry with us on the voyage south and sent them along as a slideshow set to music on a DVD. The mortuary where they hosted his closed-casket visitation in Rhode Island agreed to offer this slideshow for Larry's visitation. Jason said the funeral director finally kicked them out because they kept watching and re-watching that slideshow. Jason called us after that. With tears in his voice, he thanked us for being a friend to his socially challenged father.

After hurricane season tailed off the following spring, we sailed *Sojourn* to the Keys with our friends Doug and Marti aboard *Tara* in honor of Larry's friendship. That's the last extended trip we'd take with our beloved little ship. We'd still sail for many more years, but either shorter sorties on *Sojourn,* or longer trips on boats we'd charter, often with Doug and Marti. We'd fly to various faraway destinations, pick up a boat, and sail for a few weeks at a time. For several years, we plied the waters from the British and US Virgin Islands all the way down to Grenada, less than 200 miles from South America's northeastern coast, island-hopping and exploring various ports in between.

Two more memorable chartering experiences outside the Eastern Caribbean remain anchored in my memories:

- Three weeks sailing the Greek Cyclades Islands in the Aegean Sea aboard a 65-foot ketch with three other couples, and,
- Two weeks in the San Juan Islands on a 55-foot motor

yacht with Doug and Marti in the current-infested Pacific Northwest.

More stories!

Chapter 56

Inspired in Chandler

Seven years and countless mini-adventures later, in 2015, we still owned our condo in Southwest Florida, an artifact of berthing *Sojourn* in Burnt Store Marina. The condo was our land base a hundred yards from J dock in the south basin where we kept her.

But having sold the boat, which was bittersweet, we bought a bus in which we'd travel most of the time for almost a decade. She was our *land yacht,* our new (to us) motorhome, a lovely 10-year-old Newmar Mountain Aire.

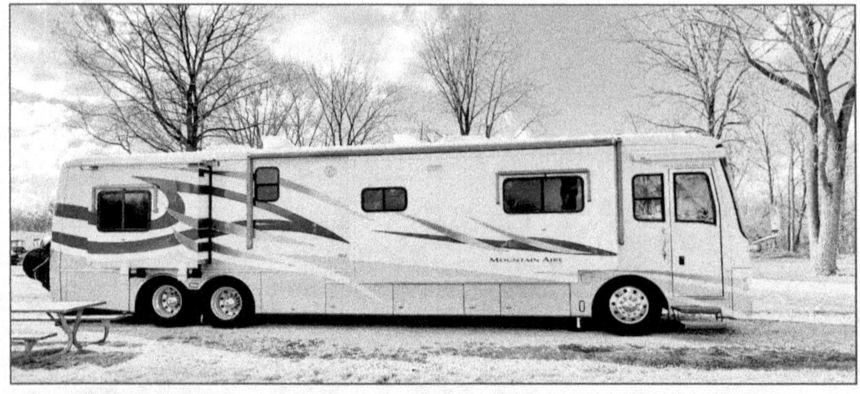

During the decade we owned "Ma" (acronym for "Mountain Aire" and a short name for our land-based "mother ship"), we had her re-skinned with a new fiberglass exterior, re-painted with 5 custom colors, including striking gradients. And we remodeled her inside and out. Here you see her "reincarnated" under our hand. She never looked so good as the day we sold her last summer (2025). Like Sojourn, she also looked new after our stewardship.

At 43 feet long with three axles, air shocks, air brakes, and four slide-outs, pushed along by a rear-situated 400 HP Cummins diesel engine with an efficient side-radiator, she promised to be powerful, comfortable, and stable on the road.

We felt certain that she would handle steep mountain grades, too. Even when towing our enclosed 10,000-pound, 29-foot cargo trailer that housed our car and two motorcycles, we were road-ready and roadworthy.

During the years we towed our cargo trailer, our composite length of 72' rivaled the length of most 18-wheel, big-rig trucks.

By this time, seven years after retiring and three years after Kay and I achieved sobriety together (that could be a book by itself, which I explore in my novel, ***Dangerous Dreams***), we launched into the next phase of our retirement.

Remember, I shared with you Kay and I learned Transcendental Meditation back in 1972? Well, isn't it then most ironic that I lost my focus on TM back in 1982 just when I needed it the most during my chaotic corporate career-climbing years? What was I *thinking*? Focus is often a fragile wisp of elusive vapor.

As the chaos mounted during that period, my alcoholism, an insidiously progressive disease—some politely call it an *allergy*—overtook common sense and had grabbed me in its clutches. I now foolishly think how much more I could have accomplished if only.... I surrendered the advantages in life that TM could have rendered.

It wasn't until 2012, four years after I retired and three years before this visit to Chandler, that Kay and I earned back the gift of sobriety. Together. And since beginning to meditate again, I'd regained crystal clarity of thought. I'd also rekindled a desire for the old rebel still deep inside to once again discover a new purpose—with my old passion. And focus.

We spent that winter of 2015-2016 in Mesa, Arizona, and attended our first RV *rally* in nearby Chandler. Rallies are monumental affairs where hundreds—or thousands—of RVs (recreational vehicles) gather in one place for most of a week. Onsite vendors offer everything from food and drink to every accessory imaginable for the RV lifestyle.

This rally was sponsored by FMCA, the Family Motor Coach Association. The sheer logistics impressed us. They provided substantial but necessary electrical power to 3,200 busses via dozens of electrical generators. Each of those units was the size of a small semi-tractor-trailer. Ongoing transportation via chauffeured golf carts to various events, and the events themselves, like concerts, were numerous and diverse.

Not to mention that a rally like this offered a stellar opportunity for *like-minders* to start or renew friendships. Some of those friendships grow and last a lifetime. That rally took over the entire Old West Town and its hundreds of acres in Chandler. *We were a small city*.

Most rallies also offer seminars on a wide range of specialized topics. One seminar I attended on a lark focused on creative writing, hosted by an accomplished writer, published author, and motivational speaker named Judy Howard. I'd always possessed more than a casual interest in writing. So I thought, *What the heck?* What I didn't expect? This would become yet another defining moment in my life.

~

I WALKED into the smallish room. About a dozen folks milled around. Another half-dozen clustered around this crazy-looking wild woman toward the front of the room. She wore a crumpled and tattered cowboy hat that had seen better days. And jeans that still had some life left in them. She waved her arms as she spoke. *Oh, boy.* The others hung on her every word. *This should be interesting if she's the speaker.*

The appointed time arrived. Everyone sat down, and quiet descended. *Cowgirl* looked to be at least as old as me. She'd been around, too. Before she said a word, her infectious laugh reverberated around the room at some joke she didn't bother sharing. Then, in a cream-and-spice voice, she announced, "Hi. I'm Judy Howard, and I tell lies for a living."

Say what now? I liked her already. She bubbled with excitement as she described embarking on an inspired journey. "Grab your keys to fire up your inspiration engine! Check your writing roadmap and rev up your creativity. But watch out for potential potholes and emotional detours!"

Yeah, an unabashed extended metaphor. I guessed she enjoyed racing cars. I later discovered that she did. I'd also learn later she traveled the country in a small motorhome by herself with a life-size biker dummy and a cat named Sportster for protection—and for company. But that's yet another story.

Okay, I thought, *this fascinating woman is offering me a new purpose.* I decided right there I was going to be an author, too, dammit!

~

THAT WAS TEN YEARS AGO. Since then, with Judy's casual, continued mentorship and a pant-load of sweat equity fed by endless research, I've published 14 novels—that's make-believe—telling my own lies. Plus, I've published a handful of other titles.

Besides teaching me how to better tell convincing lies, Judy also inspired me to teach my own writing and publishing seminars, which I've since taught all over the country, many at other RV rallies.

I am under no delusion. That seminar in Chandler's Old West Town in 2015 was yet another pivotal moment in an already eventful life. Thanks, Judy, my old friend.

JANUARY 2026 UPDATE: Fast-forward a decade, and look what happened because of that moment of inspiration back in Chandler in 2015:

I've independently published 19 books so far, with two or three more always in progress, not including this memoir.

Chapter 57

Dark Days

I IMAGINE LATE 2019 THROUGH MOST OF 2021 REPRESENTED A dark time in everyone's lives, not just Kay's and mine. It was a time of tumultuous controversy and fear, with a multitude of questions concerning medical expertise and legality. Unprecedented in my lifetime.

My irrational childhood fears returned to haunt me, as if they possessed a life of their own. Was this *the end?* Was some invisible bearded deity punishing us for past transgressions?

I remember thinking, *If this is not the Apocalypse, what will remain after this sustained period of collective terror leeches the humanity out of our souls? Will I always view the next person as a carrier of "the deadly virus"? Or will I once again be able to welcome my fellow human beings in a close embrace? Ever?* I had never felt so hollow, especially since I came from a family of huggers and a polio pandemic survivor!

Perhaps it was serendipity that we had not yet sold the condo, even though we weren't there but a few months out of every 24. But during that time, campgrounds, and RV resorts had either closed or enforced so many restrictions that we chose not to subject ourselves to that craziness and loneliness away from our comfortable and familiar home, *not* on wheels. Kay and I placed our bus in storage and hunkered down in our very own COVID *bunker*.

As a self-diagnosed germaphobe, even before the pandemic, *this*

insanity sent me right off the charts. Of course, we got *the jab*. I'd remember my mother extolling the virtues of credible science mitigating nature's risks to humanity. My siblings and I had suffered through *none* of the myriad diseases she and many of her contemporaries did during her lifetime. Gotta be more than luck. Mom was a nurse. Of course, we got vaccinated!

Further, she'd suffered social isolation as a polio-stricken child before they knew how the disease was spread. So, most people assumed the worst—that it was airborne. Family stories tell of parents instructing their kids to hold their breath as they *ran* past a house known to have been infected. My mother grew up as a lonely child. I now better understand that.

There was good news, too. America learned how to wash its hands properly. And how to keep their fingers away from their faces. And it was okay to wave, or elbow-bump, or knuckle-bump instead of shaking potentially infected hands. We'd become... civilized.

On a more personal note, Kay and I focused on our natural health and fitness like never before—our COVID armor, we joked. Blessed to have our own gym equipment in the condo's large lanai. We'd meditate together each morning. After that, Kay hopped on our elliptical exercise machine for thirty minutes. I focused on my yoga routine and ran through my free-weight regimen. Then we'd trade places. We'd eat nothing but nutrient-dense, pesticide-free, GMO-free, plant-based whole foods as much as possible. We also stayed well-hydrated and went for frequent walks or bike rides around our beautiful two-mile marina shoreline.

I was no stranger to face masks. In my business travels years earlier to countries like Taiwan, Singapore, and China, as well as some larger cities in Europe, masks were everywhere. I guessed we were finally catching up with the rest of the world.

We emerged from our cocoon in early 2021. We drove the motorhome from Southwest Florida almost 600 miles to the Alabama border, towing our little Toyota Yaris to pick up our new Jeep. Kay called to make a campground reservation. The owner insisted we leave the money in her mailbox upon our arrival. She'd fetch it later. The most natural thing in the world.

Every Walmart now offers wet wipes for sanitizing grocery carts. Social distancing in public lines no longer requires a separation stripe painted on the floor. We just do it. Even after the politicized nonsense about how harmful and/or ineffective masks were, nobody now cares if we don a mask. New normals.

The world did not end; the Biden administration effectively worked with other nations to bring us back from the brink of a catastrophic global supply chain meltdown, and hope re-emerged on a less-bleak horizon. This episode proved our collective fragility and that of our lifestyle.

It also proved how dependent we are on each other. Silly lines called borders drawn on maps, and medieval attitudes about what those lines mean? We *still* behave like petulant children blustering about the schoolyard, bullying anyone different from us, for fear of them capturing more than their fair share of the marbles. It breaks my heart that we as a species still wallow in this vain emptiness, ostensibly even within our own relatively enlightened society. Or so we believe.

However, I cannot disguise my *profound* disappointment—nay, *disgust*—observing our own country's devolving direction since the beginning of 2024. It seems we've entered yet another age of darkness. Yet I will always seek the light.

I have concluded that the human species will *forever* produce bullies, tyrants, and territorial man-babies to hijack our... *humanity*. Throughout my long life, I've leaned on the following mantra many times: Within any population, there will be 10% assholes. Any less than that is a bonus, and I will seek the remaining 90% as *my people*.

Chapter 58

Leopold's Jolt

You *THINK* YOU KNOW SOMEONE QUITE WELL WHEN YOU LIVE and travel with them for five or six years in a three-hundred-square-foot home on wheels—a bus. And then you hunker down with them during a dark time in a sunny condo. But how well do any of us see what's in anyone else's heart? Kay and I never dreamed how unpretentious and uncontentious our marriage would become. To a fault. Most of the time, that is.

I blame my weakness on the pandemic's dark days, but not in the way you might think. I will openly confess the needle in my moral compass may be flawed, but Miss Kay would need to confess her own frailty. That is not my story to tell. I *will* say *this*.

During our fifty-two years of marriage—by 2021—Kay and I have experienced the best and the worst of times together, like any healthy relationship. Now we have two middle-aged children and three adult grandchildren. But that does not mean we are immune to temptation. Here's what happened. Don't judge us too harshly.

~

Rewind to October 2019, when we came off the road. You already know from this journal's previous chapter we felt it prudent to stay put through much of 2020. But I'd like to say a few more words about our time in *the bunker* to set up this next episode.

Spending time *at home*—although the bus seemed more like home than the condo by then—gave us the opportunity to re-evaluate our default lifestyle. Years of moderate-to-severe hedonism had left us obese and sedentary. Both being burgeoning septuagenarians, we decided we must make some serious lifestyle changes, so we did. Better late than dead.

So, toward the end of 2019, Kay and I examined our hearts and put our heads together. After all, we're both pretty smart people. And passionate. Turns out we're even decisive now and then (Kay more than me). This was one of those times. How could we best combat the creeping virus destined to blanket the globe? We committed to doing whatever it took to squeeze every drop of juice out of every day remaining to us. After all, who knew when we might hit a tree or a bridge pillar at 55+ MPH?

Yes, we faced our mortality and spat in its eye. Respectfully. We decided we would not go gently into that good night, and we plotted a bold new course together. By the way, at this point in our lives, we did most everything together. We even finished each other's sentences. First order of business? Boost our immune systems. But how? Exactly?

The dramatic changes we made in our daily lives might surprise you. We were *all in*, as they say. Even shed the many social norms that built much of our lifelong belief system about our health. We shocked our family, friends, and neighbors. It started with the decision to whip our bodies back into shape. What better way to recapture our *joie de vivre*—our zest for living—across every dimension of our remaining days? At least, that's why we *thought* we were entertaining such madness.

. . .

Our first step was to treat food as medicine—we ate to live, we no longer lived to eat. So we turned our backs on what our parents and polite American society taught us growing up. Such as the *need* to regularly consume meat and potatoes, eggs, cheese, seafood, sweets, and to drink lots of cow's milk. Like you, they taught us that these foodstuffs were good for us, even essential. Remember the old food pyramid from elementary school, even high school? Oh, but that wasn't enough, was it? Like I said, we were all in.

After some research, we also turned our backs on processed foods and anything that was not grown organically, even before that became all the rage. We even shed our dependence on artificial stimulants—caffeine and refined sugar—two of the chronic villains that happily disguise toxic fatigue, screw up blood glucose levels, and feed inflammation, which is at the root of so many other maladies, including cancer.

After retirement and achieving sobriety, I ate and snacked my way to 240 pounds. Kay can tell her own story. I not only felt sluggish, I easily contracted colds and the flu.

With the decision to stop treating our stomachs like junkyards or graveyards came the decision to eat nothing that once had parents. In eight short months, Kay lost 80 pounds. I lost 65. Our physical appearances transformed over the course of our 2020 quarantine. And by April 2021, two butterflies emerged from their COVID cocoons of the darkest fear, uncertainty, and doubt we'd ever experienced.

A year later, we both not only looked a lot better.
We felt great!

Once again, we hit the road with new energy, new bodies, and new attitudes, perched on the precipice of pious arrogance and transported by a new confidence. But after only a few months on the road, our confidence got us into serious trouble.

Whether Kay cheated first, or I did, is of little consequence. We were living in places like summertime Virginia Beach and the Outer Banks of North Carolina, where tanned and near-naked bodies populated the beaches and RV resorts on sunny days.

They gathered at beachside establishments or put themselves on display, hiking or skating on the nearby boardwalks, or in village coffee shops, ice cream kiosks, and surf shops. It seemed the dark days had ended.

But then innocent young-people-watching turned into something more than a spectator sport. This is where we first slid from feelings of envy and futility toward the sordid somewhere in the tourist-infested Hatteras National Seashore.

. . .

I FOUND out Kay had snuck a chocolate-coated ice cream bar—a *dairy* product bathed in a *caffeine-* and *sugar*-laden confectionary. Conversely, she discovered I was encouraging the attentions of a local barista and her over-priced *caffeinated* concoctions. We once again began to embrace the horror.

Soon thereafter, whenever I indulged in a hot Venti Bloodshot Red-Eye—a twenty-six ounce Starbucks dark roast with two additional shots of espresso—she *expected* me to buy her an ice cream. Tit for tat. Quid pro quo. We indulged in these resurrected transgressions and addictions *together*, the very definition of co-dependence. We openly endorsed and enabled each other's frailties. *What were we thinking?*

A CRISIS of confidence ultimately spanked us soundly in the quaint village of Beaufort, North Carolina. By mutual consent, we found ourselves at Leopold's. This establishment has long been known from Oglethorpe Avenue to Bay Street for the best ice cream on the planet. Waiting in a long line out on the sidewalk and halfway down the block was a compulsory part of the ritual.

As Kay stood there, waiting, I scurried down Broughton Street to score my gi-normous hit of concentrated caffeine, *my* drug of choice once more. I returned to find Kay caressing Leopold's infamous and most iniquitous *Socialite Chocolate Sundae.* Sounds innocent enough, right?

They built this monstrosity atop a moist (nay, *wet*) chocolate chunk brownie half the size of a loaf of bread. Despite its generous dimensions, they'd buried it beneath a bottomless serving of chocolate double-chunk ice cream. *Chunks?* That was laughable. Those chunks were darkest chocolate and milk chocolate *as big as your thumb to its first joint!* They drowned the entire affair in peppery gourmet chocolate syrup and a heavy hand-whipped cream dented by substantial Swiss chocolate *shavings*. You know, the kind of sensuous chocolate so dark and rich and sweet that your cheeks cramp and your teeth hurt as it melts in your mouth, causing beads of sweat to involuntarily pop out on your forehead, just to embarrass you? They'd dusted the entire affair with several ounces of Vienna cocoa.

This was yet another defining moment in our relationship and in our marriage. We were confronting a culinary crisis. After this dietary debauchery, we called for a self-induced intervention.

This felt too familiar. Nine years earlier, Kay and I had hit a similar bottom—also together—born of similar mental cravings and physical obsessions. We have remained sober—alcohol free—since then. Leopold's helped us catalyze the gravest of galloping gastronomic insanity by bequeathing us profound nausea and gut-jabbing jitters respectively, as if we had jones'd for heroin and overdosed. Either by accident or by intent matters not. We suffered from a diminished tolerance after over a year of abstinence from such iniquities. We were once again granted the gift of desperation.

Unlike so many others who sated themselves *during* their COVID quarantine, it was our escape *from* our self-induced year-long COVID quarantine that yanked the ripcord on our co-dependent free-fall. It was *only after* we came out of our bunker that we realized we needed to renew our vows to one another—and not just our wedding vows.

Thank you, Leopold's, for a sorely needed kick in our collective posterior! I think I shall forever remember that afternoon as *Leopold's Jolt,* yet another notable tick of the clock.

Chapter 59

From the Heart

I RECALL ANOTHER POIGNANT MOMENT, A CONFUSING ONE, IN February 2023, maybe even an *event*. I'm still not really sure. We'd been parked at the Voyager RV Resort outside of Tucson, Arizona, with our motorhome since New Year's Day.

I can be *such* a baby, strong and resolute one moment, but a flaccid weakling wallowing in a sea of sorrow a second later. It's all of my own making, of course. Seems incomprehensible, but in the moment? Vast and without depth.

YESTERDAY MORNING, for example, Kay and I ate a hearty breakfast —a protein smoothie with organic protein powder, fresh spinach, apple, banana, frozen papaya, strawberries, peaches, and mango. I threw in a raw carrot for good measure and sprinkled the finished product with raw, unsalted sunflower seeds.

I usually accompany that with some additional protein—an ounce of mixed nuts, also raw and unsalted: almonds, walnuts, a few cashews, some pistachios, a couple of Brazil nuts, and pumpkin seeds.

I top off this medley with 5 desert palm pitted dates sprinkled with wheat germ.

Loaded up and cocky about maintaining my fighting weight since 2021—though I never fight—I dressed to work out at the gym in the resort with Miss Kay. The sun was shining. The temp hovered in the mid-eighties, and life was good.

We pedaled the half-mile to the gym; we both worked out hard. Kay hit an elliptical and free weights. I walked a couple of miles on a treadmill at an aggressive 4 MPH on a 6-degree up-slope. Did a hundred stomach crunches on an exercise ball. I worked up a decent sweat and drank some water. We both treated our bodies right and drove home on our bicycles—back to the bus.

As we pulled into our site, I developed a hollowness in my stomach. Too soon to be hungry. Took the five steps up into the motorhome. Airy. We'd left the windows open with two rooftop vent fans drawing fresh desert air into the interior. Delightful. Already eleven-thirty, Kay said she was hungry. I was not. A little lightheadedness concerned me. Just a little.

"Go ahead, hon. I'm going to stretch out for a bit." Not dizzy or anything; maybe I was just tired. And sore from my aggressive workout. Yeah, that must be it. But I thought about my recent brief bout of atrial fibrillation—an irregular heart rhythm—a few months ago....

Kay's voice sounded like worry as she stuck her head in our bedroom as I lay there stretched out. "You okay?"

"I think so." Took the pulse in my neck. Seemed regular enough. Wait, was that an extra beat thrown in for no good reason? *Shit.* And another. Got up off the bed and grabbed my portable ECG device. Works with my iPhone. I placed both of my index fingers on top and rested the bottom against the top of my naked left knee.

I bought this device after my last A-fib episode. Supposed to be as accurate as a six-lead electrocardiogram to measure my heart's electrical activity. Result? "Unclassified." *Oh, great. Not helpful.* At least it told me this did not present as A-fib, but... something else. Also not what I expected—normal sinus rhythm. *Good, right?* But doubt chewed away at the periphery of my consciousness.

Ten minutes later, I checked the pulse on the left side of my neck with my right middle finger—regular. No extra beats. Took another ECG measurement with the *KardiaMobile* device. Normal sinus rhythm. *What the heck?* Okay. At least I've been on a daily low-dose aspirin since my A-fib experience the previous March, so my risk of stroke remained low. Theoretically. I worried.

Now, if I were a stronger and more confident person, I'd probably think something like, *Nothing to worry about. Might as well get on with my day.* Instead, I frittered away the rest of the afternoon, waiting for the other shoe to drop, as they say. I worried some more. I let fear command my actions, or more accurately, my inactivity. Was it an excuse to be lazy? Nope, not my style.

I took a thirty-minute nap. Better. Still, I worried. Then, it bothered me I wasn't a stronger person. I'm in the best shape of my life; all my bloodwork is damn-near perfect; I'm eating healthy, not drinking or smoking, and I'm exercising regularly. The doctors might suggest it's a genetic anomaly. Thanks, Dad. After all, I'm a fit seventy-three, and I have so much more I want to accomplish. After this bullshit day, guilt washed over me. What a baby!

You see how this goes? I gotta consider I'm not the only old fart to go through this. Instead of being grateful for suffering nothing more than a sense of uneasiness and a few queasy moments with a little lightheadedness for all of a half-hour, I wallowed. In self-pity, doubt, fear, and guilt for most of a valuable and otherwise perfect day. I've already lived longer than my father. I'm almost three decades downrange from the age of his first major cardiac event. And all I've had to put up with is a little short-duration A-fib now and then.

Doctors say A-fib is diagnosed in one out of nine men over sixty-five. And some of those live with *ongoing* A-fib and its crappy symptoms. My few episodes each lasted just a few hours and then back to normal sinus rhythm and feelin' sassy. Easy. *So what the heck, Geno? Get on with it! Life is good. Just live it. And deal with the bumps in the road. They're trivial!*

The previous Christmas—of 2022—I had experienced my first *cardiac event* when I was the same age as when my dad died of his third major heart attack. That was on my mind. Scared the hell out of me. Kay had called an ambulance to haul me away to the hospital. But they sent me home after several hours of tests and consultations with two cardiologists, a bottle of baby aspirin, and a hearty, "Welcome to the A-fib club, Mr. Jurrens."

I've always known that my dad suffered from heart disease, and I had convinced myself that he had caused his own problems with poor diet and little exercise. As a farm boy, he'd been raised on red meat, dairy, and lots of saturated fat in his diet. I've mentioned this before in the early chapters of this journal.

So both he and my mom had always been heavy people. That wasn't me, except for several late pre-retirement and a few post-retirement years. I've already confessed that to you as well. Other than that, I've been a gym rat most of my life, as I was determined not to follow in their faltering footsteps. I was even a racquetball fanatic for a few years. They could not know what we've learned in subsequent decades. How could they? Nobody worried about such stuff a century ago when they were born.

So what the heck is *my* problem?

~

May 2023 update: I learned from a brain scan at the Mayo Clinic in Rochester three months after this little episode that there is evidence I had suffered a very minor stroke in the recent past. They said it should have been asymptomatic. I'm now wondering if that stupid pity party for which I alone showed up in Tucson the previous February was indeed that event. My only symptom since then seems a slight hit to my sense of balance. I'd previously ascribed that to peripheral neuropathy from back and foot surgery. I suppose it's possible....

January 2026 update: I'm happy to report I've not had an episode of A-fib (irregular heartbeat) for over a year. I attribute that to continued diligence to stay well-hydrated and a vegetarian focus on eating nutrient-dense foods. Huh. Knock wood!

Chapter 60

Salton Sea

Since retiring, Kay and I have been blessed with quality time exploring America at ground level for quite a few years now. We've lived in the tropics, low desert, high desert, mountains, plains, on the coasts of two oceans, on barrier islands, sounds, estuaries, rivers, national parks, Great Lakes, and the northern and eastern Gulf Coasts. We even sailed for a few weeks on the Aegean Sea in the eastern Mediterranean.

Each venue presented us with magnificent scenery, exposure to unique cultures. And we're *so* grateful to have met many fascinating people who shared with us their unique dialects, attitudes, food, customs, and humor. I have not included such wonderful experiences in these pages as I found each of them wonderful but... predictable. Besides, I've blogged extensively about each delightful place we visited by boat at ***OurSojourn.wordpress.com***, by motorhome at ***BigRigRoads.wordpress.com*** and later, at ***GKJurrens.com***

~

In the autumn of 2024, however, nothing made such a profound impact on me as the Salton Sea, clearly the *weirdest* place I've visited in almost ten years of RV travel in Canada and 42 of the United States. I include a focus on this most bizarre venue in these pages because it left such an indelible impression on me—a surreal *consistency of contradictions.* Not unlike my own *trouble with thinking.*

An iconic work of art on the beach at Bombay, California.

The Salton Sea is the site of one of America's worst environmental catastrophes. But there's good news, too.

An underground group of *conspirators*—their own characterization—gathers to explore their creative and intellectual freedoms. How *very* American! This biennial event lasts months and features a renegade celebration of art, music, and philosophy that takes place on the literal edge of western civilization to amplify the largely unknown and ignored ecological crisis that is the Salton Sea.

This event is unpublicized before, during, or after, and remains cloaked by enigmatic circumstances I can't fully comprehend. They call it the *Bombay Beach Biennale,* or *BBB.* Sounds like the premise for an Odd Thomas novel by Dean Koontz, doesn't it? One of my favorite authors, by the way.

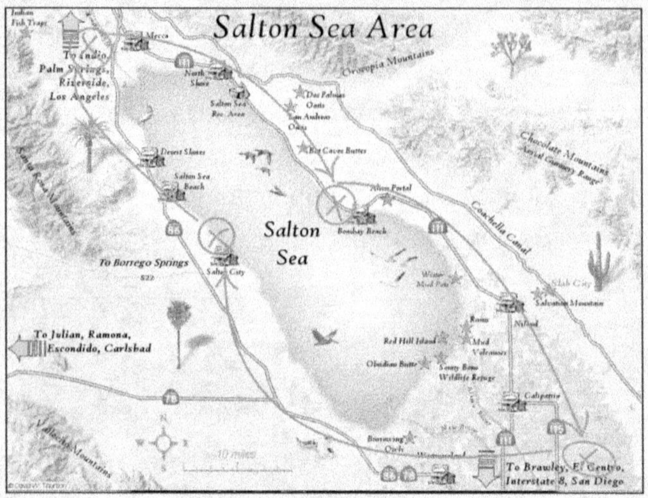

I spent just one existential day circumnavigating the Salton Sea in Central Southern California. Covered a lot of ground in a single morning and half an afternoon, but I only scratched the surface of this drab-chic area. My sortie comprised about two hundred miles with a lot of stops, mostly photo ops and short discussions. Popped the Jeep into 4-wheel-low for some beach mileage.

That Wednesday served as a suitable capstone moment to what was to be our last major exploratory RV trip up and down the West Coast. We enjoyed eight years of *most-time* RVing and *full-timing* for the last few years after selling our Florida condo, our only remaining real estate.

We'd seen so much splendor across our great nation. But it was time for me to experience something... different, eclectic. And did I ever get my wish! Keep reading about my experience in a unique and bizarre place that wears its hardships on its philosophical shirt sleeves. Sorry about the cliché, but it glows with brilliant relevance. You'll see.

So, why did we park our RV in a town a hundred miles east of San Diego that week? I'd read that almost nobody goes there anymore. It hinted at what a dystopian post-apocalyptic landscape might look like <u>if we continue to fail as our beloved planet's stewards</u>. It also signaled one possible destination for our future as a species—a grim one. I had to see it for myself. Primary research. Maybe that's the author in me.

Yup, that's our bus on the right, nestled between two hedges and tall palms.

Rio Bend RV Resort, west of El Centro, California, offered us a pleasant experience for three days while I ventured off to explore the Salton Sea area on my own. Kay harbored no interest in this visceral experience. But she made it happen for me.

This park was as close as we could get to where they didn't explicitly warn us about arsenic in the RV park's water supply. I kid you not. They still advised us to bring our own water, which we did.

I would soon discover how dramatically different the Salton Sea shoreline was from this delightful little desert oasis, questionable drinking water notwithstanding.

~

With 115 miles of shoreline, the Salton Sea was once a popular waterfront playground in the 1950s for throngs of tourists, movie stars, and politicians. Its genesis was an accident of nature. Its fate would be defined by gross mismanagement of natural resources. For many *decades*. Here's what happened.

A levee on the Colorado River broke in 1905 under the onslaught of floodwaters. That filled this below-sea-level basin, the *Salton Sink*, which lies on the San Andreas Fault within the *Salton Trough* between four different mountain ranges.

It took several years to repair that collapsed levee—to redirect the precious water to other more affluent areas in Southern California and Arizona. Of course, water is liquid gold in these parts. And this is an impoverished area. The water followed the money, of course, away from those unable to pay dearly for it.

But by then, this large lake—they call it a *sea*—was the real deal at fifteen miles wide and thirty-five miles long. This is larger in surface area than the Dead Sea between Jordan and Israel, by the way. It then continually shrank over subsequent decades. With no inlets or outlets, this landlocked sea stagnated. Desert conditions caused it to recede through evaporation. This has created a toxic chain reaction of catastrophic events in the entire area. And it's been getting worse every year.

The salt primarily comes from agricultural runoff, which carries salts and minerals from irrigation practices, plus from the natural evaporation of water that leaves salts behind. Ancient salt deposits in the lake bed add to the increasing salinity over time as the water continues to evaporate.

Kay had originally booked an RV site for us in a nearby town called Thermal, just north of this salty and dead sea. They definitely advised against drinking their arsenic-plagued water. Period. *Arsenic? The frickin' poison?*

I allocated just one day to venture around this significant geographical area, so I only experienced a fraction of what the area offers. That exposure, however brief, left an indelible impression that exists to this day, over a year later. I promise I'll tell you why.

Chapter 61

The Shore

So, I drove our Jeep from El Centro, north along the sea's western shore, and stopped at Salton City, population ~5,000. I found it to be a rather unremarkable small town to which the sea had distanced itself.

This ancient sign, at least seventy-five years old, pointed the way to the Salton City Beach. Or so I thought.

I'm guessing this mobile home near Salton City Beach (but no longer anywhere near any water), augmented with a deluxe covered patio, could be purchased with any reasonable offer. May need some T.L.C.

I meandered eastward down crappy roads windswept with powdery sand, but couldn't even get within a half-mile of any water. So, I snapped a few pictures, backtracked to the two-lane highway, and headed farther north. Like most tourists, I'd imagined.

I continued on up through the city of Coachella and had lunch in Indio with the sea now a ways in my rearview mirror. I found Indio to be a lovely city southeast of the affluent Palm Springs area, but still only twenty miles from the north shore of the sea. During lunch, I asked my server about it. She said, "No idea. Nobody ever goes down there. It's nothing." She was wrong, as I'd find out when I drove down its eastern shore. Just... wow!

On the eastern shore, Bombay Beach, California, is the second-lowest community in the United States. First, the statistics. It's 220-ish feet below sea level. The only place lower is Death Valley at minus 280-ish feet. Like the area in general, the population of Bombay is also in decline—at 231 in 2020, down from 295 in 2010, and down from 366 in 2000.

This place—not quite a ghost town—was downright eerie, although the temps hovered in the pleasant mid-seventies. The locals don't use the word *Beach* as part of the town's name anymore. Either it's too anti-climactic or serves only as high-camp humor for cynics, as reflected in some of their beach art. More on this later.

They named the only bar, the most active place in town when Bombay was a famous water ski destination back in the 1950s—***The Ski Inn***. Now, though, they just call it ***The Skinn***.

A handful of locals hunched over the bar inside. None had any interest whatsoever in talking with outsiders like yours truly. I thought it was rude. They likely just thought it was Wednesday. Message received, but not understood.

Numerous artists—painters, sculptors, multimedia creatives, poets, philosophers, lecturers, and other invited participants—gather and stay in town for several months each year while they collaborate on art and events, culminating in their invitation-only celebratory weekend. Wait, isn't the BBB supposed to be every *other* year? Their version of a joke, I guess.

This event includes a world-class philosophy conference with major scholars from universities such as Oxford, Harvard, and others. Activists, artists, writers, and independent researchers also present topics related to the festival's theme. Who knew? Is that not so... Californian?

The art seen everywhere around town on any and every surface, especially down on the beach, seemed to me rather... *on the nose...* philosophically, at least, to the uninitiated, unwashed masses (all 8 of us that day). Bear with me for a moment. I gotta get this out.

MUCH OF THE art I explored by driving my Jeep around Bombay's beach, some of it rather large scale, seemed to represent one of two different schools of philosophical thought in media that seemed a fusion of graffiti, sculpture, and diorama, or of philosophy and satire.

First, some artists offered *existential* expressions as they visually portrayed the theory that emphasizes the existence of the individual as a unique agent with free will and total responsibility for his or her own acts. Although such an individual lives in a universe devoid of any certain knowledge of right and wrong. Grim, right? As they say in the infomercials, ***but wait!***

Nihilists define relentless negativity or cynicism, suggesting an absence of values or beliefs. Yeah, this place is really *out there.* Fascinating, and unique in all the world, say I. The undeniable allure of the obscure.

These heady concepts seemed uniquely appropriate in this place, this incredibly hostile environment. I couldn't avoid the sensation of skulking around in the brilliant but fractious mind of Albert Camus, author, and philosopher, who explored existentialism, or absurdism. Talk about *trouble with thinking*!

Sorry, I'm kind of a philosophy geek, even the negative stuff, as it helps me to better understand the darker side of humanity so I can better appreciate and seek the lighter side.

Is this graffiti, art, or a satirical political statement visited upon this once-luxury vehicle? Eye of the beholder, baby!

Neither do these artists help us answer such questions. They seem to portray quite the opposite of self-serving narcissism – they not only don't seek credit, they seem to revel in keeping us plebeian tourists guessing. Consistent. Refreshing. I love it! Even the neighborhood behind the car above seemed part of the artist's *canvas*.

I EARLIER MENTIONED TRYING to chat with a few locals at the only bar in town. But I guess they're *really* tired of explaining what perversion attracts them to this bizarre community. After all, it perches on the edge of a huge body of toxic water that emits poisonous vapors and swirling clouds of unhealthy dust. A nihilist's genuine paradise, I guess, even though that's gotta be a most absurd oxymoron. Bottom line? I've never felt more okay as an outsider.

I'm told the somewhat unpleasant smell on the shore results from high levels of hydrogen sulfide overpowering the lake's low oxygen levels, but I'm no chemist. To make matters worse, the surrounding area—Imperial County to the south—faces clouds of dust regularly billowing their way from the dried-up portions of the lakebed. Not so bad until you realize that fine dust contains toxins such as arsenic and selenium. They say the effects have been disastrous for locals. I get it. After just one day there, I couldn't stop coughing.

Update December 30, 2025: *I've been plagued by a chronic cough ever since spending the day on the beach at Bombay over a year ago now. My imagination? Something else? The docs at Mayo say my lungs are clear and have failed to explain this cough. Tests continue. Maybe I am cursed for frivolously flirting with such a hellish place (wink)!*

One of my author friends, Judy Rinehimer, suggested the case of Valley Fever I contracted in 2017 in the Arizona desert might be the culprit, and did the toxic air on that beach cause a flare-up? I' got my blood tested again. Thanks, Judy. Nope. Still a mystery, but I like a good mystery.

In hiking along the seashore, I found two contrasting textures underfoot. One was rough. I'm told they're countless desiccated or petrified fish carcasses. The other, sand so fine and smooth, puffed up like powder around my shoes as I walked. Thankfully, the wind went elsewhere that Wednesday. I'm still not sure if I breathed something that irritated my lungs. Arsenic? Selenium? Another dubious self-diagnosis.

God, I sound like a wimp. Hey, I'm just reporting my experience. I've always been fascinated, and sometimes feared, what I cannot see, but that which my fertile mind *can* imagine. An author's plague.—one of many.

I GUESS you *really* gotta wanna live here, but I would never claim to understand why. Could be I'm just a Luddite. Oh, by the way, down by the shore? Dense hordes of tiny flying bugs assaulted me. Their only apparent purpose? Keep the pesky tourist population down to a manageable minimum? Dunno. They died as soon as they found their prey, landing either on the hood of the Jeep, in my hair, on my camera lens, or in my beard. Thankfully, they were not the biting kind. Had to get the car washed the next day to scrub off their futile (nihilistic?) but persistent (existential?) little carcasses.

Yup, the vibe here is one of neglect, but also of intense intellectual curiosity, and understandably fatalistic.

I imagine those who invested big in premium Salton real estate in the 50s and 60s not only lost their shirts financially but likely also their hope for humanity. Especially those who have known little else, perhaps.

Event prep?

Looked like a few boys were setting up for some sort of event. They were up on a roof next to where I took the photo above, so I didn't try to talk with them (most unlike me!). Oh, and they didn't want to be photographed. *That* they made clear with their body language. Hmmm....

Chapter 62

The "Beach"

Now for some really fun stuff. And it was *AWESOME.* I planned to drive the Jeep up over the berm or dike that rises between the town and the sea. I doubt its purpose is to keep water at bay since the sea has been receding for decades. It's more likely a measure to protect the town from the toxic dust clouds, maybe the odor, and bugs, too. Not really sure. Nobody talked.

I saw a sign for an *art tour,* but I preferred to strike out on my own. There was nobody around anyway. Artists depicted their work in various media everywhere. So I just drove around, stopping frequently to take pictures. I poked around town, as well as down on the beach. Other than a handful at *The Skinn* bar, I only saw one obvious local out and about. And she wanted nothing to do with me. Okay, then.

I'd considered posing as a reporter or photojournalist from the L.A. Times to get folks to open up, but thought better of it as an ethical consideration. Besides, I lacked credentials and a fancy enough camera. No shortage of attitude, though.

There were steps over the berm. Ramps up and over elsewhere enabled me to drive my Jeep to the mile-long beach.

Though there were no locals out and about on the beach, I saw a handful of tourists like me—only 8 by my count in three other vehicles... all day. That was it. I thought, *What do the locals know that we ignorant tourists don't?* Perhaps what I learned on the internet *after* visiting this charming little burg's erstwhile beachfront? Who knew this adventure would entail a health risk? But that added an element of authenticity and adventure to this disaster site!

No, this isn't a working lemonade stand. It is an artistic display on a dune overlooking the beach. It is a signpost for positive thinking during the darkest of times, and getting darker in these parts, despite an insistent sun. The sign says, "Life gave us lemons, so we made lemonade." Unexpected!

Huh? The smaller sign to the right warns, "The last car parked here is still missing."

Bombay is NOT a small beach! Makes my Jeep Grand Cherokee look small, doesn't it? Like Utah's salt flats.

Down here on the beach? That's where a collection of unique art pieces perches on the precarious shore of this noxious, long-dead sea.

This piece is called "Open House."

I found this small label on a larger display – an old newspaper dispensing machine, the kind we used to see on every city street corner (see below). It says, "Capitalism: The Problem Not the Solution." Clearly an indictment of our country's late-stage capitalism.

On the outside of an ancient newspaper vending box, I spotted the small sticker . It featured a much larger signboard emblazoned with just two words: "FREE" on the front, and "FACTs" on the side. Thinking it was an antiquated version of FAQs, I pulled the handle to open the box. Inside? Empty. Too *on the nose*? Dunno. I'm just a dumb tourist.

It looked to me like this *artwork* was at least forty years old. Ahead of its time? Not for me to say. Like I said, just a tourist over here.

Above is the FREE FACTs dispenser, numbly sinking into the sand at the base of an elevated aircraft sculpture constructed of 1960s car parts. Probably some meaning to that, too. If so, it escaped me. I guess if you know, you know.

Okaaaaay, so what the hell is IID? Infinite Improbability Drive (for you Hitchhiker's Guide to the Galaxy fans)? Maybe. Not.

My favorite guess as to the meaning of the sign above after researching IID? This artist blames (ever so bluntly) the area's maladies on the *Imperial Irrigation District.* Acidic homage to the politicians who so mismanaged this environmental disaster? Over time, they've re-routed the area's fresh water to those with the cash-ola to pay for it. That fits with the spirit of the BBB held bi-annually (and yes, sometimes annually) here in Imperial County. And I suspect the word *Imperial* was intended to have two meanings. I think I broke the code!

The sign above declares, "Drought Resistant Landscape." Yeah, all long-dead.

I think this hints at the insanity of unrealistic (or perhaps any) expectations.

The human species invariably seeks a greater level of happiness, of satisfaction, when not stuck in what neuroscientists call *rumination,* a thought loop that dwells on negativity. You guessed it–there's no water in that faucet above. Fake news? Alternative facts? Stuck in a misery loop? No happy ending? Double entendre where two meanings are portrayed—one risqué, one ironic? Like I said, this whole place feels so dystopian; so dire; so grim.

Uniquely Salton Sea! As the water, shore, and air above it continuously devolve into a toxic waste dump for pesticide and fertilizer runoff from the surrounding fields of Imperial County (thousands of overdeveloped acres), the ocean will nevertheless prevail. A satirical symbol of foolish hope? But the sea returns the favor by inundating the same land that's poisoning it with toxic dust. Destructively symbiotic!

Perhaps the ocean, a hundred miles away, is the only thing man's screw-ups cannot completely annihilate? Or is this pit of despair too distant from local corrupt politicians? Definitely a political statement, but did I get it right? No idea. I'm not invited to the BBB, you see, nor am I willing to subject myself to or seek out their entrance requirements.

The Bombay Beach Marina. Note the two hand-drawn red circles in this image are at least two tiny gnat-like airborne bugs that found my tiny iPhone lens before immediately expiring. They swirled all around me everywhere on the beach, but not in town (on the far side of the berm).

I strolled through the *marina*, including where water should be. Paddle boats and canoeing were once popular activities here in the 1950s and 1960s. Fabulous shore-side resorts have long-since flourished and then laid to ruin.

This marina is obviously staged like one huge artistic composition and has been there for many years. I'm guessing this is another nihilistic statement, lamenting joyful activities gone awry as the environment failed us arrogant humans, or something like that. For the record, that is ***not my philosophy***.

I felt so weird walking through and around it. Even though boats were faithfully tied to docks, the actual water was at least fifty yards away, and receding more every year as this small sea continues to evaporate. But there was water where I stood in my lifetime. I envisioned myself as some distant-future archaeologist strolling around in my own ancient past. Weird, right? Allure of the obscure, baby!

Although it probably wasn't necessary, I was glad to engage the low-range four-wheel-drive lock feature of the Jeep as I rambled around down on that huge beach. Some sections were softer than others.

I saw another car and a van down there, too. But I ventured farther than that smattering of other tourists. I don't know how many sculptures and standalone creative displays are down there, but I'd guess dozens, all spread out. These photos are the only way to even try to convey this experience that I found both dismal and exhilarating. Color me... unusual.

Check out the rough and hard and lumpy texture of the beach as I got closer to the current shoreline. Petrified fish bodies? Darn treacherous for the ankles.

I thought that was an actual bird out there in the photo above. But the thing never moved. Because it wasn't a bird at all, but a small carefully placed steel sculpture. In fact, I didn't see *any* wildlife. At all. The water looked... syrupy. Birds don't even fly *over* this area.

After spending a few hours in Bombay, I drove down the rest of the eastern shore and back to our campground west of El Centro in

Seeley, California. To the lovely Rio Bend RV Resort. A stark contrast. Quite the day!

I GOT WHAT I NEEDED, and more: a first-hand experience of what felt like a post-apocalyptic landscape, a unique experience visiting an area very much off the beaten path. Nothing in my seventy-five years of life compared. But once was enough.

For those of you who have been here, I trust you can relate to my brief experience. The area continues to devolve, I'm told. I found it both sad and heartening. The creative philosophical types that spend time here, either full or part time—I missed the secret party—give me hope that no matter how bad things get, we as a species transmogrify existential lemons into nihilistic lemonade.

Chapter 63

RO-buki

If the Salton Sea and its environs didn't strike you as obscure enough, try this on for size. Yes, we'd shuffled on down the asphalt, and the timeline, having moved our home yet again, for perhaps the two-hundredth time in 9+ years. This time to South Central Arizona, 60 miles north of Nogales, Mexico.

Today is Friday, February 12, 2024, a Friday to remember, *and* my favorite day of the week, except for starting a sea voyage, as you already know. My obstinate fingers refuse to obey commands issued by my brain. It isn't their fault. They, like much of the rest of my body and mind, suffer from a lifetime of prodigious use and abuse. And it seems I'd fallen prey to a minor stroke in the past year. Now, I make amends to both mind and body.

It isn't exactly cold out here, nor uncomfortable. Then, the clouds part at last, and the sun shines like a beacon of relentless hope. Sixty degrees in the desert in February should be a balm to any arthritic soul. Even mine. And I am now less troubled than most.

But after an hour out here in the shade of bamboo and rice paper panels, I *am* sore. And stiff, as if my bones and joints hint at a lust for petrification, like prehistoric wood. Even within earshot of one burbling fountain aerating the pond nearby that hosts an array of koi, I suppress the urge to quit.

I'm not accustomed to perching precariously on the edge of a low, backless chair for this long. Aware of my taskmaster staring at me, his expression changes ever so slightly any time my spine yields to anything but a board-straight posture. He says nothing. He just continues to blow. Wanting to please this charismatic little man, I'm doing my best from within this seventy-five-year-old carcass!

Very unlike my former selves, I am now drawn to all things spiritual. Because I face my own fragile mortality every time my heart does a tap dance that sets me on my bony posterior—with no warning. When did I become such an old codger? Each time I dwell on the age my father died, years younger than me now, I thank him for passing along to me a genetic predisposition to heart failure. He's bequeathed me with a sense of clarity. And purpose.

This is not a curse, my friends, but a lifelong gift to face one's mortality in a visceral manner and just... smile. I see that now. On such occasions, it occurs to me how much unfinished business I have yet to transact. I ponder that. Often. No, not religiosity. Rather, each breath is indeed a treasured endowment I must honor. So yes, I am drawn to what I now sense, but cannot see. I call it *extrasensory appreciation*.

Sometimes, a few clustered days in my life become a nexus for subtle spiritual experiences, a metaphor that represents my desired trajectory for my remaining years. Sound corny? As the years drift by ever faster, like a roll of toilet paper drawing toward its end, I'm edging more toward... personal authenticity.

I'd like to share an example of one such extended metaphor with you—this past long weekend. Let's roll back one day from live bamboo forests and burbling fountains. No Thursday in memory evoked such a visceral appreciation for my personal place in the universe. Deep in the bowels of the Arizona State Museum on the U of A campus, a(nother) dream came true. I felt the subtle presence of ancient Anasazi ghosts—sixth-century warlike Native American minstrels. And no, that is not an oxymoron.

This museum granted three others and me a private viewing within a room-sized, climate-controlled storage vault of perishable historical artifacts. Among other priceless artifacts, we examined in some detail four *basketmaker flutes* known as *rim-blown* instruments. Now, I'm no archaeologist, but I fancy myself a musician—perhaps just one more delusion—and this was a profound experience for someone with as fertile an imagination as mine.

These famous seventh-century Ancestral Pueblo flutes are the oldest known wooden musical instruments ever discovered in North America. Under the watchful eye of the young perishables curator, Dr. Ed Jolie, I placed my nose within an inch of one of these revered artifacts.

I *smelled* its fifteen-hundred-year history compressed into one second of supervised breath. Based on the instrument's wear patterns, my still-fertile mind imagined some ancient musician performing in his now-considered-unusual left-hand-down playing style, no less—*like my own renegade style*—breathing out haunting music on these difficult-to-play instruments. My extrasensory appreciation *connected* me to that ancient flute player. I *saw* him placing the notch in the flute's rim between his yellowed front teeth. I sensed the natural stench of his breath as he exhaled to prepare for a huge diaphragmatic inhale.

Rim-blowns require a lot of breath with controlled exhales to power this type of instrument, central to so many spiritual ceremonies of its day. Even now. Then, I imagine the tone floating from the end of this hollow tube toward the appreciative ears of a small group of acolytes squatting around a campfire. Mindless mesquite smoke swirls on a gentle desert breeze. An errant wisp demands that my musician squint against the invasion of such a tendril as the *Mother's Breath* shifts ever so slightly.

A THROATY TONE, these Pueblo flutes, the tuning of which sounds strange to our modern ears. I said as much to Dr. Jolie. He looked shocked as we three non-academics told *him* how these flutes *sounded* a millennium-and-a-half ago and what their magical ambience must have inspired. "How could you possibly know what these flutes sounded like?"

As I stared at these artifacts in their full-extension storage drawer, I said, "Ed, I've crafted three such flutes myself based on well-vetted plans for these 'Broken Flute Cave' flutes." This formal name describes their geographical origin, a cave in the Prayer Rock Valley of northeastern Arizona, within the Navajo Nation. It was discovered during an archaeological expedition led by Earl H. Morris in 1931. Yeah, I'd done my homework.

Rather fond of the sound of my own voice and proud of schooling this young PhD, I rambled on. "I modeled them from a material I call *urban ebony*—PVC pipe painted black. While their sound can't precisely model a carved *wooden* flute, their similar sound, and original tuning based on the design of *these very flutes,* is truly enchanting, Dr. Jolie."

My friend, Bill Brinkerhoff, chimed in. "Yes, and you see the notch in the rim of each flute? That allows the performer to interstitially anchor the flute to his front teeth for more control of his or her embouchure. That enables more rapid transitions between the instrument's lower and upper registers, or octaves. Some players can achieve a third octave."

We could see Dr. Jolie's professorial wheels spinning. We watched as he visibly twitched. He blurted, "I must publish a paper on the *musical* qualities of these famous flutes post-haste!"

We smiled. Bill chided, "Well, Doc, they ***are musical*** instruments."

Yep, even museum curators blush.

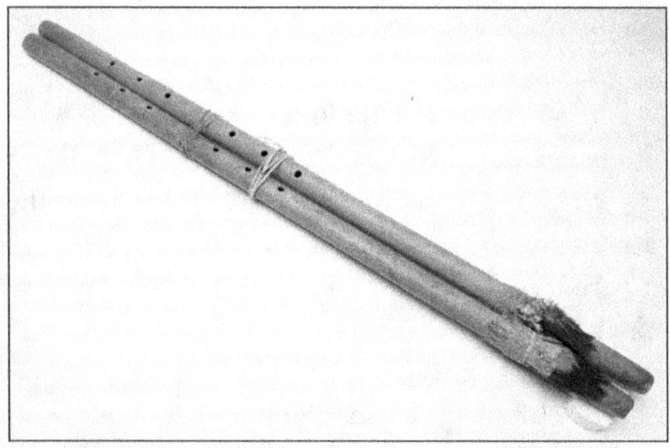

Ancestral Pueblo Flutes from Broken Flute Cave
(photo credit: Arizona State Museum)

THEN, one day later on Friday, a small group of local musicians invited me to participate in a *RO-buki,* a Japanese term that means *to blow* RO. In the rather obscure American subculture surrounding the *Japanese* flute community, there is a bamboo instrument called the shakuhachi—also an ancient rim-blown flute, much like the ancient Pueblo flutes I'd admired the day before. The word *RO* describes the lowest—or fundamental—note of that frustrating instrument, which also possesses an enchanting voice.

I won't bore you by trying and failing to describe the subtle techniques and variations that surround *RO* and the other notes of this flute's pentatonic—five-note—scale. But each note boasts a name of honor. They are *TSU, RE, CHI,* and *RI*. All the other notes and a near-infinite tonal variations, along with their unique nomenclature, ascend or descend from each of these, as do their degree of difficulty.

By the way, Western musical notation can't even pretend to represent the subtle (and strange to the Western ear) musical capabilities of this ancient instrument. Though some composers and musicians try. Some for a lifetime. Some traditional shakuhachi masters instruct their students to *only* blow *RO* and its variations for an entire *year* before progressing to the other notes!

Like the Native American rim-blown flutes, each flute is tuned to what Western music would consider a specific musical key.

Once again, I feel connected to the past. The shakuhachi's historical connection to ancient Japanese warriors—the samurai, is not unlike the North American Anasazi. Through a paranoid emperor's edict, the samurai lost their *katanas*—their swords—which lore suggests carried the soul of its master. The emperor's Sword Abolishment Edict of 1876 prohibited them from carrying swords, marking the end of the samurai's status as a specialized warrior class in Japan, *at least on the surface.*

They were *not* prohibited from roaming the land, and many served as spies for their own feudal masters as a sort of underground resistance to their maniacal emperor. Does any of this sound familiar?

Evolving from a lifetime of training in discipline, adaptability, flexibility, and close-quarters combat, they adopted the shakuhachi flute as a musical pretense. Why? Because a yard of hard, round, inch-and-a-half-thick bamboo with sharp edges on one end and a heavier root-end at the other still made for a nasty *stealth* weapon. And these erstwhile warriors learned to play their *weapons.* So says the lore. Fascinating, is it not? But back to the shakuhachi as a musical instrument.

Fine shakuhachi flutes are handcrafted out of old bamboo by expert craftsmen.

My first *RO-buki* remains crisp, as I now relive it. Deep within the center of the Yume Japanese Gardens in Tucson, seven of us sit in an intimate circle, perched only on the forward edge of our low chairs. Backs straight, breathing so very deeply, up from our diaphragms and expanding our rib cages with every breath, but without hiking up our shoulders. A dizzying exercise in itself.

We repeatedly blow *RO* and sustain it for as long as we are able. This is an ancient meditation practice originating in China and later migrating to Japan thousands of years ago. Yes, another trip into the past during this special weekend, but from another continent and an even earlier age. Obscure enough yet for you, dear reader? And here's that infomercial that once again says, ***"But wait!"***

MY EYES SQUEEZE shut in concentration as I struggle to produce *any* sound with my shakuhachi of composite construction, an "authentic replica." I dare to look up at our leader. The little man is one of the revered international rock stars of the shakuhachi world. Sensei Alcvin Ryuzen Ramos lives in a retreat in rural British Columbia when not traveling to perform or on pilgrimages to various monasteries in Japan. He and his on-stage performance partner, Brandy Wood, from South Florida, blow *RO*. We all blow *RO*. We make every attempt to match their incredible clarity and sustained purity of sound. *Impossible! How do they* ***do*** *that?*

I am privileged to be here with some fascinating new friends. Of note, Allan, the gentleman to my left, is about my age and a lifetime practitioner of Zen. He has played the shakuhachi for many years. Although he, too, remains frustrated with this maddening instrument that demands both humility and sustained focus.

Across from me, I later learned that Goya, a Tucson native, crafts Japanese swords for ritualistic Samurai combat. Many of his clients live in Japan, and he travels there frequently. Lis and Kai are heavily involved in the local shakuhachi community. I scored my invitation to this *RO-buki* through Lis, a fellow member of a local Native American-style flute circle. We're all honored and humbled to blow *RO* with Alcvin and Brandy. We look forward to their concert the following day.

With deliberation, Alcvin moves on to the next higher musical note—*TSU*—with an expressive and explosive breath of air, perfectly controlled. Of course, there's a Japanese term for this technique that I have yet to memorize, much less accomplish.

Then Alcvin switches back to RO, but now sustains an improbable note with crystalline clarity in the instrument's second register, or one octave up from *otsu,* the previous lower octave. They call this elusive higher octave *kan.* He changes only his embouchure. He motions for us to rise from our chairs *while still playing.*

We stand, still blowing (or trying to blow) *RO-kan*, or *Ha.* Each of the shakuhachi's notes is imbued with its own personality, its own story. He now wants us to... *follow him through this circuitous Japanese garden while blowing RO-kan?* Like the Pied Piper?

Now, please understand that it is difficult enough for a relative newbie like me to get *any* sound *at all* out of a shakuhachi. I'll sit concentrating with pinched eyes, forming and keeping the precisely correct embouchure—the shape of the mouth and lips. Then, I struggle with achieving and maintaining the right orientation of my embouchure to the flute's *utaguchi*, or its razor-sharp mouthpiece. And then *changing* that orientation by a few millimeters to achieve a different tonal variation, *or* to ascend to *kan*—the higher octave—without losing all sound, or worse, sound like a squawking Canada goose. I kid you not, it's a bitch.

And now, to continue generating not just any sound, but the precise note and timbre as Sensei... while *walking*? Over irregular ground? Around the edges of rock-rimmed ponds, and weaving our way through a dense stand of tall green bamboo trees? Talk about demanding humility *and* focus! I'm surprised they didn't ask us to sign a liability release.

I struggle to process it all. Nevertheless, the others and I rise to the challenge, at least to the best of our individual abilities, which are now better than I thought possible. We're making sound, and the more experienced of us are even blowing and sustaining *RO-kan as we walk!* Sensei has thus instructed us without uttering a single word. This goes on for more than an hour. My back burns. The peripheral neuropathy in my lower extremities commands me to leave, to quit. I do not.

Afterward, one student complained that every note was a struggle. Sensei said, "There is great fulfillment in this struggle, in every successful breath." How very Zen! But I think I understand. After this experience, I feel... fulfilled and joyful to have been part of something special. Something... obscure. Something... spiritual? Perhaps this is the genesis of yet another lifelong journey, at least what remains of it.

At home later, this old septuagenarian falls into a deep sleep for a two-hour afternoon power nap in his La-Z-Boy recliner. But I muster the energy to rise and eat a hearty supper. Kay asks, "What are you still smiling about?"

I do not intend for my reply to sound condescending, although it does. "You wouldn't understand, my love."

Chapter 64

Intercontinental Culture

THEN SATURDAY ARRIVES. I AWAKEN TIRED BUT ENERGIZED. Concert day. In the circular kiva* of an old local church, Alcvin and Brandy transport us on a magical musical journey. It begins with traditional Japanese compositions of another age and then leads us forward in time to more progressive pieces in this versatile instrument's cultural history. Unlike my trials by fire with this instrument, Kay's ear can't appreciate much of their music. That's understandable. But she listens with respect. I better appreciate it having some small idea how challenging it is to master this instrument like they clearly have.

We see their sheet music in Japanese notation. Beautiful, but incomprehensible to the untrained eye. They guide us through myriad moods until the concert climaxes by offering us serene and startling moments with a final piece. They bring to the stage their local friend, Machu. I've seen him perform at Native American flute

* A kiva is a large, circular, underground room used for spiritual ceremonies and as a place of worship. The term kiva derives from Native American Pueblo heritage. This feels like a fusion of cultures.

festivals. He shares his amazing talent on one of his seven-foot Australian Aboriginal didgeridoos.

Together, the trio performs a piece that I can only describe as... tribal. Perhaps primal. Feral. And Sensei throws his entire body into his part of the performance. Yes, a fusion of Eastern and Western and aboriginal musical cultures that flirts with a... jazz fusion? *Incredible.* The didgeridoo is an astounding instrument developed by the Aboriginal peoples of northern Australia at least a thousand years ago. Besides my applause along with everyone else's, I offer only one boisterous word of appreciation as I stand: "*Whaaaat?!*"

I leave that concert with one of Alcvin's own authentic bamboo Shakuhachis, and a commitment to receive lessons from the man himself. I *so* need guidance. And it starts the following day.

I EXPERIENCED a delightful workshop on Sunday with Sensei and just seven students, including my humbled self. We sit in an old warehouse transformed into a rustic and unpretentious gallery in downtown Tucson called *Solar Culture.* It also serves as a small performing arts venue that once embodied the heart of Tucson's art scene with several resident artists. But there is no heat in this erstwhile warehouse. It's fifty-six degrees in the sun and feels colder inside. I'm wondering if this is how shakuhachi acolytes pay their—our—dues. But this ain't the blues!

After three hours of exercising, whispering, screaming, laughing, and practicing new performance methods, my face smiles... again. I aim my Jeep's autopilot for the motorhome, now profoundly exhausted. My head is impossibly crammed with shakuhachi tips and techniques, along with peripheral pearls of philosophical wisdom. And I have now consummated my bond with my new SunRoot Shakuhachi Jiari flute. But alas, it is no easier to play than my much cheaper replica!

. . .

There is no describing with mere words this delightful afternoon. Yet another unique experience in an obscure setting with dear new friends from Tucson, British Columbia, South Florida, Oahu, and Moscow, by way of Dublin. The spirit of the shakuhachi and its merciless demands connect us in revered international humility and a subtle sense of joy.

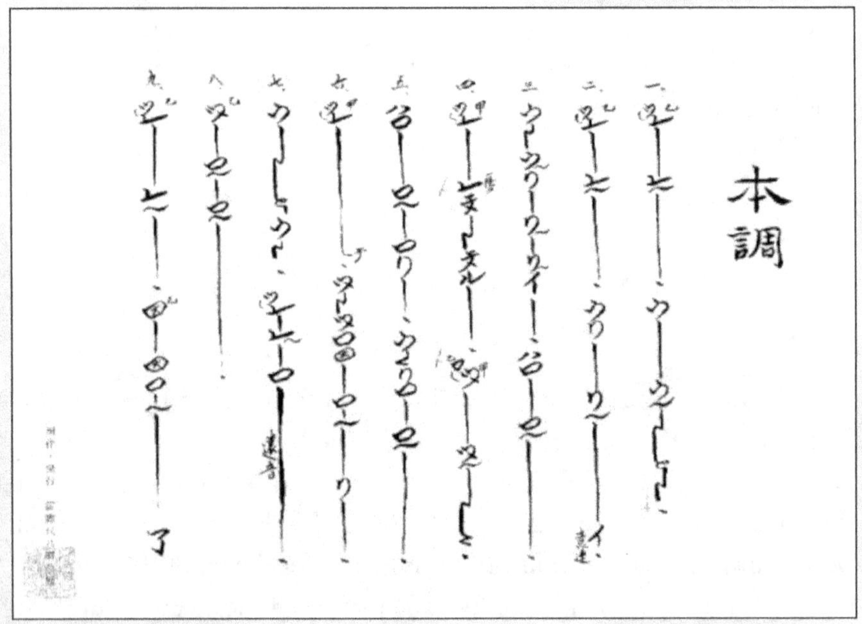

I offer you an example of traditional shakuhachi musical notation. This is a traditional piece I've been studying for a couple of years now, called Hon Shirabe. Any wonder why this (or any) Westerner struggles with such notation? But this instrument demands more frequent and consistent practice than I have given it.

I arrive home minutes before the 2024 Puppy Bowl "kicks off," and in plenty of time to prep our traditional vegan pizza —our guilty pleasure—prior to the kickoff of Super Bowl LVIII. These twin "bowls" are Miss Kay's favorites, not mine. We watch them together. Call this part of this recovering alcoholic's living amends.

Once I hit my La-Z-Boy as this long weekend winds down,

however, Kay's offering three-to-one odds that I'll awaken right about half-time. A decent wager.

Oh, did I mention I peddled my books for several hours at Voyager RV Resort's Market Daze on Saturday until minutes before heading across town to the shakuhachi concert? Yeah, that includes hauling three heavy boxes of inventory to and from the venue in the rain and wind. But meeting so many lovely people, many of whom have become fans of my modest literary efforts, is gratifying. A nod to that other obscure passion that still holds me in its clutches—writing.

One hell of a weekend that began and ended with smiles. And so my journey of personal authenticity spins off of the toilet roll ever faster.

Chapter 65

Aging paradox

So toward what single point have all these key moments in my life coalesced? I recently celebrated my seventy-sixth birthday in late November 2025, and I'm doing pretty damn well. I weigh 169 pounds at not quite six feet tall, and am strong enough—for an old guy, that is; although I'm also (finally) wise enough to know my limitations. But here's the rub.

I'm young in my mind even though my body tells me some things are no longer to be attempted. Takes too damn long to heal. Alright, already, I'll listen to my body and set aside my pride. This is no doubt true of anyone fortunate enough to live a long and eventful life with a healthy mind. I've chosen to optimize my mind and body for my remaining years as a deliberate decision backed up with a specific plan. Right now, I've already lived longer than both my parents.

One of my few regrets? Not spending more time with family earlier in all our lives. That is now more important to us than ever before. Kay and I have renewed our efforts to do so.

We now discuss how many years of life we think each of us has remaining. We don't immerse ourselves in a morose or fatalistic mood. It's simply pragmatic planning. What vacations do we still wish to take? Do we need to consider different living conditions? If so, under what circumstances? What do we still really want to experience or achieve?

Yeah, we're planning and prioritizing our bucket list for the next 10 to 15 years, for both of us together, *or* one of us as the sole survivor. Oh, and we ensure our wills, living directives, and trust are up to date. But that's about it. We both wishes to be cremated. And for all I care, flush my ashes down the nearest toilet. Kay prefers hers sprinkled on the Mississippi River. And neither of us wish to be sustained past the point where we feel the quality of life has eluded us at last.

The reason we gave up traveling full-time and bought a townhouse in Rochester, Minnesota, during the summer of 2025 originated with this mindset. It's a nice house that features all of our day-to-day living requirements on one floor. Although it also offers us a finished lower-level family room, den, a third bedroom, and a third bathroom, plus a large hobby room. We were surprised that it fully met 27 of our 30 specific requirements.

But it lacks a fenced-in yard for a dog, which we don't yet have, and gave us more square footage than we needed. I'll be able to plant a few flowers and herbs outside. Other than paying a bit more than we'd planned in this white-hot real estate market, I won't have to worry much about lawn care or snow removal. That's awesome, especially if Kay's lingering wanderlust still draws us away for trips to warmer climes in the winter, or visiting family or friends in the summer who may live afar. If she recovers nicely from four significant surgical procedures in 2025 and early 2026. *Only* two for me!

But, as they say, hope springs eternal. Nor will we now need to worry about a mortgage should one of us pass, thanks to the sale of our Florida condo and our motorhome.

So, the paradox? As we continue to think of ourselves as adventurous seniors, we also must plan for our ultimate and inevitable journey toward our demise, hopefully still in the distant future.

Chapter 66

Toward the end

INDULGE ME WITH A FEW LAST WORDS ON THIS TRIP DOWN MY personal yellow brick road. A few health issues stack up despite our best efforts to stave them off with slavish obedience to the rigors of physical, mental, and spiritual fitness. However, I'm pleased to report that the longer I live with my recently discovered but manageable maladies, the more I accept them. After all, they *are* (advancing age is) inevitable as I approach my expiration date., now visible over the hopefully distant horizon.

They say those who fall prey to personal vanity must suffer pain. I can only speculate, as someone not cursed with abundant beauty or grace. Beautiful people who desperately cling to the illusion of youth must be a glum lot as they age and wrinkle. That ain't me. My heart is heavy for them, speaking as someone who is unfettered from anything resembling a vanity quest (at last). And that's saying something for someone whose ego remains as healthy as ever. Besides, I'm rather proud of my abundant wrinkles and scars. Each tells a story.

I will close this chapter of my full life's pivotal moments so far by thanking *everyone* in my life. My wonderful friends, my dear family, my readers, my AA sponsor, and my treasured mentors, both before and after retiring from IBM, those both living and at rest. I'm filled with gratitude because you've all graced my life with not only your presence, but with your friendship.

Most of all, I'm brimming with gratitude for a robust life enriched by an argumentative young gymnast with the muscular legs and scintillating but infuriating intellect. Thankfully, she still kicks my egoistic ass regularly. She's the guilty party who gave us our wonderful children and grandchildren. Well done, old girl! And may you always be my most brutal and honest critic!

Speaking of my much better half, we're so blessed to have shared countless adventures together. Kay now cares for me when I'm *broken,* and I care for her when she is. When we're both *down,* we still lift each other up, now sometimes with a little outside assist. I'm grateful that we kiss and hug often. I'll sneak in a little boob squeeze or ass pat here and there, like Daddy did with Mom long ago in *their* later years.

Kay pinches *my* now-flabby ass at every opportunity where a public display of our mutual *affliction* won't embarrass me too much. Or as we gaze at each other once in a while with misty eyes. I kid you not. We hold hands wherever we walk together so neither of us slips or falls, though we may still stumble, physically or emotionally, especially these days.

We open doors for each other, and we scratch each other's backs, which lately conjures drools and eye-rolls. Yet she's *still* the most exasperating *and* brilliant woman I've had both the pleasure and frustration of disliking *and* passionately loving over the years—now going on six decades—with every fiber of my not-so-humble being.

We took this photo a few years ago, likely circa 2008.

If you've made it this far in this journal, dear reader, you now have a sense of how delightfully screwed up and content this old fart has grown. Life is messy. It offers texture and spice. It demands our attention. It kicks us in the butt. We fall down. It expects us to rise again, and we may only be rewarded with nothing but the next challenge, and hopefully, another lesson learned. That is the heart—and the joy—of it.

My sincerest wish is that, like me, you allow yourself the opportunities to become as screwed up and content as I am. I pray that if you haven't already done so, figure out, like I did too late in life, how to (re-)wire your brain, your neural pathways, for seeing the pure joy in every messy and fleeting moment.

Thanks for touring with me through a selection of key moments that represent what I consider a fortunate life pretty damn-well lived. Even though it often felt like traversing a mine field.

I DON'T SO MUCH FEAR DEATH
AS I FEAR WASTING LIFE.

The End?
Nope.
Not Yet.

Chapter 67

Art Gallery

THIS MEMOIR CANNOT BE COMPLETE WITHOUT SHARING A FEW of my artistic endeavors beyond words on a page. I'm particularly proud of my drawings, creative photos, digital paintings, and watercolor paintings. There's no room to explore with you my body of poetry in this volume, so you might be interested to explore my book, ***The Poetic Detective,*** for eclectic verses, more original images, and eclectic essays.

I hope you enjoy the following selections curated from my sporadic artistic efforts over the years. ***Please note that none of these images were created using artificial intelligence.*** This collection merely paints a window into what I *think* I can do. Let's start with a few of my favorite original drawings.

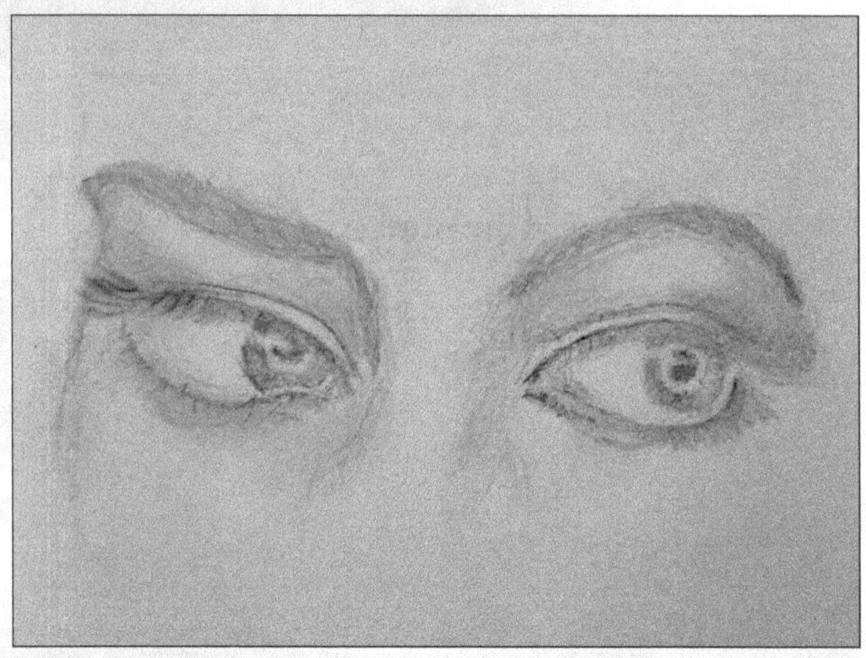

APPREHENSIVE (pencil). **See an acrylic interpretation of this drawing in the coming pages.**

CAVEMAN (pencil & charcoal)

ON THE PROWL (pencil)

CHIAROSCURO **(charcoal), a study in contrasting light and shadow.**

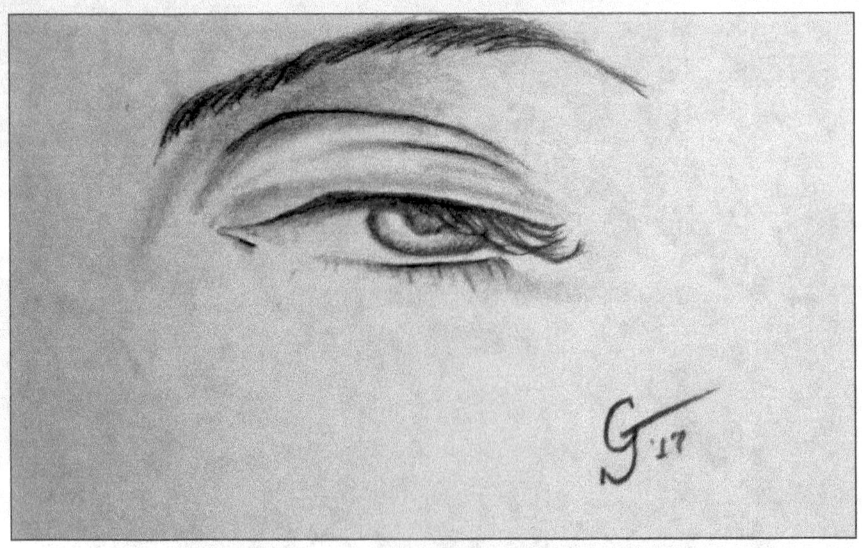

BORED (pencil)

CREATIVE PHOTOS

For several years, I focused on the elements of creative photography: composition, color, contrast, mood, presentation techniques, modeling techniques, and selecting evocative subjects. Of course, there is a story behind each image.

HONEY, I'M HOME!

HOLLOW HEART

BELLO'S FINAL BOW

DIGITAL PAINTINGS

To paint digitally, I use a computer stylus as a paintbrush and the screen as my canvas. Once completed, I may print the image on paper, canvas, metal, or just keep as a digital file in my archives.

I start with a high-quality photo as a reference, just like I do for drawing or painting with acrylics, oils, or watercolors. But I use a variety of computer-based tools (think different digital brushes). Note this is still all me as the artist, and not A.I. doing it for me. In fact, A.I. didn't really exist back then.

Nick Page's On-Stage Head-bangin' Mood

Setting Sojourn's Stern Anchor

ACRYLIC PAINTINGS

For a short time, I flirted with acrylic paints on canvas.

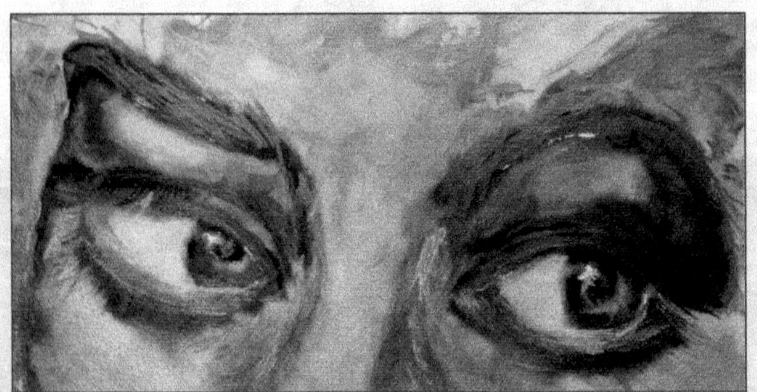

EYE OF THE STORM. I leveraged the first drawing in this gallery (APPREHENSIVE) as a model for painting these eyes.

SEÑORITA BONITA

WATERCOLOR STUDIES

Over time, I settled on watercolor as my painting medium of choice. Not only is watercolor tricky, its unique beauty and transparency enable lovely results not possible with any other medium. Plus, sheets of paper were easier to store on the bus than stretched canvases.

GERIATRIC hippie (not a selfie!)

I FEATURE the following image in my book of poetry and essays, ***"The Poetic Detective"***. I'm actually rather pleased with this wet-on-wet composition.

INTO THE STORM

THIS PRECOCIOUS KITTEN's headshot employs several techniques to achieve a level of abstraction that makes the composition more... "atmospheric"?

BUDDY

TO MARKET. While sailing in the southeastern Caribbean aboard a 65' catamaran with a huge sloop rig, we visited the port of Soufrière located on the west coast of Saint Lucia, a volcanic island which is part of the Windward Islands chain. It boasts a rich history, having been colonized by the French and was once the original capital of the island. I captured this Soufrière street scene in watercolor.

This cowboy art is fun and good practice for capturing the expressive anatomy of these bull riders.

COWBOY WAY

I LIKE THIS ONE. Annie still hangs in *Sojourn's* head (bathroom) even though she now belongs to a new captain and crew.

ANNIE

A TOUGHER GIG is painting a shiny surface with interest:

TEA TIME

On the path to painting convincing subjects. I suspect this young wrangler might have been a young lady in disguise.

HURTS SO GOOD

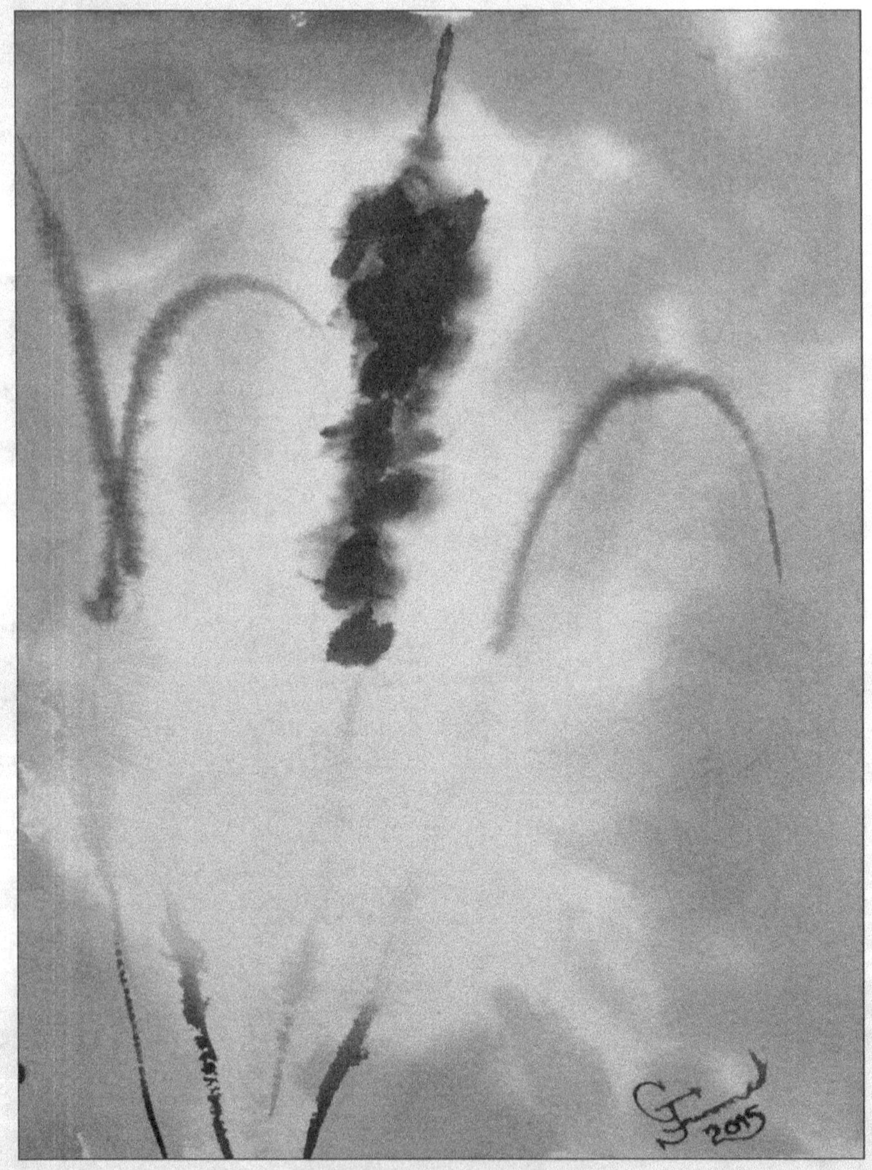

EXPLODING PUSSY WILLOW

A British Coastal Farm

COCK OF THE WALK

THIS ROOSTER STRUTS his stuff in brilliant colors. This style of using pure watercolor paint right out of the tube and onto the paper takes me well outside my comfort zone, but I'm pleased with the result.

UNUSUAL SUSPECT

Unusual Suspect is my latest watercolor effort (January 2026). My objective? To achieve the loose "atmospheric" and semi-abstract style of British watercolor artist ***Jean Haines.***

Epilogue

JANUARY 2026 UPDATE:

By the way, our first winter "up north" in over two decades served up a few surprises. For example, I'd forgotten how to tread lightly on ice. The technique is known as the *Minnesota Shuffle*.

The second snowfall of the season melted. Mother Nature topped it with a dusting of fresh powder. You know what's coming. I slipped and fell on my butt in a lightning-fast second. Broke my wrist and hyper-extended my right shoulder. Lesson remembered, characteristically, too late.

So naturally, I purchased ice cleats *after the fact*. And the real irony? They recommend installing them on one pair of shoes and then using only those shoes to venture down the icy driveway 's slope to the mailbox. I installed them on my *tropical boat shoes!* Even God loves a good gag.

You know what? It's just one more adventure, isn't it? I'm grateful I didn't break a hip and start a free-fall that happens to so many geriatrics. *Jeez, am I really geriatric, now? Okay, so be it!*

. . .

We'd set aside the summer of 2025 and the winter of 2025-2026 for selling the bus, buying a house, catching up on medical issues, and spending time with family. 2026 burst onto the scene yesterday, as I write this epilogue, and we've already spent more time with our family than we have in years. After Kay's back surgery coming up in six weeks, we then plan to take the summer off. At our age, that means *no major medical procedures during nice weather!*

As we erstwhile SCUBA divers always say, "Plan your dive, then dive your plan." Nevertheless, so far, my ***fall*** notwith***stand***ing (is that a pun?) we're "diving our plan"!

Boat and motorhome ownership are now in our past, along with countless other ***subtractive*** *life changes.* However, my bride and I are already planning our next adventures of shorter duration that require less physicality—more ***additive*** *life changes.*

Maybe a month in Copenhagen. Or Malaga, Spain. Or London. And Kay wishes to spend a month haunting the Smithsonian.

Watch this space, y'all!

Other Books by GK Jurrens

Historical Fiction (Great Depression Era Crime)

- Black Blizzard: A Lyon County Adventure (also audiobook edition with virtual voices)
- Murder in Purgatory: A Lyon County Mystery

Aubrey Greigh Mysteries

- Voodoo Vendetta - Culture That Kills (also audiobook edition - self-narrated)
- Dancing With Death - Who Will Die? Or Disappear? (also audiobook edition - self-narrated)
- Rogue's Gallery - Beyond Evidence (also *theatrical* audiobook edition with cinematic music and sound effects - self-narrated and produced)

Sam Travis Adventures (in collaboration with my friend, Lt. Tom Kasprzak (ret.) of the Massachusetts Environmental Police):

- Lethal Game - Bears Under Siege (also audiobook edition - self-narrated)
- Lethal Trail - No Body Is Safe
- Lethal Bounty - A Dirty Secret
- Lethal Catch - Crossing the Line

Contemporary Autobiographical Fiction (Drama)

- Dangerous Dreams: Dream Runners: Book 1
- Fractured Dreams: Dream Runners: Book 2

Futuristic Fiction Mash-Up (Paranormal Romantic Mystery Thrillers)

- Underground, Mayhem: Book 1
- Mean Streets, Mayhem: Book 2
- Post Earth, Mayhem: Book 3
- A Glimpse of Mayhem: Companion Guide to the Mayhem Trilogy

Non-fiction

- The Poetic Detective: Investigate Rhyme With Reason
- Why Write? Why Publish? Passion? Profit? Both?
- Moving a Boat and Her Crew (out of print)
- Restoring a Boat and Her Crew (out of print)

Chapter 68

About the Author

GK JURRENS WRITES WITH UNDILUTED passion. He's published 19 fiction and non-fiction titles to date (eBook & paperback editions of each). These include 14 action-oriented novels across five series, one book of poetry and essays, one book on the craft of writing and publishing, one companion guide to his trilogy of futuristic paranormal romantic mysteries, and two nautical coffee table books.This memoir is number 20. Plus GK has created four audiobooks, three of which he narrated (so far).

He also teaches writing & publishing seminars nationwide, as well as hosting periodic book signing events.

<u>THIS AUTHOR'S VISION</u>: To create gritty fictional realism based on true stories with social relevance set in the past, present, or future to:

- Protect wildlife and the environment,
- Fight crime and corruption,
- Solve quirky, character-driven mysteries.

WITH UPLIFE PRESS, GK has independently published:

- Outdoor Environmental Adventures (in collaboration with retired Lt. Tom Kasprzak of the Massachusetts State Environmental Police)
- Historical Crime Fiction (1930s America)
- Modern Murder Mysteries (near future)
- Contemporary Autobiographical Fiction
- Futuristic Paranormal Romantic Mysteries (22nd century)
- Science Fiction (22nd century)
- Poetry & Essays
- Writing & Publishing
- Nautical Travelogue & Sailing Yacht Restoration
- And now, a memoir.

Until recently, GK and his wife lived and traveled in a motorhome as their *only* home. They wandered their beloved North America as a source of endless inspiration. They've lived in 42 states in the last decade for a few weeks to a few months at a time.

After studying Liberal Arts and Electronics Engineering Technology, GK earned a Bachelor of Science degree in Business and a Master of Science degree in Management of Technology from the University of Minnesota.

Six years of government service (US Coast Guard Search & Rescue, Marine Law Enforcement, Reserves) and a successful three-decade career in global high-technology (IBM) preceded more than a decade of voyaging on America's waterways aboard a fifty-one-foot pilothouse motorsailer. Besides America's inland waterways, GK and his wife Kay have cruised the Gulf of Mexico, the Florida Keys, and the Eastern Caribbean from the British Virgin Islands to Granada, near the coast of Venezuela.

Plus, brief forays sailing through the Greek Cyclades Islands in the Aegean Sea, as well as the San Juan Islands in the US Pacific Northwest, offered Gene and his wife Kay more unique nautical challenges, *and* inspiration.

With multiple works always in process, GK continues to write with a sense of urgency, and of course, passion. Always. He embeds contemporary social issues in each of his action-oriented stories.

~

Selfie of the author with Miss Kay, his much better half.

www.ingramcontent.com/pod-product-compliance
Lightning Source LLC
LaVergne TN
LVHW020040110826
845155LV00029B/572

* 9 7 8 1 9 5 2 1 6 5 4 3 6 *